"A very timely work to help strengthen our understanding of what it means to be a professional fighting force in the twenty-first century."

> —**Lieutenant General Rick Burr**, AO, DSC, MVO, Chief of the Australian Army

". . . a great volume composed of varied perspectives that provide insight and historic context so we can maintain and cultivate our profession for the coming decades."

> —**Major General John Kem**, USA, Commandant, U.S. Army War College

". . . a conversation that not only reflects on where the profession stands today, but perhaps more importantly, how our civilian-led institutions adapt our military to the future nature of warfare and the increasingly heavy responsibility placed on the individual citizen-service member."

> —**Daniel Feehan**, former Principal Deputy Assistant Secretary of Defense (Readiness)

"*Redefining the Modern Military* astutely describes why both competence and character are vital to leadership in the military profession."

> —**Lieutenant General Robert L. Caslen Jr.**, USA (Ret.), former Superintendent, U.S. Military Academy

"Today's true military professionals will find much in this collection to set their necessarily ambitious, but essentially pragmatic, reform agendas."

> —**Lieutenant General Sir Paul Newton**, KBE, CBE, MPhil, UK Army (Ret.), Director, Strategy and Security Institute, University of Exeter, and former Commander, Force Development and Training

"This book fuels the necessary conversation to make every curious reader a better warrior. Bravo Zulu!"

> —**Rear Admiral Peg Klein**, USN (Ret.), former Senior Advisor to the Secretary of Defense for Military Professionalism

"[A] must-read for anyone who cares about professional military education or civil-military relations."

> —**Jim Golby**, PhD, former Special Assistant to the Chairman of the Joint Chiefs of Staff, Special Advisor to Vice Presidents Joe Biden & Mike Pence

REDEFINING THE MODERN MILITARY

The Intersection of Profession and Ethics

EDITED BY

NATHAN K. FINNEY AND TYRELL O. MAYFIELD

NAVAL INSTITUTE PRESS
ANNAPOLIS, MARYLAND

NAVAL INSTITUTE PRESS
291 Wood Road
Annapolis, MD 21402

Library of Congress Cataloging-in-Publication Data
Names: Finney, Nathan K., editor of compilation. | Mayfield, Tyrell O.,
    editor of compilation.
Title: Redefining the modern military : the intersection of profession and
    ethics / editors, Nathan K. Finney & Tyrell O. Mayfield.
Description: Annapolis, MD : Naval Institute Press, [2018] | Includes
    bibliographical references and index.
Identifiers: LCCN 2018019223 (print) | LCCN 2018028683 (ebook) | ISBN
    9781682473641 (epub) | ISBN 9781682473641 (mobi) | ISBN 9781682473641
    (ePDF) | ISBN 9781682473634 (alk. paper)
Subjects: LCSH: Military ethics—United States. | Military education—
United States. | United States. Army—Military life. | Military
    socialization—United States.
Classification: LCC U22 (ebook) | LCC U22 .R39 2018 (print) | DDC
    174/.9355—dc23
LC record available at https://lccn.loc.gov/2018019223

∞ Print editions meet the requirements of ANSI/NISO z39.48-1992
    (Permanence of Paper).
Printed in the United States of America.

26 25 24 23 22 21 20 19 18   9 8 7 6 5 4 3 2 1
First printing

Book design and composition: Alcorn Publication Design

To the officers and noncommissioned officers who live and breathe the profession every day—in peacetime and in war.
And to Rebecca and Jennifer—the keepers of the flame and the foundation of our lives. Thank you for your enduring patience, love, and support.

CONTENTS

FOREWORD

Just short of a decade ago, the US Army began a journey to rediscover its professional roots during war. After years involved in the daily grind of two wars, there was a recognition that, like in past wars, our institutions and our people became singularly focused on the daily operations that combat demands. But this external focus came at a cost: the sustainment and maintenance of what makes modern militaries truly unique—their profession.

The Army's introspection was not the first time it had conducted such an assessment. Following the Korean and Vietnam Wars, in particular, our military took a long, hard look at itself, measuring against both unspoken and explicit standards of professionalism. Such studies, including works ultimately published by Samuel Huntington and Morris Janowitz, as well as reports commissioned by Gen. William Westmoreland and others, established the foundation for the modern military as a profession.

Building on that foundation, this book, compiled by two serving military officers, ably uses these seminal texts on the profession to assess the applicability of the ideas on leadership, ethics, and the military profession put forth a half century ago. How these ideas relate to today's armed forces, how the character of war has changed, what we expect of our combat leaders, and how we prepare them for the hazy ethical situations into which they will be thrust is worth considering.

One of the key elements defining a profession is the way it educates its members, both through structured education and through self-development. This book provides significant material to think through the profession of arms in the twenty-first century, and therefore would be significantly useful for faculty in both professional military education institutions and in civilian institutions focused on educating our nation's future leaders. The concepts of professionalism and the ethical foundation on which today's military leaders must stand are articulated here in a voice of contemporary experience, which resonates in new ways.

As we continue into this century, our international environment will be one typified by transitions between war and peace. Our men and women—our military professionals—will need to be even more knowledgeable about their role in society, their function in conflict, and their responsibility to the state and the citizenry they serve. Continuing to assess how we conduct ourselves as servants of our nation, and where individual leaders fit into its ranks, is a critical task in the maintenance of our profession of arms. The more members of our military professions engage, understand, and question the foundations of their own profession, as the authors in this book have done, the better prepared our men and women will be for the future. We owe it to ourselves, in the profession of arms, and to our nation, to ensure we are educating and developing leaders of consequence that use their time on this earth to make it matter. Make every day matter.

Martin E. Dempsey
General, U.S. Army, Retired
18th Chairman of the Joint Chiefs of Staff

ACKNOWLEDGMENTS

We would like to thank many who helped us along the long road to publication. First, we thank Richard Ganske, Eric Murphy, Mikhail Grinberg, and the rest of The Strategy Bridge team who supported the initial idea that led to this effort, as well as allowing us the time and room to pursue it to completion. Next, huge thanks to Adam Kane at Oklahoma University Press who was an initial champion of this effort and who provided counsel over pints and across oceans for more than three years. Also, thanks to Dr. Wade Huntley of the Naval Postgraduate School who patiently listened to Ty think aloud and who offered gentle guidance and helped bring order to a wide constellation of ideas. Of course, we must thank our contributors, each of whom provided not only unique perspectives and experiences, but a significant amount of time and patience as we worked through this project. Without them, literally, this work would not be possible. Finally, we would also like to thank our reviewers; anonymous as you were, you challenged our ideas, sharpened our work, and thickened our skins—we're sorry we could not come up with a better title.

Nathan Finney and Tyrell Mayfield
Honolulu, Hawai'i, and Carlisle, Pennsylvania

REDEFINING THE MODERN MILITARY

Assessing the Modern Military Profession

Nathan K. Finney and Tyrell O. Mayfield

More than fifty years have passed since the publication of seminal texts that fundamentally changed the conversation on professional Western militaries. Samuel P. Huntington's *The Soldier and the State* (1957), Morris Janowitz's *The Professional Soldier* (1960), and Sir John W. Hackett's *Profession of Arms* (1963) quickly became benchmark publications that framed the discussion of the military as a profession, its place in Western societies, and modes of civil–military relations.[1] These texts emerged during the brief window between the Korean and Vietnam Wars—the last two wars that America would fight with conscripted forces—a critical and opportune time for the American military. First, these writers saw on the horizon profound changes in the way America would train, organize, and equip its military. Second, the deep introspection in the military following the victories of World War II and, maybe more important, the perceived failures of the Korean War, helped shape Western militaries going forward. Finally, in the wake of the professional and ethical failures in the Vietnam War, these texts were well placed to help shape new, modern, professional militaries.

Many of the chapters in this volume pick up where Huntington left off, using his work, and that of Janowitz and Hackett, as a base on which to build their arguments. These texts are beginning to show their age as the complexity of modern military operations and the demands placed on the practitioners increase. Huntington published his text the year Sputnik was launched—much has changed. The base domains of air, sea, and land no longer encapsulate the entirety of environments or mediums in which military operations are conducted. Sputnik literally took the fight into orbit, opening an entire new domain that nations sought to monopolize for both commercial and military advantages. This technological leap into space led to what now must be seen as the inevitable networking of systems that created the first domain of conflict created by humans—cyberspace.

The early writers on military professionalism focused on the development and organization of the profession of arms. While this remains a central theme in conversation, the change in the environments in which militaries operate, their relationships with the societies they serve, and the increasing interconnectedness of the world demand that we look again at the concept of profession.

As Andrew Abbot points out, change remains the one constant in this equation. Much of what has really changed are the responsibilities for modern, professional militaries: a decrease in domestic policing functions, increased global interconnectedness (soft power), and the leveraging of global systems by non-state actors.[2] Similarly, Stanley Hoffman tells us that when the major actors in the security situation change, when their capabilities change, or when their intentions change, we must reconsider our own posture and purpose.[3] The end of the Cold War, the collapse of the Soviet Union, the rise of non-state actors, the proliferation of weapons, and the use of global communications and transportation systems by non-state actors to challenge the status quo of nation-states suggest that the time has come to reevaluate the military profession.

Patterns of Professional Introspection

Professional introspection by the military tends to follow a recognizable pattern. In times of war, the military and national security professionals justifiably focus on the fight at hand, employing the professionals developed between large conflicts. Once those conflicts are completed or brought to a manageable level of stability, the military goes through a process of assessing its previous performance—both organizational and individual—followed by reorganization to address identified shortfalls and build on successes. Depending on the conflict, its intensity, duration, and effects on society, the military's assessment may be cursory, meaningful, or penetrating.

Similar, if less robust, assessments of the military profession occurred following conflicts in the Balkans and in Operation Desert Storm. These operations, largely quick and bloodless, created a sense of vindication following the Vietnam War and the subsequent reforms that the military had adopted. Because these successful conflicts heightened the standing of the military within American society, citizens and decision-makers in the United States paid little attention to professional introspection. These so-called quick-win conflicts, coupled with the end of the Cold War, led the United States into a period of drawdowns in the size of all branches of the military. With fewer personnel to manage and proportionally larger budgets per service member, professionalism became in some ways easier to ascribe as an attribute of the military. This smaller, more technical, increasingly professional force was the military that the United States went to war with in 2001.

Today, rhetoric inside and outside the military often describes the US military as the most professional and combat-experienced force the world has ever seen. This oft-lauded force may not see introspection as required at this point, though strategic failures in our most recent conflicts suggest this self-congratulatory tone rings hollow. Inconclusive results following nearly two decades of conflict in Iraq and Afghanistan indicate it would be naïve—perhaps even dangerous—to believe that a fresh round of professional evaluation is not forthcoming. Whether the military addresses these issues first, or if civilian leaders ask the questions, remains to be seen.

On the other hand, despite continued support by the American people, the effects of the longest series of wars in modern Western history has created ample material for a professional assessment of the relationship between the American military, the state it protects, and the society it serves. The Army's Profession of Arms campaign, examined in the chapter by Casey Landru in this volume, could have been the beginning of the military describing its norms and standards to its citizens, but there is still a need for a deep dive into what the military profession means in the twenty-first century. This will require the military to unflinchingly reflect on its own performance across the past two decades and ask serious, tough questions of itself, or cede the ground for others to ask.

This book serves a unique function in that it begins this challenging task of self-assessment for the military profession going into the twenty-first century. Crafted by military officers with recent experience in modern wars, academics who have trained and educated this generation of combatants, and lawyers and civilians who serve side by side with the defense enterprise at all levels, this volume seeks to begin the process of reevaluation for the twenty-first century.

The Military Profession

The assessment in the previous discussion must begin with a definition of what a profession is, and how the military fits within that definition. It must also address how the military views itself, and how it is viewed by those it serves. Each chapter in this volume addresses an aspect of the military profession and the professionals within it. Most arguments, and the definitions that support them, revolve around those postulated by Huntington, Janowitz, and Hackett, but chapter authors were not bound by them. While these three foundational authors remain the bedrock on which modern discussions about the military profession are built, this volume delves into the military profession in the twenty-first century and compares today's reality with the ideas of prominent thinkers from the mid-twentieth century, illuminating the trajectory the military profession has traveled so that we can better anticipate the path it must follow in the future.

This volume employs a multidisciplinary approach, drawing on the disparate backgrounds of the authors. Each author brings to the discussion a unique perspective on the military profession; the chapters address the professional issues facing all levels of the institution. Yet, despite the diversity of opinion, readers will find that there is a convergence of views among the authors about certain aspects of today's military profession, including the areas of ethics, mentorship, and education.

However, readers will also see that just as Huntington, Janowitz, and Hackett disagreed at points, the extent, form, and manner of professionalism found in the military is not universally agreed on by our authors. Readers will find the assessments on the military profession range from the military doctrinal view, to a belief that professionals are defined in part by knowing when to diverge from rules and regulations, to the increasing importance of both ethics and education as the cornerstone and backstop of a professional force.

Professional Ethics

The first and arguably most important aspect of a military profession is its sense of a professional ethic. It is this ethical core that provides direction in the absence of orders or clear guidance. Modern militaries that represent liberal democracies are unique in that they draw on volunteers from across the citizenry, and therefore represent a part of the whole. The society's collective ethical standards, however, are subordinated by military ethics in the training and development that military members undergo.

When ethics prevail in the face of moral challenges, we see individual professionals held up as the standard. When military members are found ethically wanting, the professionalism of entire institutions, and the systems that sustain them, is questioned. As discussed by Rebecca Johnson and Pauline Shanks-Kaurin in Part I, ethics seem to serve as both the first line of defense in maintaining order and the last line of defense in preserving honor. Ethics also prove difficult to teach, because instilling an idea in someone that they must subsume their own identity into something larger and more important than themselves is a task to which not all are equal.

Professional Education and Mentorship

Even with an understanding of the elements of a profession and the ethical constraints in play, a military force cannot be professionalized without ensuring that its values and norms are inculcated into each service member. In today's modern force, the primary methods of ensuring professionalization are mentoring and education. While education is an attribute that mid-twentieth-century writers focused on extensively, the emergence of mentorship as a professional responsibility is new. The importance of mentorship in the development of individuals is easy to see, yet the process for formalizing successful, sustainable mentorship programs within professional military forces continues to be elusive. Part II explores the mechanisms used to educate and mentor the military professional.

Professionalization begins with education as a requirement for accession (whether through basic training or a university education) and continues through various levels of staff schools, as Simon Anglim discusses in his chapter. Formal education is only one aspect of this process, however. Throughout a career, professionalization is reinforced with mentorship relationships, through both interaction and example. Ray Kimball dives into this aspect of the profession in his chapter.

The US military is primed for a deep examination of its role as a profession. History clearly indicates what is coming. World War I saw a review of mobilization and fighting formation performance, resulting in new combat formations, the integration of air power and armor into combined arms maneuver, and the resultant requirements on its professionals to implement each of these on the battlefield. The professional result was less based on organization and more based on mentorship, as could be seen by Fox Conner's impact on those that would lead change into, during, and following World War II. Following that second conflict in Europe, reviews of the military profession like S. L. A. Marshall's *Men Against Fire* led to significant changes in the understanding of soldiers on the battlefield and significant changes in how the military equipped itself and trained for war.[4]

The near-disaster of Korea led to the greatest period of professional introspection, as is detailed above. Finally, the President's Commission on an
All-Volunteer Force (the Gates Commission), the Astarita Report, and
the review of the profession by William Westmoreland following the
Vietnam War resulted in the end of conscription and set the course for an
all-volunteer military. Other Western militaries similarly struggled with
professionalism in an increasingly complex military, yet more civilianized,
defense context that resulted in forces that are less conscription based.

In the turmoil of America's longest series of wars, fought almost
exclusively as part of a larger, Western coalition, the issue of the military
profession is once again ripe for discussion. The time has come for the
military to grapple with the technological advancements and challenges
of the asymmetric nature of war that has dominated the past two decades.
Professional militaries owe it to their practitioners, their governments,
and the citizens they serve to shape their force for the next war. This volume seeks to begin that conversation in hopes our military will not fight
the last war against our next adversary.

Western, professional militaries remain works in progress, and the
leaders that are shaping them today have themselves been shaped by a
conflict no less than the near-disaster of Korea or no less controversial
than Vietnam. Just as the leaders coming out of that conflict, from junior
to senior ranks, increased the professionalism and capability of our military, so will our leaders of today shape our future force.

Notes

1. Samuel Huntington, *The Soldier and the State: The Theory and Politics of Civil–Military Relations* (Cambridge, MA: Harvard University Press, 1957); Morris Janowitz, *The Professional Soldier: A Social and Political Portrait* (New York: Free Press, 1960); General Sir John Hackett, *The Profession of Arms* (London: Times Publishing, 1963).
2. Andrew Abbott, "The Army and the Theory of Professions," in *The Future of the Army Profession*, ed. Don Snider and Lloyd Matthews (New York: McGraw Hill, 2005), 5.
3. As quoted in James G. Stavridis, Ervin J. Rokke, and Terry C. Pierce, "Crafting and Managing Effects: The Evolution of the Profession of Arms," *Joint Force Quarterly* 81 (2nd qtr., 2016): 5.
4. S. L. A. Marshall, *Men Against Fire: The Problem of Battle Command* (New York: William Morrow, 1947).

PART I

CHAPTER 1

Questioning Military Professionalism

Pauline Shanks-Kaurin

Introduction

In what ways is the military a profession? If the military is a profession, discussions about ethics, obligations, and responsibilities of members of that profession will be rooted in that understanding of profession. If the military is not a profession, however, then military ethics will be rooted in other sources of values. In short, is the military profession the source of ethical understanding and values for the military?

First, I examine the nature and content of military professionalism in the North American context. Second, I turn to different understandings of military professionalism, asking whether it is a matter of descriptive fact or an ideal to aspire to and work toward. Third, it is necessary to examine military professionalism considering the prominence of asymmetric conflicts and military missions other than conventional combat. Finally, I will conclude with future directions and issues that need attention for professionalism to work, especially in the context of asymmetric, nonconventional, and non-kinetic warfare. I argue that we should understand claims about military professionalism as aspirational, and that disagreements about the topic are essential demonstrations of and affirmations of military professionalism; they show the profession struggling to define its boundaries, identity, and role in a time of change, exactly what a profession does when faced with new challenges.

The Nature and Context of Military Professionalism

Why Professionals?

To begin, why would we think about the military as a profession and what might that mean? This question is not asking whether members of the military can display professionalism, such as doing a job well and in accordance with certain basic standards. When I refer to a profession, I have something quite specific in mind: (1) a body of expert knowledge on which basis (2) the public accords certain privileges in exchange for (3) an understanding that the members of the profession will self-regulate and (4) operate for the common or public good. Historically, medicine, law, and the clergy were the main professions. Therefore, to say the military is a profession is to say that it commands an expert body of knowledge, to which people are admitted and regulated by the profession (and not primarily by outside authorities) and given special privileges and trust of the public with the idea that they will serve the public good.

Professional Codes

Another point worth considering is that professions also have their own distinctive codes of ethical conduct generated from the nature and identity of the profession. It is not happenstance that medical professionals "do no harm" as the ethical principle, because that comes from the very identity of their profession as healers. To talk about the military as a profession is to say that the ethical values (and not simply the laws and procedures to which military members are subject) are generated from the identity and nature of the profession. They are not merely contingent, but also evolve organically from the nature of that profession; loyalty and courage are not virtues or traits that might be replaced with any others. These traits are essential to being a member of the military; one cannot be a good member of the military and fulfill one's role without them. As Sir John Winthrop Hackett observes, "What a bad man cannot be is a good sailor, soldier or airman. Military institutions thus form a repository of moral resource that should always be a source of strength within the state."[1]

The implication here is that because they are rooted in the basic tasks, function, and self-regulated understanding of the community of professionals, these ethical values do not change as technology changes or as the conditions in which the profession practices change. This provides a certain kind of rootedness and consistency that we can observe across time, culture, and context. To be a medical professional means to heal; to be a member of the clergy means to bring the presence of the divine and administer the community of faith in ways that we can recognize as having a great deal of consistency. Given this, we need to look at what it might mean to be a military professional in a similar way: Is there a similar sense of rootedness and identity that provides the foundation for military professionals?

Challenging Classical Views

The classical view articulated by Samuel Huntington and expanded on by Morris Janowitz identifies the officer corps as the locus for military professionalism based on intellectual skills—a blend of theory and practice—and professional responsibility: "The modern officer corps is a professional body and the modern military man a professional man." In contrast, this view presents enlisted personnel as technicians, members of a vocation rather than a profession. Lacking the intellectual skills and responsibility of the officer, "they are specialists in the application of violence, not the management of violence."[2] At some level, what is being referenced here is the greater level of education and training for officers; Janowitz notes the importance of the skill of intellectual criticism, insisting that the soldier is an intellectual officer as opposed to the military intellectual. The officer is a soldier first.[3]

We might wonder if this is still true, considering the case of noncommissioned officers (NCOs) and the greater access to higher education in Western society. Is there a difference between education and training that is significant enough to translate into professionalism for one group and not for the other? Hackett raised this question in the 1960s, problematizing the relationship between officer and NCO, even as he affirmed this distinction. "There is much to be said for a reexamination of the pattern of distribution of responsibilities between officers and NCOs."[4] He suggested that some of the tasks that junior officers currently were occupied with could be shifted to NCOs, on the grounds that some of these tasks did not make use of their intellectual capacities and skills.

What then is the specific content of military professionalism? Huntington suggests that the supreme military virtue is obedience, but notes obedience might conflict with morality and professionalism.[5] More-recent accounts by Sam Sarkesian and Thomas Gannon note that the basic elements of military professionalism are integrity, loyalty, commitment, trust, honor, and service; Sarkesian and Gannon appeal to Janowitz's view that military honor is the crucial part of professional military ethics.[6] We can see both of these perspectives reflected in the Core Values movements in the military; regardless of the different incarnations, these movements reflect a list of moral values that include many of the elements listed above as constitutive of military ethics and professionalism.

Sarkesian and Gannon also note that individual conscience and individuality are basic elements in professionalism, which can cause any professional stress on integrity and institutional mission/goals to be in tension with any kind of dissent or criticism, with the latter being viewed as out of bounds or disloyal.[7] Honesty and obedience are seen as primary here, which is reflected in the consternation caused by the release of the recent report on lying in the military that demonstrated the tensions between these two virtues, as well as the tension between individual judgment/ discernment and institutional mission/goals such as unit cohesion.[8]

In addition to the above elements of military professionalism, we should include the following elements of the Uniform Code of Military Justice (UCMJ); the Laws of Warfare (including the Hague and Geneva Conventions); and principles of the Just War Tradition and the moral principles that are the foundation for them, like minimizing unnecessary suffering and the aim of war being the restoration of the just peace. In the current environment, these elements have become incorporated to some degree; some see them as congruent with the warrior ethos that frames the military identity. The idea of the warrior ethos reflected in the Core Values, the Soldier's Creed, and various other documents and living practices defines the function of the military, particularly informing military-civilian relations and considerations about the resort to and proper uses of force.[9] At its core, the military sees itself as oriented to the defense of the nation using violence in combat as necessary to that end.

As early as the 1960s, however, Janowitz was raising the issue of the degree to which the warrior ethos and combat model of the military were in fact still applicable, questioning whether the military was headed to more of a constabulary model and what that would mean for the future of the profession.[10] His account anticipates the discussion that we find later in this chapter from Martin Cook's treatment of the future of the profession relative to nonconventional wars. Hackett had also noted the changing aspects of warfare: "Limited wars for political ends are far more likely to produce moral strains . . . than the great wars of the past."[11] Sarkesian and Gannon noted a similar issue in the 1970s, writing that the ethical questions in the profession were linked to the purpose of the military force and to what degree war was a political matter, especially for the officer corps.[12]

From the above discussion, we can see that there is a sense of professional identity rooted in a common mission and shared self-conception undertaken at the permission of society for the common good. There is a clear moral code and framework, which despite the civilian control of the military and legal constraints are largely self-regulating. The military is self-policing in the sense of who it admits to its ranks and in the sense of what constraints they are subject once they are members. This sense of professional identity is rooted in the warrior ethos, military tradition, and history, as well as the purpose of the military in relation to the democratic society it serves. On the surface, it seems that the military does fit the classical model of a profession.

Aspirations of Professional Status

This all seems straightforward, so why might one think that the military is in fact not a profession? While the officer corps and possibly NCOs fit this description, what about the lowest level of military members? Aren't they just doing a job that the military trained them and pays them for? Another issue emerges, not so much in terms of rank or education, but more in terms of experience and age: Is there any meaningful sense in which we could consider eighteen- to twenty-two-year-olds to be professionals, whether enlisted or officers freshly commissioned? Traditionally, professions like medicine, law, and the clergy involve education, but also long training/apprenticeship processes to acquire and practice skills, as well as to develop intellectual capacities and knowledge.

Both points raise a distinction critical to the discussion: this issue is not a matter of whether it describes some empirical reality of military service in the twenty-first century. If this is the question, it is a brief discussion and the answer is no, the military is not a profession. However, I take the question to be a more prescriptive or aspirational claim. We ought to think of the military profession in this way. Huntington, Janowitz, Hackett, and the more recent work by Don Snider all argue that the military is actually a profession (although Snider recently worries it will not continue to be); these authors try to establish the definition and boundaries of that profession.[13] I am arguing for an aspirational understanding of military professionalism, which means that the descriptive claims will be true to varying degrees. It further means that since it is a profession by aspiration, what this looks like need not be static and stable (although there will be a recognizable core) and will be continually under development and negotiation within the community of practice.

If we think about a military profession as an aspiration or goal toward which to work, we can acknowledge two things. First, the development of the military as a profession, as with other professions, is a work in progress. It is a process and not a destination that we say that we have arrived at when x, y, and z conditions are obtained. Rather, the military, like the other professions discussed, is always in the process of becoming a profession, just as individuals are always in the process of becoming professionals. To push the individual analogy further, Professional Military Education, one kind of professional development, looks different depending on the stage of career, whether one is an officer/NCO or enlisted, and on the nature of one's specialty within the military.

Given this aspirational idea of the profession, the community must continually reflect on its profession; discuss the identity, function, and the ethical standards that go with that identity; and inculcate new members into the profession. In this process, there must be room for critical questioning and reassessing of this identity and the ethical values. The degree to which the members can and do engage in discourse about the nature of the military identity and in what ways they are professionals signals the kind of aspirational approach to the profession. For example, the protests on social media several years ago objecting to possible US military intervention in Syria and debates about the integrations of female, and lesbian, gay, bisexual, and transgender (LGBT) members into the military could all be viewed as another form of this kind of discussion. Second, it means that the ethical values of the military are rooted and grounded in a way that is fundamentally different from the ethical values of other vocations or jobs, like business, fashion, or child care. If the military is a profession, then the ethical values of the military must be grounded in the nature and identity of the military as a profession and will therefore be generated internally. This is a theme that appears in popular culture, such as in the film *A Few Good Men*, where one of the characters notes that as Marines, they were expected to protect the weak, which they had failed to do.[14] The horrors of the events at My Lai during the Vietnam War are rooted in the description of the killings as "a Nazi kinda thing"—that is, something that seemed at odds with the internal values of the American military.[15]

Development from Within

An aspirational approach will see the generation of these values and development in members of the profession as a process internal to the profession, and not one coming from outside. For example, loyalty has a particular meaning in the military profession, some elements of which are stable (loyalty to your fellow soldiers, loyalty to the Constitution, and loyalty to one's oath), some elements of which may alter over time and even come into conflict with one another (as in the case of whistleblowing on a fellow soldier who has violated some rule or principle). The meaning of these different ideas of loyalty can be understood only internal to the profession, and the conflicts or tensions they produce must be resolved internally as well.

Similarly, courage will be understood in direct relation to the warrior ethos and the role of the military in the defense of the nation; notions of moral courage are often viewed as secondary, though still important. Integrity and/or honesty likewise are generated as values by the need for trust, both within the military and with the larger society; there is a direct correlation between perceptions of integrity, trust, and combat effectiveness.[16] As the role of the military changes, how one understands these basic virtues will change as well. We see this reality in discussions about the role of soft power in the military and by calls to reexamine whether the warrior ethos is still sufficient and appropriate in the kinds of conflicts the military now faces.[17]

Professionals: All, Some, or None?

This returns us to the question of exactly whom we ought to consider a professional in the military. Numerous authors have suggested that, at a minimum, officers (especially the middle and upper ranks) and NCOs are professionals, whereas lower enlisted and possibility junior officers are not, especially if we consider the issue of experience. To complicate things further, I would highlight the idea of the strategic corporal.[18] This is the idea that because of technology and the asymmetric, rapidly fluid, and decentralized nature of modern conflict, combat turns out to be in practice much less hierarchical than in conventional wars; the strategic corporal makes crucial tactical decisions with important ethical implications and does not simply execute orders given by others (e.g., officers). If this idea is to gain traction, it requires important elements of professionalism—adherence to a moral code, a degree of independent judgment and discretion, trust, and orientation toward a common good—that the classical accounts locate solely with the officer corps.

Thinking of professionalism as aspirational is an easier challenge to accommodate. We might think about professionalism as a sliding scale, a matter of degrees or as a developmental model, rather than an all-or-nothing judgment that could be quite destructive to command climate, trust, and unit cohesion. On this account, we have rigorous expectations of professionalism depending on things like rank, experience, and level of responsibility. This also opens the possibility that professionalism may look different at different stages of one's career and as one takes on or changes roles within the military, as opposed to one universal idea of professionalism that is imposed on a wide variety of people and contexts. This is not to argue that professionalism is relative; rather, we need to consider that professionalism has some core overlap, as well as pluralistic aspects.

The Future: Asymmetric Professions?

Given the above, the military is aspirationally a profession with the trust of the public, tasked with protecting the American homeland and interests by bringing war-waging expertise to bear on that function, having been given license to kill and destroy property. There are rigorous and specific requirements for admission and certification to be a member of the profession, and the military largely self-regulates with its own justice system to which its members are subject, and its own ethical code. The new challenges that the military faces, the new contexts in which it wages war, necessitate ongoing and critical discussions about the nature and identity of the profession and the ethical values that derive from the profession.

The Contemporary Military Landscape

There are a variety of issues and challenges in the contemporary military landscape, including sexual harassment and assault, women in combat roles, transgendered and homosexual members of the military, high-level leadership scandals that raise issues about a double standard for flag officers and those who are well connected, post-traumatic stress disorder (PTSD), and moral injury. Conflicts are also taking different forms with counterinsurgency and other doctrinal challenges to the nature of kinetic warfare, but a new focus on non-kinetic forms of warfare is emerging with a variety of actors, some of them non-state. Some commentators insist the military is focused too much on battles and not enough on wars; the military needs to think of itself not just as managers of violence, but more as managers of effects.[19] Many of these issues are not just new challenges but are challenges to the very core of the military identity itself: the warrior ethos. To think through what is necessary to address these changes, I turn to Martin Cook's account because he directly addresses both military professionalism and many of the challenges to it under discussion in this piece.

In considering the components of professionalism, Cook notes that there are elements of the nature of the military that are timeless, while other elements are connected to certain contingent historical or political conditions. In terms of the more static conditions, he argues that there are two core elements of professionalism: (1) obedience and subordination of soldiers to legitimate civilian political authority, and (2) the role of the officer corps in rendering military advice to civilian authorities. In addition, Cook argues that intellectual independence and some critical capacity is an essential part of military professionalism; society gives the right to make independent judgments in a particular area of expertise and to self-regulate within that domain.[20]

Cook does not necessarily locate the warrior ethos as a part of the military profession's timeless, unchanging aspects. He also notes that the identity of professional military members is formed by stories of great sacrifice and ancestors that demonstrate certain traits and virtues contemporary military professionals are to take inspiration from and emulate.[21] If part of professional military education involves reflecting stories of sacrifice, heroism, and courage, those stories will to some degree be rooted in the historical circumstances in which they occurred. For example, Hugh Thompson's story at My Lai is heroic, but it is also rooted in the Vietnam War context in important ways.[22]

Cook indicates that professionalism can be maintained in a stable environment, but what happens when this is not the case? He notes the military profession is in flux because stability is more lacking now than it once was. He points out that the tasks of professionals increasingly depart from those professionals' collective self-understanding, in this case of the warrior ethos, asking them to take up missions that do not fit neatly into that ethos. He observes, "Precisely because the reasons for these deployments do not clearly link up to the moral core of professional self-understanding —that is, defense of the vital interests and survival of the American people and state—many officers worry that they are eroding their core warfighting competencies and wonder if this is 'what they signed up for.'"[23]

Cook wonders if this understanding of professional identity is in fact timeless or if it is instead rooted in certain historical contingencies, like the Cold War, and whether what needs to happen is professional reflection about identity and serious thought about how the profession might need to change to adapt to the new circumstances, and how best to develop capacities to engage in these new missions. Is the central task of the military changing and what does this mean for professionalism?[24] Is it unprofessional for military members to claim that this is not what they signed up for, or are these objections and questions precisely the mark of the professional?

In the end, he argues that it is the job, especially of the officer corps, to raise exactly these kinds of questions and to come to grips with the new challenges and kinds of missions. For him, asking these questions and engaging in critical inquiry is part of the task of the professional. Critical inquiry is a mark of professionalism and will be instrumental in reshaping some aspects of the military while maintaining certain core professional tasks and elements. Cook argues that questioning military professionalism is, in fact, the professional thing to do.

Questioning the Future of Professionalism

There are three important questions for future exploration and discussion that I would add to Cook's analysis. These questions all point to the core need for what I term professional judgment and discretion, which is essentially the kind of questioning, critical thinking, reflection, and analysis that I have highlighted in this discussion of military professionalism.[25] Traditional accounts have thought of these as the exclusive domain of the officer corps; this assessment needs to be broadened in the ways indicated earlier.

First, to what degree is intellectual capacity (professional judgment and discretion, including historical understanding, critical thinking, and the ability to think and act strategically) still central to military professionalism and is it still primarily the domain of the officer corps and/or NCOs? It seems that for all members of the military, critical thinking, some level of appreciation for strategy, the Just War Tradition, ethics, and cultural literacy are necessary, given the strategic corporal phenomenon. Traditionally, the officer corps had college education or the equivalent, but as more members of society attend college (including community college and different sorts of vocational training), more enlisted personnel come into the service with some college-level education. I think these new facts erode the line traditionally drawn between officer and enlisted on the grounds of differing intellectual capacities, without even getting into the issue of how experience develops intellectual capacity.

Second, what is the impact of technology on military professionalism? Officers and to some degree NCOs are managers of violence, and enlisted personnel technicians are the appliers of violence, but I have already highlighted the idea that the military is involved in the management of effects. It seems likely that changes in military technology have begun to and will continue to blur this distinction, and this blurring will bring additional complications. An example of this blurring would be unmanned aerial vehicle or drone pilots. Are they just executing orders given to hit a specific target, or are they part of a larger feedback loop including judge advocate generals, others in the chain of command, and personnel on the ground who all collaborate or have input in whether, when, and how to strike a given target? We might also wonder if cyber-war or other non-kinetic aspects of conflict also create some the same confusion, and whether some personnel in the military are managers and technicians of violence, as well as managers of effects. If this is the case, it complicates the argument that only officers and senior NCOs are professionals and speaks to the need for many more military personnel to understand and be trained in the intersection of tactics and strategy. Given the strategic corporal argument and the so-called CNN effect, virtually any action taken in the field of conflict can have quite wide-ranging impacts.[26]

Third, how does the rise of counterinsurgency, asymmetric war, and other forms of unconventional conflict (which tend to be more decentralized and less hierarchical) change, or the professional conception in the military, especially in terms of decision-making processes and ethical reflection? We need to reconsider whether the military is still hierarchical in a sense that supports the officer-centric model of professionalism. In my view, the most salient question becomes, who has the responsibility? The literature of moral agency and its relation to the Just War Tradition, including discussions on moral injury, makes it clear that far down the chain of command, people feel and have responsibility in profound ways.[27] If current conflicts are more like the Vietnam War in the level of decentralization that obtains, then we could look to that experience to show how the idea that officers were the professionals and that the enlisted personnel were not professional became highly problematic and in fact led to a crisis of identity that resulted in the current all-volunteer force and a renewed focus on professionalism.[28] If we shift and broaden our ideas about who is a professional, then I think that has implications for what level of ethical reflection and rigor we expect from members of the military and how we go about training for these expectations.

Conclusion

These three questions give some idea about the kinds of things that professionals in the military ought to consider going forward and highlight several concerns. First, it is critical to see professionalism in the military as an aspiration—a continuous process to be undergone to varying degrees by all members, not as a description of a static, universal reality as most conventional accounts claim. Second, this involves taking seriously the problem of decentralization of decision-making within conflict along the lines of the strategic corporal model. Third, experience needs to be added as a more central aspect or requirement for professionalism, expanding out from intellectual capacities, education, and responsibility that traditionally limited military professionalism primarily to the officer corps. Finally, I affirm Cook's argument that critique, some forms of dissent, and individual judgment are, in fact, marks of the profession. The discourse on professionalism needs to come to terms with the ways institutional pressures and cultures can undermine these marks of professionalism. The report about lying in the military should be seen in many ways as the canary in the coal mine, alerting us to the level of attention that conversations about professionalism require in the current, complex, and changing environment.[29]

Notes

1. Sir John Winthrop Hackett, "The Military in the Service of the State," in *War, Morality and the Military Profession*, ed. Malham M. Wakin (Boulder, CO: Westview Press, 1979), 124.
2. Samuel P. Huntington, "Officership as a Profession," in Wakin, *War, Morality and the Military Profession*, 11 (first quote), 22 (second quote).
3. Morris Janowitz, "The Future of the Military Profession," in Wakin, *War, Morality and the Military Profession*, 65.
4. Sir John Winthrop Hackett, "Today and Tomorrow," in Wakin, *War, Morality and the Military Profession*, 97.
5. Samuel P. Huntington, "The Military Mind: Conservative Realism of the Professional Military Ethic," in Wakin, *War, Morality and the Military Profession*, 40.
6. Sam C. Sarkesian and Thomas M. Gannon, "Professionalism: Problems and Challenges," in Wakin, *War, Morality and the Military Profession*, 135.
7. Sarkesian and Gannon, "Professionalism," 137.
8. Leonard Wong and Stephen J. Gerras, *Lying to Ourselves: Dishonesty in the Army Profession* (Carlisle, PA: Strategic Studies Institute, 2015).
9. For a general overview of these issues see Michael Walzer's *Just and Unjust Wars: A Moral Argument with Historical Illustrations* (New York: Basic Books, 1977), esp. chaps. 3 and 4.
10. Janowitz, "The Future of the Military Profession," 53.
11. Hackett, "Today and Tomorrow," 123.
12. Sarkesian and Gannon, "Professionalism," 130.

13. Don Snider, "Professionalism and the Volunteer Military: Will Army 2025 Be a Military Profession?," *Parameters* 45, no. 4 (Winter 2015–16).
14. *A Few Good Men*, dir. Rob Reiner (Culver City, CA: Columbia, 1992).
15. Michael Bilton and Kevin Sim, *Four Hours at My Lai* (New York: Penguin Group, 1992), 1–24.
16. Pauline M. Kaurin, "Identity, Loyalty and Combat Effectiveness: A Cautionary Tale," International Society for Military Ethics (formerly Joint Services Conference on Professional Ethics, or JSCOPE), 2006, http://isme.tamu.edu/JSCOPE06/Kaurin06.html.
17. Pauline M. Kaurin, *The Warrior, Military Ethics and Contemporary Warfare: Achilles Goes Asymmetrical* (London: Ashgate Press, 2015), 83–96.
18. Lynda Liddy, "The Strategic Corporal: Some Requirements in Training and Education," *Australian Army Journal* 2, no. 2 (Autumn 2004): 139.
19. Stavridis, Rokke, and Pierce, "Crafting and Managing Effects," 4–9.
20. Martin Cook, *A Moral Warrior: Ethics and Service in the US Military* (Albany: State University of New York Press, 2010), 55, 62–63.
21. Cook, *A Moral Warrior*, 69.
22. Trent Angers, *The Forgotten Hero of My Lai: The Hugh Thompson Story* (Mount Pleasant, SC: Arcadian, 2014).
23. Cook, *A Moral Warrior*, 75.
24. Cook, 76–77.
25. Pauline M. Kaurin, "The Missing Link in Military Ethics Education" [blog], 28 July 2016, https://queenofthinair.wordpress.com/2016/07/28/the-missing-link-in-military-ethics-education/.
26. Piers Robinson, "Media as a Driving Force in International Politics: The CNN Effect and Related Debates," E-International Relations (17 September 2013), http://www.e-ir.info/2013/09/17/media-as-a-driving-force-in-international-politics-the-cnn-effect-and-related-debates/.
27. Jeff McMahan, *Killing in War* (New York: Oxford University Press, 2011). See esp. his revisionist critiques of the moral equality of combatants.
28. Richard Gabriel and Paul Savage, *Crisis in Command: Mismanagement in the Army* (New York: Hill & Wang, 1979).
29. Wong and Gerras, *Lying to Ourselves*.

CHAPTER 2

The Military Profession
Law, Ethics, and the Profession of Arms

Jo Brick

The function of the profession of arms is the ordered application of force in the resolution of a social problem.

General Sir John Hackett

Introduction

The issue of whether military forces deserve the mantle of the term "professional" can be determined when juxtaposed against other widely accepted professions such as law or medicine. A comparison of the fundamental characteristics of the legal profession and the armed forces reveals common characteristics that distinguish professions from other occupations. The inherent characteristics of a profession are the following:

- The depth of knowledge in a field gained through enduring dedication to learning and experience.
- The monopoly over a specific area of expertise or skill, which makes members distinct from the wider public who are not members of the profession (or laypersons).
- This depth of knowledge creates a knowledge or information deficit (or knowledge gap) between the members of the profession and laypersons.
- This knowledge gap creates a duty in the professional to act in the interests of their client and society as a whole, rather than in self-interest.
- This duty is monitored through self-regulation against a predetermined framework for accountability—that is, a professional code that applies to the entirety of the profession.[1]

The military profession is entrusted with the use of force to resolve social problems, most often in the pursuit the national interests. However, the nature of the relationship between the military and the state is inherently linked to the very existence and security of the state. This linkage elevates the nature of the relationship between the military and the state to a special status, akin to what is commonly referred to in legal jurisprudence as a fiduciary relationship. The issue of whether the relationship between the military and the state is a fiduciary one as a matter of law is not discussed in this chapter, but the fiduciary law framework provides a useful lens to view the importance of this relationship.

Trust forms the foundation of all fiduciary relationships and is preserved through a system of accountability that applies to all members of a profession. This system of accountability ensures that members of the profession carry out their fiduciary duties. The system of accountability consists of legally codified standards of behavior that are accompanied by ethical standards. This code provides practical guidance to members of the profession as they deal with the complex social problems for which they are responsible. Legal and ethical standards act as a balance against the advantage that members of a profession have over laypersons and ensure that they act in accordance with their fiduciary obligations and not to further their self-interest.

Professionals will sometimes face situations where the law and ethics are opposed. In these complex circumstances, the professional is expected to harness his deep knowledge and experience to make a decision. Mike Denny explores this point in more detail in chapter 4, where he discusses the need for professionals to understand their field to enable them to determine when to break the rules. This is what it means to be professional. However, the complexity of contemporary operations and the pressures on individual soldiers, sailors, and airmen at the tactical level of military operations warrant greater emphasis on engendering moral fitness in military professionals so that they are better able to deal with the legal and ethical dilemmas they are likely to confront.

Military "Professional"?

General Sir John Hackett's seminal work, *The Profession of Arms*, provides an account of the development of professionalism in military forces. The origins of military professionalism are generally founded on the development of standing armies in the service of nation-states. The conclusion of the Thirty Years' War and the Treaty of Westphalia in 1648 led to a period of relative peace between great powers in Europe. Hackett finds that by the

nineteenth century true professionalism had emerged in the armed services, with a particular focus on developments in Germany. The reforms
in the German army that led to the increased professionalism of officers
included movement away from service based solely on aristocratic lineage, to an officer class that had to demonstrate ability by passing a series
of examinations as a precondition to entry into military institutions. The
establishment of the Kriegsakademie in Berlin also institutionalized
education as a key foundation of professionalism, because it enabled the
acquisition of knowledge in the art of war and facilitated the continuing
education of officers in warfare.[2] These reforms were replicated in other
countries, such as France and the United States, to varying degrees and
over different timeframes. Samuel Huntington provides a perspective
on the development of professionalism in the United States in *The Soldier and the State*.[3] The reforms of military forces that commenced in
Europe in the nineteenth century allowed military forces to obtain a
fundamental characteristic of professions: deep knowledge and skill in
a specialized field.

Knowledge and specialization are what distinguish professions from
other occupations, as emphasized by Hackett, who said that professions
are occupations that have "a distinguishable corpus of specific technical
knowledge and doctrine" and "an educational pattern adapted to its own
specific needs."[4] As the Kriegsakademie example demonstrated, many
military forces that consider themselves to be professional have dedicated
training institutions that serve to indoctrinate new members into the profession and facilitate continuous education for its members. As a result,
members of the military profession are able to obtain a monopoly over
expertise or skill within the specialized field surrounding warfare and the
use of force.

The monopoly over the use of force possessed by state-based military forces means that those who are not members must rely on the military for advice, or on an application of the military's specialized skills, to
resolve matters where military force may be appropriate. In the case of
military professionals, these matters are manifested in the maintenance of
national security and the protection of national interests. The military's
monopoly over the knowledge and skills regarding the use of force creates
a position of advantage over the nation and its citizens, resulting in an
imbalance in the relationship between the military and wider society. In
liberal democracies, this imbalance creates a relationship of trust between

the military and the state, which, as discussed later in this chapter, creates a fiduciary relationship between the military and the state.

The relationship of trust between the military and the state is based on an understanding that the military will employ its monopoly over the knowledge and skills to use force only in the furtherance of the interests of the nation. It is a principal–agent relationship akin to that between a doctor and patient, or a lawyer and client. These relationships of trust are considered to have a special status because the agent offers socially important services that involve entrustment by the principal of property or power in the agent. Fiduciary law, which governs such special relationships of trust, provides a useful lens through which the civil-military relationship can be examined. Under fiduciary law, the relationship between the agent (the fiduciary) and the principal is characterized by the vulnerability of the principal in this particular relationship. This is because of the great dependence that the principal has on the fiduciary and the significant loss that the principal may suffer if the fiduciary breaches the relationship of trust. In a fiduciary relationship, "the risks [to the principal] are serious, and the harm they might cause can be significant; [the risks] are very difficult to uncover or prevent."[5]

The fiduciary relationship between the military and the state is manifested in two ways. First, this relationship is demonstrated at the strategic level where military leaders provide advice to civilian leaders regarding the use of military force as an option for resolving a particular national problem. This strategic level interaction is central to Huntington's thesis.[6] The state trusts that the military will provide advice regarding the use of force in the furtherance of the national interest. A breach of this trust relationship has grave consequences for the state, such that its legitimacy is jeopardized by the threat of a military that is not responsive to its needs or might use its expertise to undermine the state (as in a military coup).

The second manifestation of the fiduciary relationship exists at the individual level. The state trusts individual members of the military profession to use their expertise and to behave in a manner that is consistent with the interests of the state. Individual discretion is central to this level of professional decision-making. Professionals are also expected to use their specialized knowledge and skill to exercise discretion when solving the complex problems that are entrusted to them. The exercise of discretion is also the hallmark of fiduciary relationships, where the principal allows the fiduciary to exercise discretion that affects the interests of the principal.[7] Individual members of the profession are expected to exercise their personal judgment, which lies at the heart of what it means to be a professional. In the context of the military profession, individual members are trained to make decisions and to exercise their personal discretion where possible. Making decisions and exercising discretion are central to leadership and initiative, two fundamental characteristics of military organizations.[8]

The exercise of discretion by military professionals must always be focused on the interests of the principal (the state) rather than on serving personal interests. For example, Don Snider emphasizes that the discretions exercised by military professionals are moral in nature because the effects of individuals making decisions are likely to affect many people, and not just the interests of those in the fiduciary relationship.[9] A system of legislative and ethical codes is a means of ensuring that the conduct of military professionals is consistent with the interests of the state, as the principal, as well as to mitigate any collateral effects on those who are not a party to the fiduciary relationship. This system of legislative and ethical codes is a means of keeping the military profession accountable and is consistent with the legislative and ethical codes that govern professions generally.

Professionalism, Law, and Ethics

"Our profession is distinguished from others in society because of our expertise in the justified application of lethal military force and the willingness of those who serve to die for our Nation. Our profession is defined by our values, ethics, standards, code of conduct, skills and attributes. As volunteers, our sworn duty is to the Constitution. Our status as a profession is granted by those whom we are accountable to, our civilian authority, and the American people."[10] The position of advantage enjoyed by a profession due to its monopoly over a particular field of expertise is mitigated by legal and ethical obligations, and duties that bind the behavior of its members. As General Dempsey highlighted, the trust relationship between the military and the state is also underwritten by a framework of professional accountability consisting of legal and ethical codes. These codes serve two purposes: first, to situate the relationship between the military and the state, including when the military can use force; and second, to establish standards of conduct for members of the military force when conducting military operations.

The Use of Force

In liberal democracies such as the United States and Australia, the first purpose is achieved through a cultural paradigm of civil control over the military. Huntington's theory of objective control is arguably the most popular theory of civil–military relations and, at the very least, is a starting point for scholars in this field. Under Huntington's theory of objective control, which creates a strict division between political and military activities, professionalism of the military force is effectively a prerequisite for vesting that force with the trust to conduct its activities without civilian interference.[11] The subservience of the military to civil authority is also reflected in legislative frameworks that limit the role of the military in a domestic setting. In Australia, for example, the Australian Defence Force cannot operate domestically unless the government calls it out under Part IIIAAA of the Defence Act 1903. This legal mechanism is discussed in more detail elsewhere but is an example of how legislative frameworks situate the relationship between a professional military force and the state.[12]

Standards of Conduct

The second purpose establishes duties and obligations that are intended to guide how members of the profession are to behave when undertaking their duties. In the legal profession, for example, standards of conduct are contained in legislation and codes of conduct about avoiding conflicts of interest and ensuring that trust funds are managed in a particular way to maintain accountability. In the military profession, the legal and ethical frameworks assume a much different focus, as they are heavily influenced by a nation's foreign policy activities. The actions of an individual military member may result in strategic or political consequences for the state. These factors add a thick layer of complexity to members' legal and ethical considerations when they execute their duties. The military professional, as a fiduciary of the state, must therefore harness her knowledge and skill to ensure that she exercises the discretion entrusted to her in a manner consistent with legal and ethical paradigms as a guide for navigating complex strategic or political situations.

Legislative frameworks and professional standards are merely starting points for determining the ethical responsibilities of military members. Military forces in liberal democracies are governed by disciplinary codes that establish the boundaries of behavior. These codes are generally contained within legislation that covers purely disciplinary offenses (such as absent without leave) and criminal offenses (such as murder, assault, and sexual offenses). These legislative codes are intended to apply to military forces at all times, including extraterritorially when forces are deployed overseas. Some examples include the UCMJ for US forces, and the Defence Force Discipline Act 1982, which applies to the Australian Defence Force.[13] Overlaid onto these legislative frameworks are international humanitarian laws of armed conflict, which are intended to regulate the behavior of belligerents at war. For example, belligerents must not target civilians; medical personnel; or wounded, sick, or shipwrecked persons.[14] These domestic and international legal frameworks form the outer boundaries of behavior for military forces outside of, and during, military operations. However, the law discloses only part of the solution to complex problems encountered in military operations. Laws apply only when they are enforced, which is usually after the fact (i.e., after an incident has occurred). Ethical frameworks are therefore comparatively more useful than law because they provide guidance for future behavior at the point of dilemma rather than ex-post (retrospective operation). The identification of ethical responsibilities does not rest solely on professional codes of conduct because identifying these responsibilities is very much the product of individually based considerations such as personal, family, or cultural values that influence individual behavior.

Reliance on purely legal frameworks to guide behavior has its limitations. A. Edward Major, who explores the role of law and ethics in command decision-making, discusses this issue.[15] According to Major, "Moving from decision making based on wisdom, experience, and ethics to an undue reliance on the law is all too expedient and common in society at large." When grappling with the complexities of a particular operational scenario, the military professional must rely on his own judgment and not solely on legal principles. The law sometimes filters out much unethical behavior, but the law is not a comprehensive or detailed guide for behavior that addresses the details of a moral dilemma in a particular situation.[16] An inherent part of professional behavior is the exercise of discretion and judgment in complex circumstances; a professional must harness all relevant considerations, including individual values, to address those details.

Ethics

The Ethics Centre (formerly the St. James Ethics Centre), an institution focused on the study, discussion, and teaching of ethics in Sydney, Australia, states that ethics is concerned with several issues, including,

"Asking one simple question—'*what ought I to do?*'"[17] The question of what one ought to do can be answered only when taking into account a person's perspective on a particular issue. It is easy to answer an ethical question on, say, detainee handling while we are in the peaceful confines of a cafe in Canberra or Washington, DC. It is an altogether different matter if we are infantry soldiers answering the same question after a fierce battle in the dusty and oppressive heat of Kandahar Province. This is not to condone or justify any behavior that runs counter to the law or professional military codes, but rather to highlight that human emotion can cloud rational judgment when determining ethical issues.

While the law dictates behavior, in the lonely, unobserved, and isolated pockets of areas of operation throughout the world, soldiers, sailors, and airmen must make their own individual judgments about their ethical responsibilities by relying on their personal ethical framework. Professional codes of conduct are merely one consideration that coalesces with a multitude of others (such as personal morals, institutional culture, training and experience, personal biases, societal expectations, and legal obligations) to form an individual's framework for ethical decision-making. At the end of the day, each military member has personal limits that cannot be crossed. A more serious question to resolve one's ethical responsibilities is to ask, "Can I live with myself if I do this?" The Ethics Centre proposes some other questions that can be used to frame a particular ethical dilemma:

1. Would I be happy for this decision to be headlining the news tomorrow?
2. Is there a universal rule that applies here?
3. Will the proposed course of action bring about a good result?
4. What would happen if everybody did this?
5. What will this proposed action do to my character or the character of my organisation?
6. Is the proposed course of action consistent with my values and principles?[18]

Major's comments, relevant to a military context, are consistent with the Ethics Centre's approach: "Ethics, by definition, involve an internal, in-depth searching of one's value system and soul, as well as an extensive review of cultural norms, political climate, the law, and the implications of one's actions against those of the unit, those of the military, those of our country, those of our enemy, and those of world opinion."[19]

It is important to understand that legal frameworks can provide broad guidance only for individuals, and that professionals must adhere to their own codes of conduct. Professionals must have an awareness of ethical frameworks, which are more useful guides for behavior at the point of dilemma. This is highlighted in United Nations (UN) peace operations in Srebrenica and Kibeho, both of which provide useful examples regarding the exercise of professional discretion in highly sensitive and complex operational settings.

Srebrenica

During the Bosnian War in 1993 the government of the Netherlands decided to send battalions from its airmobile brigade to ostensibly protect a Muslim safe area in Srebrenica. Subsequent rotations of the battalion encountered a number of issues, including a vague mandate. In 1995 Dutchbat, a Dutch battalion under the command of the UN, was responsible for guarding the enclave of Srebrenica, a UN safe area.[20] The Dutchbat, commanded by Lieutenant Colonel Thom Karremans, was in an invidious position of having to morally protect the enclave while lacking the military capability to do so. The enclave was under threat from Bosnian Serb forces, and the UN headquarters (UNHQ) ordered Karremans to withdraw his forces. Karremans made the decision to act in accordance with his legal obligation (to comply with superior orders and policy), but the resulting ethical dilemma rendered him unable to protect those in the enclave from being rounded up and, as the world later learned, falling victim to genocide.[21] This case demonstrated that while a clear legal "answer" was available—that is, Karremans' decision to follow the UNHQ order—it was unhelpful in resolving the complex ethical dilemma that unfolded before Karremans' Dutchbat.

Rwanda

Richardson, Verweij, and Winslow discuss the dilemma facing General Tousignant in Kibeho, Rwanda. Canadian General Tousignant was the force commander of the UN Assistance Mission in Rwanda during the Kibeho massacre in April 1995. Prior to the massacre, UNHQ in New York ordered him to withdraw from Kibeho, but General Tousignant did not withdraw his Zambian battalion. Arguably, this decision reduced the number of casualties due to the presence of the Zambian battalion. He believed that he was responsible for the safety of the civilians in Kibeho, and this was the reason for his decision to leave his forces in that location.

He said, "Rationalizing a decision not to follow directions from UN Headquarters on a moral issue does not in any way remove the question of ethical dilemma and certainly does not relieve the Commander of his responsibilities towards his superiors. Not to execute a lawful command is rarely justifiable and it is clear that I defied an order from New York at Kibeho."[22] General Tousignant was not held accountable for his refusal to follow orders. His actions are an example of an ethics-based (rather than law-based) approach to exercising command discretion.

The examples of Srebrenica and Rwanda provide insight into some of the legal and ethical dilemmas that must be navigated by military professionals at the forefront of military operations. The examples are from a UN peace operations context; these examples are accompanied by their own unique challenges that are usually centered on the mandate and its subsequent impact on rules of engagement. Daniel S. Blocq examines the ethical issues that arise during UN operations, particularly in relation to the protection of civilians. He argues that the operational, legal, and political frameworks associated with UN operations do not offer any ethical support for peacekeepers.[23] The same could be said for such frameworks as they apply to other types of operations such as conventional war fighting. Arguably, it is not the role of these frameworks to provide ethical guidance.

As previously discussed, these legal and policy frameworks draw the outer boundaries for the behavior of a military force in a particular operation. The ethical background, values, and training of individual members of the force are what fill the gaps and inform the individual's exercise of discretion, including whether or not to use military force, in a particular situation. For this reason, ethical codes—rather than legal frameworks— are more useful in guiding behavior at the point of dilemma. The practical utility of ethical codes highlights the need for greater focus on increasing the moral fitness of professional military forces.[24]

Ethics Training and Moral Fitness

The profession of arms is guided by a "warrior ethos [based on] values of honor, duty, courage, loyalty, and self-sacrifice." This ethos binds members of the profession of arms to a covenant of trust to serve society and is intended to make the use of military force an effective instrument. Although legal codes have a role to play in maintaining operational effectiveness through the disciplined use of force, H. R. McMaster argues that "ensuring ethical conduct goes beyond the law of war and must include a consideration of our values—our ethos." This ethos is cultivated by upholding the professional culture of the military force and through realistic training that integrates applied ethics education that is considered essential in steeling individual members against the psychological and moral stresses of military operations.[25]

The concept of moral fitness is explored by Richardson, Verweij, and Winslow as an important component of military professionalism, particularly in the context of peace operations: "Moral fitness . . . points to the attitude of a person who can cope with an increase in ethical questions and dilemmas because he or she has the necessary moral alertness required. Moral fitness implies that a person regularly practices self-critical reflection."[26] Training for moral fitness should therefore include ethical scenarios that individual members can be expected to confront during operations. Training units should design such scenarios that include challenging ethical problems, as one method for preparing individuals, and to mitigate against moral injury. Alex Horton frames a discussion on moral injury juxtaposing ethical dilemmas in the TV series *Breaking Bad* with those arising in war. He defines the topic as "an existential disintegration of how the world should or is expected to work—a compromise of the conscience when one is butted against an action (or inaction) that violates an internalized moral code."[27] Practical or scenario-based training allows military professionals to grapple with ethical dilemmas prior to confronting such scenarios during operations so they are prepared for the "existential disintegration" Horton describes. This is consistent with Gen. George C. Marshall's argument that "a good officer must learn early on how to keep the beast under control, both in his men and himself."[28]

Conclusion

"What battles have in common is human: the behaviour of men struggling to reconcile their instinct for self-preservation, their sense of honour and the achievement of some aim over which other men are ready to kill them. The study of battle is therefore always a study of fear and usually of courage, always of leadership, usually of obedience; always of compulsion, sometimes of insubordination; always of anxiety, sometimes of elation or catharsis; always of uncertainty and doubt; misinformation and misapprehension, usually also of faith and sometimes of vision; always of violence, sometimes also of cruelty, self-sacrifice, compassion; above all, it is always a study of solidarity and usually also of disintegration—for it is toward the disintegration of human groups that battle is directed."[29] As Keegan's words starkly emphasize, war is a complex human endeavor that incorporates the breadth of human emotion. War also requires a lifetime of dedicated learning to comprehend and master. Members of the military forces must dedicate themselves through a cycle of study, experience, reflection, and writing to understand how to use military force to achieve national objectives. The military profession is entrusted by the nation with the ordered application of force to achieve national outcomes. This trust is founded on a number of key factors that form the foundations of a profession: that the members of the military profession possess a monopoly over a high level of skill or knowledge in the use of military force; that the military force must use that knowledge and skill to further the interests of the nation rather than of the profession or its individual members; and that the trust between the profession and the nation is preserved through a system of accountability that ensures that members of the profession are acting according to professional codes (legislative and ethical).

The most important aspect of the military profession is the relationship of trust between military forces and the state. This relationship of trust can be described as a fiduciary relationship between the military force (the agent) and the state (the principal). The fiduciary relationship of trust is also underwritten by legislative and ethical codes that govern how military operations are conducted, and how military forces behave while they conduct those operations. Legislative and ethical codes are a key characteristic of professions and ensure that their members conduct themselves in a manner that serves the interests of their principals. Whereas legislative frameworks, such as disciplinary codes or international law, provide the outer boundaries of acceptable behavior for military professionals, ethics provides more-detailed guidance for behavior at the point of decision.

Examples from Srebrenica and Rwanda demonstrate that there are times when legal and ethical frameworks are opposed. As these case studies show, military professionals in such circumstances must formulate a solution that navigates these legal and ethical conundrums. More important, these case studies demonstrate that while legal frameworks are important in regulating behavior, the ethical factors and the question "Can I live with myself if I do this?" are drivers of individual behavior that are more important in complex circumstances. Military professionals must be trained in facing the inevitable ethical dilemmas that arise in the course of military operations. Increasing moral fitness in military professionals is an important means of preventing moral injury. Training in the laws of war is, of itself, not enough. The law is easy; ethics is hard.

Notes

1. Hackett, *The Profession of Arms*, 9.
2. Hackett, 99, 102, 101–3. See Charles E. White, *The Enlightened Soldier: Scharnhorst and the Militärische Gesellschaft in Berlin, 1801–1805* (Westport, CT: Praeger, 1989). White's book examines Gerhard Johann David von Scharnhorst's establishment of the Militärische Gesellschaft (military society) and its role in fostering professionalism in the Prussian army.
3. Huntington, *The Soldier and the State*.
4. Hackett, *The Profession of Arms*, 9.
5. Tamar Frankel, "Fiduciary Law in the Twenty-First Century," *Boston University Law Review* 91 (2011): 1289, 1294 (quote).
6. Huntington, *The Soldier and the State*.
7. Matthew Harding, "Trust and Fiduciary Law," *Oxford Journal of Legal Studies* 33 (2013): 86.
8. See Mike Denny's discussion in chapter 4, this volume, on how professionals exercise discretion and how they know when to break the rules.
9. Donald Snider, "Renewing the Motivational Power of the Army's Professional Ethic," *Parameters* 44, no. 3 (Autumn 2014): 8.
10. Gen. Martin E. Dempsey, *America's Military—A Profession of Arms White Paper* (Fort Myer, VA: US Army Training and Doctrine Command, 2010), 4. General Dempsey is the former chairman of the Joint Chiefs of Staff.
11. Huntington, *The Soldier and the State*, 83.
12. Cameron Moore, "To Execute and Maintain the Laws of the Commonwealth: The ADF and Internal Security—Some Old Issues with New Relevance," *University of NSW Law Journal* 28 (2005): 523–37; Michael Head, "Australia's Expanded Military Call-Out Powers: Causes for Concern," *University of New England Law Journal* 3 (2006): 125–50.
13. UCMJ is at 10 US Code §§ 801–946.
14. See articles 10, 15, and 51 of Protocol Additional to the Geneva Conventions of 12 August 1949 (Additional Protocol I), International Committee of the Red Cross, Geneva, https://www.icrc.org/applic/ihl/ihl.nsf/INTRO/470.
15. A. Edward Major, "Law and Ethics in Command Decision Making," *Military Review* (May–June 2012): 61–74.
16. Major, "Law and Ethics," 63 (quote), 64.
17. The Ethics Centre (formerly The St. James Ethics Centre), "What Is Ethics?," http://www.ethics.org.au/about/what-is-ethics; emphasis in original.
18. The Ethics Centre, "What Is Ethics?"
19. Major, "Law and Ethics," 70 (quote).
20. R. Richardson, D. Verweij, and D. Winslow, "Moral Fitness for Peace Operations," *Journal of Political and Military Sociology* 32 (2004): 100–1.

21. P. J. deVin, "Srebrenica, The Impossible Choices of a Commander" (PhD diss., US Marine Corps Command and Staff College, Marine Corps University, Quantico, VA, 2008).

22. Richardson, Verweij, and Winslow, "Moral Fitness," 110–11, 111 (quote).

23. Daniel S. Blocq, "The Fog of UN Peacekeeping: Ethical Issues Regarding the Use of Force to Protect Civilians in UN Operations," *Journal of Military Ethics* 5 (2006): 201–13.

24. Richardson, Verweij, and Winslow, "Moral Fitness."

25. H. R. McMaster, "Moral, Ethical, and Psychological Preparation of Soldiers and Units for Combat," *Naval War College Review* 64 (2011): 19 (first quote), 10 (second quote), 14.

26. Richardson, Verweij, and Winslow, "Moral Fitness," 108.

27. Alex Horton, "Breaking Bad's Moral Lesson to Civilians," *The Atlantic*, http://www.theatlantic.com/entertainment/archive/2013/08/-i-breaking-bad-i-s-moral-lesson-to-civilians/278544/ (including quote).

28. Douglas A. Pryer, "Controlling the Beast Within: The Key to Success on 21st Century Battlefields," *Military Review* (January–February 2011): 81.

29. John Keegan, *The Face of Battle* (New York: Viking, 1976), 83.

CHAPTER 3

Evolution of Defining the Army Profession

Casey Landru

Introduction

The evolution of the American definition of the profession of arms can be traced to the post–World War II security environment and the Cold War. Prior to this, despite American involvement in both the international community and warfare, the United States had not found it necessary to maintain a large standing military. Previously, America had relied on noninvolvement and rapid mobilization around a small professional officer corps backed by a conscripted force to respond in the event of conflict. The Soviet development of nuclear weapons and a limited war on the Korean peninsula reinforced in American society the need to maintain a large standing Army and once again raised a debate over civilian control of the military that had largely lain dormant since the founding of the country.

Huntington and Janowitz

The roots of modern military professionalism can be found in Samuel Huntington's *The Soldier and the State,* in which he investigates and proposes methods to ensure civilian control over a large standing army. Huntington defines two methods of civilian control over the military, subjective and objective. All civilian control necessitates that the civilian government maintains more political power than the military. Subjective control seeks to ensure that the civilian government remains more powerful than the military. Historically under this model, civilian governments subject the military to political manipulations as one civilian group struggles for power against another civilian group. Huntington references clashes between Congress and the executive branch as an example of subjective manipulations. Both are examples of civilian political entities with control over the military, but their policies could clash. A good example of this could be the executive directing the military to save money by reducing overhead costs to fund other domestic priorities, but Congress refusing to authorize a base realignment and closure process to keep constituents in their home districts happy. In this case neither side is interested in the welfare of the military, but both are using the military as an instrument to gain political power over a competing group. Because subjective control assumes that civilian and military political goals are different, subjective control seeks to dominate military institutions so that they are not a threat to the state. This loss of military primacy eventually leads to a power vacuum in which the state loses its monopoly on violence or decreases the ability of the state to defend itself from external threats.[1]

Objective civilian control does not assume that military and civilian political goals must necessarily clash. Instead, it seeks to professionalize the military into a politically neutral body, focused entirely on defense of the state while remaining obedient to whichever civilian group maintains political control at the time. This method of control seeks to remove the military as a political actor in the affairs of the state and preserves the ability of the state to maintain a force as large as is necessary for national security.[2]

Accordingly, Huntington defined a profession in terms of expertise, responsibility, and his word "corporateness," and went on to apply this framework in terms of the military. The expertise of a profession was defined as particular knowledge in a field essential to society. In the case of the military it was the "direction, operation and control of a human organization whose primary function is the application of violence." A profession was responsible for a service essential to the function of society, which the military fulfilled by ensuring the state maintained its monopoly on violence and avoiding the use of violence for political gain, which would in turn destroy the society it originated from. Finally, Huntington's corporateness defined professions in the sense of their collective identity, their lengthy training, common work, self-regulating and certifying bodies, code of ethics, and restricted entry.[3] Huntington found that military officers embodied all of these characteristics, but that enlisted personnel of the post–World War II era did not.

Janowitz, in contrast to Huntington, nearly takes for granted that the military is a profession prior to exploring the nature of the military and how professionalism best ensures civilian control. Up front, Janowitz compares the professions of law and medicine to the military profession and draws attention to the prolonged training and specialized service of each profession.[4] He takes note of the sense of group identity and internal administration required for all professions, but his primary concerns are those factors he determines to be unique to the military profession and the implications they have for the future of the military profession and civil-military relations in an era of persistent international conflict.[5]

Janowitz identifies the changing nature of war and its increasingly technological character as factors that will narrow the gap between military professionals and civilian technical experts. This may force the military to become increasingly more involved in politics, while civilians become more concerned with the minutiae of military matters. In this state of affairs, Janowitz envisions a military that embraces partisan neutrality, but is not necessarily unpolitical. In this scenario, the military would be firm in its neutrality, but deeply committed to the democratic ideal of government.[6]

The changing nature of the military forced by the development of nuclear weapons and more-technical machinery, led Janowitz to propose an international constabulary conception of a professional military. This military would be continuously prepared to act, dedicated to both a minimum use of force and a defensive military posture, and politically educated to see the use of force in an international relations perspective rather than in terms of victory or defeat. Due to the new international order imposed by the dynamics of the Cold War, this military force would need to become experts in evaluating the consequences of the use of force on world politics, while remaining amenable to the political and administrative constraints of civilian control.[7]

Subsequently, Janowitz proposed that civilian control of the military was best accomplished through ensuring that the military remained a reflection of the society that it served. The military would still be encouraged to develop a professional identity and ethos, as well as continuously pursue expert military knowledge. However, military professionals would willingly submit to and acknowledge civilian political expertise in the employment of the military worldwide and would most importantly share the common democratic values of civilian society rather than standing apart as a warrior class.[8]

Huntington and Janowitz provided the modern military a foundation on which to develop as a profession, and despite the titles of their books using the word "soldier" in the parlance of the times, their theories cover the entire profession of arms, which includes land, maritime, and air elements. The US Army and Marine Corps, as organizations whose culture evolved historically to place primacy on people over machines, have most fully embraced the concept of the profession of arms with written doctrine. The Army has dedicated an entire manual to the concept.[9] To understand the profession of arms as a concept, this chapter will examine its evolution in the context of the American Army, keeping in mind that the profession of arms includes all branches of the modern military.

Developing the Professional Ethic and a Focus on Values

Following the societal upheaval America experienced in the 1960s and the escalating involvement of America in the Vietnam War, General Westmoreland, as chief of staff of the Army, directed the Army War College to conduct a study of professionalism in 1970. The resulting report added a code of behavior to Huntington's threefold definition of professionalism, elevating it from a facet of corporateness to equal footing alongside expertise and responsibility. Additionally, the report concluded that the Army needed to place more emphasis on values-based leadership. Junior officers especially felt that the Army leadership climate rewarded short-term solutions, "dishonest practices that injure the long-term fabric of the organization" and self-centered career-oriented behavior over the good of the unit. Officers were especially disheartened with the tendency of majors and lieutenant colonels to distort reports to further their own careers. Based on the broad implications the findings of the report had for the professionalism of the Army, the War College recommended a comprehensive emphasis on reform.[10]

In 1971 the Army again surveyed a broad section of officers on leadership and began to identify areas for improved training across the force; the Army included NCOs in its recommendations for improvement of professionalism.[11] Thus began the professionalization of the total force, resulting in the rebuilding of the hollow force of the 1970s and improved professional development education for the warrant officer and NCO corps.[12]

The Army continued to search for its professional ethic and espoused values throughout this period, developing values common to soldiers universally and values specific to the American soldier. The theme of the year in 1986 was values.[13] It would not be until 1999, however, that the Army formally designated the Seven Army Values, as they are known today.[14]

Throughout the formation of the all-volunteer force, the Army has continued to emphasize values-based leadership as an important aspect of the Army profession.

Reemphasis of the Professional Model

The Army's focus on the development of expert knowledge contributed to the overwhelming success of Operation Desert Storm, but the Army's conception of itself as a profession had not been doctrinally examined since the early 1970s. The ending of the Cold War and the proliferation of operations other than war and peacekeeping missions caused an identity crisis within the Army profession. Operations in Haiti, Rwanda, and Bosnia forced the Army to reconsider exactly what its body of expert knowledge should consist of and what roles and missions the Army should fulfill. Finally, a so-called revolution in military affairs and the debate over the role of technology in battle spurred calls for the reorganization of the structure of the Army. In the middle of these two debates, a private research study led by Don Snider, a retired Army colonel then teaching at West Point, began to reevaluate the Army as a profession. In 2000 Snider's research found that the Army as a profession had been "seriously compromised by excessive bureaucratization," but just four years later his research found that wartime demands of the post-9/11 environment had mitigated micromanagement and that units in combat had improved immensely in professionalization. The challenge remained, however, to capture and institutionalize these changes in the larger Army as a profession.[15]

Accordingly, Snider's research group posited a threefold definition of expertise, jurisdiction, and legitimacy to define the Army as a profession using new understanding of professions developed from Andrew Abbott's theories. Additionally, the group explored the identity of an Army officer, developing four criteria for an Army professional: warrior, leader of character, member of a profession, and servant of the nation.[16] Snider's research group explored these definitions at length, both defining them and analyzing the implications of their findings for the future of the Army profession.

The Army's expertise would be the development and application of expert knowledge in the management of violence. New conflicts and the return of counterinsurgency as a focus area for the Army would continue to force the development of doctrine and refinement of professional education. The Army's jurisdiction would be land warfare, and in accordance with Abbott's theory, it would force the Army to continually compete to define this jurisdiction, especially with the advent of joint operations, the increasingly interagency nature of operations, and the changing nature of warfare. Competing within a system of defense professions, the Army would need to describe and explain the role of its unique profession. This competition was envisioned as more of a competitive cooperation than a distinct effort to usurp Navy or Air Force jurisdictions. The Army would aggressively define its roles and missions, demanding ownership of land warfare while cooperating with the Navy and Air Force to incorporate joint war fighting. Finally, the Army's legitimacy derived from the public confidence of the American people and their trust in the Army's participation in the defense of the nation. Challenges for the Army in maintaining its legitimacy would be societal trends to question the expert knowledge of science-based professions and the increasing proliferation of market-based methods for the development of new knowledge.[17]

Don Snider's study envisioned an Army officer to have four identities. As warriors, Army officers were to be expert in the application of lethal force, studying and refining technical military knowledge. As leaders of character, officers would apply their technical military knowledge consistent with the moral and legal obligations of the United States. As members of a profession, officers would be experts in the leadership and development of cohesive units as well as other professional leaders. They would consciously consider the Army a profession and act as stewards of the profession. Finally, as servants of the country, officers would understand that their client is the American people, and they would be dedicated to upholding the principles of the United States as embodied in the Constitution. Additionally, professional officers would accept that they were the manifest representation of the Army within the United States and often the face of America when deployed across the globe.[18]

Don Snider's study was later issued to United States Military Academy cadets during military science courses, and his four identities of an Army officer were echoed again in Gen. Martin Dempsey's 2010 white paper on the Army profession; General Dempsey prepared that white paper while he served as the commanding general, Training and Doctrine Command. While influential, Army doctrine would continue to evolve from Snider's study and finally be codified in 2013 with the *Army Doctrine Reference Publication 1, The Army Profession*.

The Army Profession describes the five aspects of a military profession: the military profession must provide a unique and vital service to society, develop expert knowledge and practice, apply knowledge effectively and ethically, self-regulate, and be granted significant autonomy in application. The Army's unique and vital service is to provide the primary ground component of the Department of Defense. In this function, it serves to execute national policy through sustained ground operations. The Army's expert knowledge and practice in current doctrinal terms is land power. This term, "land power," invokes an idea that the Army no longer simply executes combat operations but also takes actions to prevent and shape future conflicts. To apply its knowledge effectively and ethically, the Army must conduct operations according to the Law of Land Warfare and Just War Theory.[19]

As a self-regulating body, the Army uses the UCMJ, regulations, policies, and professional military education to control its members. Additionally, the Army propagates an Army ethic so that Army professionals understand the spirit of self-regulation, and not just the letter of the law. Finally, the Army is granted significant autonomy and discretion in practice, and Army professionals are regularly called to make discretionary judgments based on years of training and experience. Seen over the course of the sixty years since Huntington and Janowitz wrote on this topic, the Army has evolved its definition of a profession to focus heavily on the moral and ethical aspects of its unique work—the application of violence. Correspondingly, the three criteria an individual must meet to be considered an Army professional are also heavily weighted toward ethical and moral factors. An Army professional must be competent and proficient in expert work. Across the Army, individuals are certified appropriately to the grade and level of work that they perform. An Army professional must also have character, defined as dedication to the Army values and to the professional Army ethic. The application of violence and the inherent lethality involved require professionals of high moral character. Finally, Army professionals are defined by their commitment. They provide honorable service to the United States, act as effective stewards of the profession, and are intrinsically motivated by a call to service.[20] Combined, these three criteria demand that Army professionals are experts in their field, including the moral and ethical obligations inherent in land warfare, with the character to act rightly under stress while remaining committed to honorable service to the nation.

The modern concept of a professional military in the United States has evolved since its formation was necessitated by the need to maintain a large standing force. It is a concept focused at the heart of civil-military relations, ensuring the security of the state, both from internal and external threats, as well as from the military itself. When compared to the other services, the Army, rooted in a historical culture that elevates people over capabilities, has most fully explored the profession of arms in doctrine. The state-sanctioned application of violence, especially in the international arena, is of great concern to citizens. Accordingly, the military must continue to develop professionals who are competent in their field, committed in service to the United States and its founding principles, and disciplined in the moral and ethical responsibilities of the profession of arms.

Professionals Have a Moral Obligation to the State

The state, as a human institution, has long been the subject of Western philosophy. Regardless of whether one considers the state of nature to be that of conflict in the Hobbesian tradition or that of reason and tolerance as Locke did, Western intellectual tradition holds the state to be "an indispensable social institution." Regardless of the philosophical tradition chosen, an armed force dedicated to the security of its citizenry has a moral obligation to preserve the state and the benefits to society that the state provides.[21] This moral obligation to the state takes form in three parts for the military professional. First, the military must preserve the existence of the state from external threats. Second, the military must preserve the legitimacy of the state by ensuring the state maintains its monopoly on the use of violence. Finally, the military must establish safeguards to protect the state from the military itself.

External Threats

Historically, the American military has existed primarily to secure the state from external threats. With oceans on two sides and hesitant (though not always benevolent) neighbors to the north and south, the United States has rarely needed a powerful standing military in times of peace. Separation by oceans and sprawling landmasses have traditionally allowed American forces time to mobilize in the event of a war. Indeed, after the conflict of World War I, the key military concern of the United States became a question of how quickly civilians, the National Guard, and other reservists could be mobilized to increase the strength of the military in the event of conflict. Following World War II, the development of nuclear weapons, intercontinental bombers, and an international rival with expressed ideological opposition to the American ideal would force the United States to reconsider its defense policy. For the first time since 1778, the United States signed an alliance and committed itself to a collective security arrangement.[22] New realities of the Cold War compelled America to view military supremacy as the best method to ensure its security and sovereignty.

Along with diplomatic, informational, and economic elements, maximizing the military element of national power helps the United States maintain supremacy over competitors. The military element includes both quantity and quality of the military forces. While quality is the predominating factor given the value placed on individual life in Western societies, an adequate quantity of military force is also required to ensure victory. Included in America's military strength is power projection and sustainability. Given the transition from a policy of isolationism to global engagement after World War II, the American military needed to be able to deploy and sustain itself anywhere in the world in support of national security objectives. Finally, integrating new technologies into a successful war fighting doctrine became essential to the expert knowledge of the military.[23] While the fundamental aim of warfare remains to compel another to do your will through force, new technologies continue to change the methods available to military forces.[24] Ensuring that doctrine captures the human element of warfare while adapting to emerging technologies remains a significant challenge for the military profession to ensure the United States remains able to protect its interests.

Internal Threats

Preserving the internal monopoly on the use of force is normally a function of police at the state and local levels in America. That the military has been called out so few times to restore order is a tribute to the effectiveness of America's federalized system of government and the dedication and professionalism of the state and local governments. However, in the aftermath of a natural disaster, when state and local forces are simply overwhelmed with the magnitude of the task at hand, the military can be sent to support local efforts. In the case of Hurricane Katrina in 2005, for instance, nearly 46,000 National Guard and 22,000 active duty personnel were deployed to provide support and restore order in Louisiana and Mississippi.[25] In such situations, military forces must act with professional restraint and be aware of all the legal considerations that govern their conduct while conducting relief operations within the United States.[26]

Unfortunately, the federalized system of government is not without drawbacks in maintaining internal law and order. At times, state and local governments might resist the will of the federal government; in such cases a professional military is obligated to ensure the constitutionally valid will of the federal government is carried out, by force if necessary. The 1957 integration of Little Rock Central High School is a glaring historical example of the federal government stepping in to enforce federal law. Following a Supreme Court decision that declared segregation unconstitutional, schools across the southern United States began to prepare to integrate racially. In Little Rock, Arkansas, Governor Orval Faubus used National Guard troops to prevent nine black students from attending classes and ignored several orders from federal courts to allow the integration of the school. Although the governor was eventually forced to withdraw the national guardsmen, mob violence erupted when the black students began attending school. Citing "extraordinary and compelling circumstances" President Dwight D. Eisenhower deployed a thousand soldiers from the 101st Airborne Division and federalized the Arkansas National Guard to restore order and ensure compliance with the court orders mandating integration.[27]

When using the military in this manner, it is extremely important for governments to have strict guidelines and maintain oversight. In the case of Little Rock, Eisenhower's focus was on the enforcement of law and order, and military force was his last resort after several weeks of diplomatic efforts. Additionally, military professionals must always conduct such operations with a goal to use the minimum necessary force. Excessive use of force can easily cause backlash, and failure to be mindful of the legal sensitivity of the operating environment can easily jeopardize both the mission and the soldiers involved.

From the Military Itself

Professional members of the military understand that democracy, while messy, slow, and unpredictable, is the form of government chosen by the American people. The threat of a standing military was of fundamental concern to the Founding Fathers and was debated at length during the drafting and adoption of the Constitution. Accordingly, as stated in the Federalist Papers, the Founders recognized that local militias would not be adequate in safeguarding the frontier or competing with European forces should those powers choose to augment their garrisons in North America.[28] To provide the necessary safeguards to liberty while still allowing the government to maintain a standing military, the Founders added requirements to the Constitution such as civilian oversight and the need for congressional appropriations every two years.

Finally, the professional commitment to American democracy and values is the best safeguard the people have from their military. With the level of technical expertise and destructiveness of military weapons, it is conceivable, but highly unlikely, that American society could resist a military takeover in the manner that the Founders intended when writing the Second Amendment. However, the American people remain protected from this scenario because their military remains a reflection of the liberal society from which military members are drawn. While the military tends to be more conservative in nature than society, professional emphasis on leadership and equality has alternatively been ahead of society in integrating personnel based on gender and race, while (until recently) behind society in allowing service members with alternative sexual orientations to serve openly. Nonetheless, military professionals embrace the concepts of democracy, liberty, and equality found in the Constitution; their loyalty to the Constitution over any one leader or official remains the best protection American society has from the military itself.

Military Professionals Have a Moral Obligation to Each Other
The moral obligation that military professionals have to each other is twofold and directly related to the unique lethality that results from the waging of war. Military professionals must be prepared to wage war ethically both for the protection of civilians on the battlefield and for the protection of their fellow soldiers. Military professionals also have an explicit responsibility to their fellow comrades-in-arms to ensure that lives are not needlessly spent during military operations.

Regarding Civilians on the Battlefield
It is fundamental to the nature of warfare that decisions regarding the military necessity of an action will be weighed against the collateral damage to civilians. In the post-9/11 era, as the unit of action for military operations has shifted from battalion-sized to platoon-sized elements, younger and younger officers and NCOs have been required to make these decisions. Operations other than war require military professionals to exercise courageous restraint and accept risk to their forces. These decisions are of

a life-and-death nature and it is necessary that they be made from a professional mind-set.

This professional mind-set will help mitigate moral injury. Moral injury, stated in simple terms, is "a violent rage and social withdrawal when deep assumptions of 'what's right' are violated."[29] Traditionally, cultural assumptions within the American military have focused on the concept of fairness as being "what's right."[30] Professional and competent military soldiers and leaders avoid civilian casualties whenever possible and ensure that the necessary and proportionate military responses minimize collateral damage. By doing so, military professionals act not only to protect civilians on the battlefield, but also to protect themselves and other soldiers from moral injury.

Regarding Fellow Soldiers

While the military professional's first moral obligation is to the United States, the second and emotionally greater obligation is to fellow soldiers. Combat is an inherently lethal environment in which competing organizations seek to use their skill and strength of arms to impose their will. In infantry combat, this environment becomes an orchestra of chaos in which only well-trained, disciplined, and adaptable units succeed. Soldiers from the lowest private to the platoon leader or company commander are required to employ deadly force. And yet the military professional must maintain control. Members of the platoon, such as riflemen or machine gunners, ensure that they place accurate fire on known and suspected enemy locations. The team leader engages the enemy while simultaneously controlling rates of fire and maximizing the capabilities of his grenadier and automatic rifleman. Squad leaders operate within their platoon leader's intent, positioning their squads not just on the letter of a command, but also using their judgment to best fulfill the spirit of the command and ensure the success of the platoon. The platoon sergeant and platoon leader anticipate further developments of the battle, adjusting mortar and artillery fire, coordinating with the company commander who may be maneuvering multiple platoons or working to bring more assets to a single platoon. The arrival of helicopters and aircraft will make the battle space three-dimensional, and the ground commander will need to coordinate different altitudes for each asset to fly at and ensure that they are clear of the multitudes of projectiles flying through space. Through it all, military professionals must use precise and distinct language to communicate a clear picture to higher headquarters, allowing commanders and battle captains at echelons above the fight to make decisions on where to allocate finite resources.

At each level of this symphony of death and destruction military professionals are responsible to make split-second decisions with life-or-death implications that will be immediately discernible. The increasingly combined arms nature of combat forces military professionals to rely more heavily on larger and larger numbers of supporting assets. Therefore, military professionals at every level from the tip of the spear to supporting depots in the United States must ensure that they are of the highest character and competence so that lives are not needlessly jeopardized. This commitment to each other transcends a single battle or firefight. To be fully realized, it is articulated over the course of each campaign, deployment, and strategic operation.

Soldiers do not find themselves in firefights all the time. There are long periods of predeployment, deployment, movement to the area of operations, routine patrols, and stretches of boredom in which they do not encounter the enemy. And yet, especially in the asymmetric battlegrounds of Iraq and Afghanistan, each action, patrol, or simple trip to the mess hall or shower possibly exposes the soldier to enemy attack and mortal danger. Military professionals at all levels must ensure that they have considered the mission and the commander's intent for placing their soldiers in harm's way and that the expected benefits outweigh the potential risks of the operation. Military professionals serve and accept responsibility from the individual level "fully knowing the hazards of my chosen profession" as embodied in the Ranger Creed through levels of command to the Secretary of Defense.[31]

The lethality of the military profession does not just manifest itself when deployed overseas in combat operations. Ensuring that units are as well trained as possible and prepared to engage in combat is just as, if not more, important as making the right decisions on the battlefield. Live-fire training exercises, for which there is no substitute, ask soldiers to employ their weapons within degrees of separation of the assaulting element. Leaders across climates use their judgment to discern the fine line between training their unit to operate day or night in any weather condition and pushing too hard and having soldiers become casualties to heatstroke or frostbite.

The specter of pushing too hard in training pales in comparison to not training well enough. Poorly trained units will fare worse in combat.

They suffer more casualties, fail to accomplish their missions, and could be responsible for other units being redirected to assist or rescue them. Additionally, poorly trained soldiers are more likely to be ill equipped mentally to deal with the stresses of combat just as they are physically. These units will likely have higher incidences of post-traumatic stress, even from relatively less traumatic experiences as other units. Lacking a physical and mental toughness of spirit, a poorly trained soldier is much more likely to feel helpless when faced with the rigors of combat, unable to fall back on the muscle memory that repetitive training imbues; such a soldier is more easily broken than one tempered in combat.[32]

Military professionals also have an obligation to be stewards of their profession, perpetuating a professional mind-set across their organizations and their subordinates. They do this by investing in the success of their subordinates and focusing guided and self-structured development. Fostering a desire to become a lifelong student of the profession of arms is the best method to ensuring subordinates will achieve future success and provide for the future of the profession.

Commanders are the frontline stewards in the profession of arms. They have great power to discipline their troops and control the careers of their subordinates. They can affirm or reject court martial decisions, administer nonjudicial punishment, and process administrative actions such as bars to reenlistment or personnel file flags that prevent any favorable actions. In the Army, professionals as low as squad leaders are responsible for writing evaluation reports, and even team leaders are responsible for sponsoring their soldiers for promotion boards into the NCO ranks. These evaluation reports and sponsorships, or lack thereof, can easily make or break a burgeoning career for the young officer or enlisted soldier. In all such cases, the judgment of the military professional must be based on sound logic and reasoning and that professional's character and integrity must be above reproach. Anything less would jeopardize the status of military professionalism in the eyes of the soldiers who are affected and in the public perception at large. Lack of faith in military objectivity can lead to reforms being imposed from outside the service, such as the UCMJ reforms regarding sexual assault in the National Defense Authorization Act of 2014.

Whereas military service has the potential to demand the ultimate sacrifice, as previously discussed, it also demands a culture of everyday selflessness that those who wish to cause bitterness in the heart of one without a professional mind-set can easily take advantage of. Military professionals accept certain restrictions on fundamental rights, such as freedom of expression, for the good order and discipline of the service. Indeed, even the US Supreme Court has traditionally granted the military wide latitude to regulate itself for the good of the service.[33] Even training exercises routinely separate military members from their families for days or weeks at a time; other functions, such as Charge of Quarters or Staff Duty will occupy their time on weekends and holidays. Professional and impartial conduct in the appointing of these duties and the restriction of behavior is essential in maintaining the morale of an organization and the status of the profession.

Conclusion

The American experience with military power has traditionally led US citizens to be skeptical of a large standing military. Beginning with the quartering of British soldiers in colonists' houses and culminating in intolerable laws enforced at the tip of a bayonet, Americans were determined not to allow the military establishment to overrule the civilian government. Bounded by two large oceans and weaker neighbors, the United States has relied on distance and rapid mobilization to secure itself for most of its history. Following World War II mobilizing civilian and reserve forces was no longer an option. The military and the government had to grapple with how best to preserve the American form of government in the presence of a large standing military that was a result of America's new superpower status.

Professionalization of the armed forces became the solution to best meet the needs of the United States. Beginning with the officer corps, and eventually expanding to all soldiers, airmen, sailors, and Marines, the military evolved as a profession to become heavily values-based due to the unique lethality of the combat environment. Working on a foundation built by Huntington and Janowitz, the officer corps continued to consider itself a professional body. Aware of a possible breaking point in the Army, General Westmoreland, as chief of staff of the Army, began to focus on professionalism with two studies by the Army War College in the early 1970s. These studies led directly to the professionalization of the warrant and NCO corps. The military focused heavily on developing organizational values consistent with military leadership and the ethical application of force throughout the 1980s and 1990s, before becoming again concerned with the whole of the profession in the early 2000s. Finally, in

2013 the Army published its latest manual on the subject, *The Army Profession*. Using this doctrine as a guide, military leaders can assess the professionalization of their organization and themselves.

In the modern military, with interdependent combined arms warfare, military professionals have two great moral obligations: one to the state and its people, the other to their fellow professionals. The military must ensure the state's survival from external threats, maintain a monopoly on violence internally, and guarantee the state's protection from the military itself. Military professionals must be competent in battle, committed to preparing for the test of combat, and prepared for a life of sacrifice during their time serving in the military. The absence of this professional mindset has the potential to be gravely injurious both to their subordinates and to themselves.

Notes

1. Huntington, *The Soldier and the State*, 81, 84.
2. Huntington, 84.
3. Huntington, 8, 11 (quote), 14–15, 10.
4. Morris Janowitz, *The Professional Soldier: A Social and Political Portrait* (New York: Free Press, 1971 [1960]), 5.
5. Janowitz, *The Professional Soldier*, 6.
6. Janowitz, 422, 420, 234.
7. Janowitz, 418.
8. Janowitz, 440.
9. US Army, *Army Doctrine Reference Publication 1: The Army Profession* (Washington, DC: Government Printing Office, 2013).
10. US Army War College, *Study on Military Professionalism* (Carlisle Barracks, PA: US Army War College, 1970), 53, 6, 13 (quote), i.
11. US Army, *2013 Chief of Staff of the Army Leader Development Task Force Final Report* (Washington, DC: Government Printing Office, 2013), 48.
12. Center for the Army Profession and Ethic, *The Army Profession* (West Point, NY: Center for the Army Profession and Ethic, 2014), 6.
13. US Army, *Department of the Army Pamphlet 600–68: The Bedrock of Our Profession* (Washington, DC: Government Printing Office, 1986), 1.
14. US Army, *Field Manual 22–100: Army Leadership* (Washington, DC: Government Printing Office, 1999), 2-2.
15. Snider and Matthews, *The Future of the Army Profession*, 7, 8, 9, 21 (quote), 32, 29.
16. Snider and Matthews, 44, 12.
17. Snider and Matthews, 49, 50–51, 55.
18. Snider and Matthews, 11, 12.
19. US Army, *Army Doctrine Reference Publication 1*, 1–3.
20. US Army, 1–4.

21. Snider and Matthews, *The Future of the Army Profession*, 393 (quote), 394.

22. Allan R. Millett, Peter Maslowski, and William B. Feis, *For the Common Defense: A Military History of the United States from 1607 to 2012* (New York: Simon and Schuster, 2012), 109, 366, 471, 472.

23. US Army War College, *U.S. Army War College Guide to National Security Issues,* Vol. 1, *Theory of War and Strategy* (Carlisle Barracks, PA: US Army War College, 2012), 152.

24. Carl von Clausewitz, *On War,* trans. Michael Howard and Peter Paret (Princeton, NJ: Princeton University Press, 1984), 75.

25. James A. Wombwell, *Occasional Paper 29: Army Support During the Hurricane Katrina Disaster* (Fort Leavenworth, KS: Combat Studies Institute Press, 2009), 4.

26. US Army, *Army Doctrine Reference Publication 3-28: Defense Support of Civil Authorities* (Washington, DC: Government Printing Office, 2013). See chapter 1 for a reference guide to legal considerations during relief operations.

27. Anthony Lewis, "President Sends Troops to Little Rock, Federalizes Arkansas National Guard; Tells Nation He Acted to Avoid Anarchy," *New York Times,* 2 September 1957, https://archive.nytimes.com/www.nytimes.com/learning/general/onthis day/big/0925.html#article.

28. Alexander Hamilton, John Jay, and James Madison, "Federalist No. 24," *The Federalist: A Commentary on the Constitution of the United States,* ed. Robert Scigliano (New York: Random House, 2000), 149–50.

29. Jonathan Shay, *Achilles in Vietnam: Combat Trauma and the Undoing of Character* (New York: Scribner, 1994), 5.

30. Shay, *Achilles in Vietnam,* 12.

31. Robert M. Gates, *Duty: Memoirs of a Secretary at War* (New York: Alfred A. Knopf, 2014), 386.

32. Dave Grossman and Loren W. Chistensen, *On Combat: The Psychology and Physiology of Deadly Conflict in War and in Peace* (New York: Guilford Press, 2008), 274.

33. Parker v. Levy, 417 U.S. 733 (1974).

CHAPTER 4

Professionals Know When to Break the Rules

H. M. "Mike" Denny

On a sunny day in mid-October 2008 in the Kunar River Valley in eastern Afghanistan I heard a large explosion in the distance and reflexively began jogging toward the small tactical operations center on our combat outpost. I was a young lieutenant, a hundred days into my first combat deployment, and I had just passed my second anniversary in the Army. Little did I realize that I was about to knowingly violate a handful of regulations. As I walked through the wooden door of the mud-walled compound turned tactical operations center, the radio squelched through the static, "Delta base, this is Delta 27, lead vehicle destroyed by IED [improvised explosive device], 9-Line to follow."

The clock was ticking, in a span of seconds several decisions needed to be made, all while a flurry of activity was occurring in the small command post. "Delta base, this is Close Combat 25 we have four MAM [military aged males] with potential weapons approximately 200m from blast site, unable to confirm PID [positive identification], need authorization for engagement."

In 2008, leading up to the Afghan surge, this type of scenario was an intensifying trend. The rules of engagement were significantly tightened and constantly being revised. Aircrews were increasingly restricted from engaging suspected militants, necessitating ground commander approval even if the commander might not have eyes on the situation unfolding. In previous months there had been several engagements by the North Atlantic Treaty Organization (NATO) attack and scout helicopters against Afghan forces that were in areas of insurgent activity. Due to these events, aircrews were increasingly unable to make immediate attacks on suspected militants without de-conflicting the action with commanders on the ground.

Many thoughts flew through my head as I weighed multiple scenarios to not make an emotional decision. *Can I even make this decision on my own? Do I know where the friendlies are? Where's the platoon leader?* The on-scene commander, a fellow lieutenant, was involved in the casualty evacuation. The company commander was thirty miles away and involved in another operation.

The Rules of Engagement briefings flew through my brain. *Was there hostile intent? Is this a hostile act? What did yesterday's intelligence summary say about this village? Was that high value target sighted near there? How many days ago?* I took a deep breath to focus on the problem. *How do I send a five line again? What is the risk estimate distance of a 2.75-inch rocket? Do I have to worry about secondary blast mitigation? What attack heading should I give the aircraft?*

I spoke confidently on the radio. "Close Combat 25, this is Delta Base cleared to engage, make attack heading northwest away from blast site, report clear of target area, initials HD, over."

Introduction

The military is a profession. As Tony Ingesson highlights in chapter 5, that fact does not mean that everyone in the military is a professional. There are many hard-working service members grinding away daily at very important jobs that do not meet the professional standard. Their jobs are important, but at the end of the day they are not empowered with the professional responsibility needed of the military profession. This raises an important question, one that this chapter will address: When does a soldier become a professional? In boot camp? On his or her first combat tour? In a classroom?

This chapter will address the transition and argue that there is a clear line of demarcation. Soldiers become professionals when they can make the best available decision even when it contradicts the textbook answer, whether that textbook is a field manual, regulation, or strategy. As this collection shows, there is no single agreed-on definition of military professionalism among the services or individual communities. In current publications, the discussion of violating orders or procedures is typically focused on two aspects. The first is indiscipline discussed as a breakdown of the moral military and undermining of the foundation of the profession. The second aspect is violation of unlawful orders, especially related to involvement in war crimes. As discussed in several texts, including *Killing in War* by Jeff McMahan, there is much discussion about preventing war crimes and command responsibility of war crimes, but no thought to violating perfectly lawful orders due to circumstances on the field of battle.

This chapter will use historical examples, texts in the field, and personal vignettes to support the thesis of the autonomous professional. Current publications on the military profession do not support this idea, but allude to it, particularly in expanding discussions on mission command and reflections on the future of the military profession. Within the medical profession there are numerous studies and articles on the degree of autonomy that should or could be granted to various members of that profession. The focus of literature on professional autonomy presents a professional whose freedom is self-serving and counter to contributions to the profession. The autonomy of professionals is also discussed as a means of self-regulation of the profession, separately responsible from a governing body. This chapter postulates that an autonomous military professional is granted the ability to make critical decisions that support the outcome of her professional responsibility regardless of personal gain or risk. Education, training, ethics, and disciplined initiative in difficult decision-making situations that place success above careerism are required for an individual to make a critical decision autonomously. It is important to stress that the primary outcome of the decisions required of the autonomous professional is not for personal achievement, but for mission accomplishment and possible victory.

To develop an autonomous professional, there is a required transcendence of the professional identity within the individual. In *The Future of the Army Profession*, the argument on the multidimensional development of the professional identity introduces research using the Kegan Developmental Scale. This scale uses a measurement to determine how people make sense of themselves and their world or the structure of identity. The correlation for this chapter is that, according to the Kegan Development Scale, Stages 4 and 5 indicate an individual that represents psychological autonomy and eventually universality of a self-authored system of values recognizing that own perspective on experience is a created convenience. More simply, professionals that develop a psychological maturity and autonomy (requiring several decades of experiences) are most capable of making independent judgment based on their values, experiences, and conscience. The professional at Stage 4 has transcended performance for tangible rewards (Stage 2) and how others feel about him (Stage 3). In the Kegan model one way a professional "constructs his understanding of his performance as a military officer [professional] is that he/she has their own internal compass for proceeding even when he is receiving ambiguous or conflicting signals from others. In short that military professional can function as an independent decision-maker, one who shapes the environment in which he operates instead of merely reacting to it."[1]

As Pauline Shanks-Kaurin discusses in chapter 1, the nature of the military profession is that ethical values are part of the identity of the profession, particularly loyalty, honor, and courage. An autonomous professional functions within these ethical values, not in violation of them. We will discuss transparency in action of the autonomous professional later; this transparency frames the potentially subversive behavior of breaking the rules as a necessary basis of fulfilling duty. Unlike medical professionals—with the creed *primum non nocere* (above all, do no harm)—the military exists solely to maintain the state's monopoly on violence. In other words, the military is designed to purposefully do harm to others. The comfort and acceptance of killing as a tool of the military professional are important because often the most trying decisions for an emerging professional evolve around the base question of right versus wrong, the act of using violence as a tool to impart your will on an enemy being the most fundamental application of this question. In a counterinsurgency battlefield, the questions of what is an acceptable level of violence for the killing of enemy combatants and what instead constitutes murder are difficult to determine and challenge many *jus in bello* concepts. While these points have merit in the discussion of the autonomous professional, this chapter will not address them in depth.[2]

Analysis of Autonomous Action

In the action described in the vignette, I decided that I was not authorized to order an aircraft to attack unconfirmed but likely enemy forces. While the risk decision for that engagement, based on the current rules, was above a gray area and time mattered. I was willing to accept the potential consequences, and believed I had the best situational awareness to make a decision. The short years of training and operational knowledge gained from professional study, combat experience, and willingness to understand my area of operations allowed me to decide. My professional responsibility required me to make an immediate decision that was professionally wrong.

The experiences of that fall day reinforced the lessons of self-improvement, as mastery of the craft can often be taught best through self-study and experience. The weapon system in this case is not important. The expertise derived strengthened the decision-making processes with regard to weapons implementation. While weapon system selection is a crucial engagement criterion, the true decision in this case was to engage or not to engage.

My individual decision—to clear aircraft to engage—was based on in-depth knowledge of the area of operations through countless intelligence briefings and discussions with local nationals and Afghan Security Forces. The experience gained through numerous skirmishes, troops in contact situations, and fire missions executed to that point led me to recognize on that sunny October afternoon I was faced with a critical decision that needed to be made quickly. This autonomy was due to my education and training as an officer and the ethics that I had internalized. Through self-study and formal learning I valued the ethics that motivate military professionals who used all available assets to snatch soldiers out of harm's way.

Mistakes happen in combat, particularly at the tactical level; although mistakes can have potential negative strategic consequences, they often develop opportunities for exploitation. The fear of negative consequences and associated inaction can damage tactical units. In this case, the action allowed for a surprising exploitation of the enemy intelligence left behind. The platoon successfully evacuated the remaining casualty and chased the trigger men to a fighting position where the platoon later killed both militants. The team of military aged males that the pair of Kiowa Warrior helicopters engaged was part of the militant group ready to ambush the remaining platoon members. The aircraft would have likely engaged the insurgent group later in the battle, when the insurgents were expected to open fire on the dismounted forces as they reacted to the improvised explosive device, generating unknown further damage to the dismounts or aircraft. Unfortunately, three soldiers died that day in the initial blast, and their loss was a heavy burden on the platoon that returned that night. Even if I faced punishment after making a decision I was not authorized to make, the tired faces returning to the outpost late that night were a reward in itself.

My situation was in no way unique in the war; junior leaders have made countless on-the-spot decisions across multiple countries during the war on terrorism. Some were good decisions and some were bad; many had far-reaching operational consequences, and plenty did not impact in the overall operational picture. One of the great fallacies of counterinsurgency is that an action where insurgents are killed has immediate and far-reaching consequences that potentially undermine the operational or strategic environment. The insurgents in this case were foreigners to the small village, infiltrating from neighboring areas. This situation cemented in my mind the need for a military professional to take career risks by exercising disciplined initiative in difficult circumstances. Combat is an imperfect informational environment; intuition can save lives. The military professional will be faced with a question in her career: "Should I disobey this order?" and this chapter will show that history and the underpinning of the American military professional answers, "Yes, when your education, training, ethics, and mission indicate it is necessary for an outcome that positively affects the mission, and the team is certainly worth the risk it poses individually."

The Autonomous Professional

The military professional not only delivers violence as a means of political will, but must also be an astute manager of violence. As discussed in "Officership as a Profession," officers are managers of violence, where enlisted members are considered less expert; "they are specialists in the application of violence, not the management of violence."[3] In the modern context of the military profession, the autonomous professional is not required to be an officer or even a leader. Specifically due to information sharing and the digital connectivity of the modern world a seemingly insignificant tactical decision has the ability to spread to strategic significance more today than ever before, where a junior soldier can make lasting impacts on the profession.

The decision of an autonomous professional to break the rules contributes to the fulfillment of her duty, as defined within the constructs of operational strategy and commander's intent. The delivery of violence as an extension of the state's political will can occur directly or indirectly. Just War Theory attempts to define the moral gray area of killing in the name of politics; however, many military actions beyond killing raise serious ethical questions to some in the field.[4] This is particularly true when evaluating deception, psychological operations, and certain targeting methodologies. Philosopher Immanuel Kant stated that actions in the name of duty are inherently moral, yet history shows that many acts performed in the name of duty have been inherently immoral. Duty to the mission, the ethical foundations of the military, and the nation ultimately guide the professional through moral quandaries. In operational environments where strategies are examined through individual tactical actions, the magnification of risk grows.

The US Army's Center for the Army Profession and Ethic has defined a profession as "a trusted, self-policing, and relatively autonomous vocation whose members develop and apply expert knowledge as human expertise to render an essential service to society in a particular field."[5] In the decade of conflict that followed the events of 9/11, increasing levels of autonomy were granted to America's most junior leaders to make decisions that might have international significance. During the Napoleonic era, the relevance of the strategic corporal was noted as the ability for even the lowest of soldiers to have great impact on the outcome of a campaign. In the information age, actions by subordinate elements are easily manipulated and magnified for global significance.

Since the Napoleonic era, the idea of the strategic corporal has been raised under various definitions. Today, modern soldiers must be in tune with operational or strategic effects of their actions as they execute missions throughout the globe. Special operations forces are an example of forces that have developed individual operators who meet many of the criteria of a strategic corporal. It is important to note that developing this strategic corporal, like the autonomous professional, is not limited to academic study and formal education.[6] To successfully grow strategic corporals requires a holistic development of professional education with self-study; operational decision-making is not necessarily limited to major combat operations. The basis for a strategic corporal is in many ways a background for the autonomous professional who will eventually be pressed into autonomy in combat.

Combat is not the only crucible for the military professional; in noncombat roles, professionals may still need to act autonomously to save lives or complete the mission. Much of the vital development of twentieth-century strategic leaders occurred during interwar operations, including limited engagements in the so-called Banana Wars of Central America. Many of the leaders entering the environment post-9/11 in America had little or no combat experience, instead drawing from experience with peacekeeping operations in the 1990s and exposure to combat scenarios at regional training centers. These experiences later were tied into various autonomous actions that occurred during the conflicts post-9/11.

The American military has long celebrated maverick leaders willing to eschew unsuccessful thinking to embrace an unpopular course of action that is ultimately successful. At the crux of this discussion is that when faced with a decision of failure or breaking the rules, these leaders break the rules, picking the course of action that cements their legend. Professionals are expected to navigate ethical dilemmas and capture these lessons to teach the next generation, much of which is packaged with myth and legend. Martin Cook notes that the identities professional militaries are often taught are developed through stories from their ancestors that exhibited certain traits and values.[7] For instance, look at the popularity of legends such as Leonidas and his king's guard at Thermopylae, an example of violating the decisions of the ruling body to fight a delaying action against an invading Persian force. The various fictional accounts of this battle live on in the reading lists of American militaries.[8]

Modern professional militaries are learning institutions that pass lessons down through the generations, and not all lessons make it to the tomes of future strategy. Field craft, tactical innovations shared over a beer, or war stories represent an important informal part of the development of a military professional. Tribal wisdom of the collective profession is a reinforcing means of valuating the formal doctrine of the profession. Many of the lessons that drove the development of the author toward the specific experience were based on personal relationships with combat-tested mentors. Over many cups of coffee, my rifle company first sergeant, with a lip full of chewing tobacco, would regale me with lessons learned from operations from Panama to Iraq. This knowledge transfer from veteran to junior leader was invaluable, and only a snapshot of the importance of storytelling in professional development.[9] The value of these mentorship relationships for burgeoning military professionals is a connection from the abstract to real experience. These relationships generate a context for the important and tough decisions to come. The empowerment granted to junior leaders in the military is underwritten by the mentoring provided by seasoned professionals. This relationship is at risk in a military that adheres to "impossible standards in a misguided, centralized attempt to limit every imaginable accident or error," and the failure to push the limits and accept more risk will limit the development of autonomous professionals.[10]

The United States has granted significant latitude in decision-making to its military due in part to its professional status. American military professionals are empowered by an oath and enabled by their expertise with the authority to make rapid decisions regarding the application of violence in pursuit of the state's goals. This latitude is increasingly governed by ever-stringent rule sets, regulations, and oversight by various command levels. Due to the increase in digital mission command influence, this means that military professionals must know when to break the rules. A self-regulating profession cannot let regulations become sacred cows preventing the fulfillment of our duty, or the winning of wars.

The Decision Point

Military professionals might train for years or decades before they are required to take the most critical of professional actions—decision-making in combat. The scenarios presented during combat operations are the focus of this chapter, where a decision requiring autonomous action necessitates an act that objectively is ethically wrong because it violates established rules or regulations. The ethical violation could be necessary at that time to achieve the state's objectives. Dwight Eisenhower served for nearly three decades before he would lead troops in combat during Operation Torch in 1942. His collective decades of training and expertise culminated in the series of decisions he made as a task force commander. The defining moment in a military leader's or soldier's career may occur early in his or her career, or after many decades in the military. An individual does not know when her defining moment will come. Military professionals must prepare continuously to be capable of making a crucial decision at a time and place not of their own choosing.

One of the most difficult decision points where the autonomous professional emerges is over the application of violence. The decision to kill a person, whether enemy, suspected enemy, or potential civilian, must be weighed deeply and quickly, and there are many competing inputs on the current battlefield that dominate a soldier's limited capacity to interpret information. The actions are simple—a short command on a radio or the squeeze of a trigger—but they require extensive training and education to ensure that the result, the death or dismemberment of a human being, is justifiable within the context of autonomous professionalism. The pressure or decision to kill an enemy has changed little since the beginning of time, but the ramifications of this action today are fundamentally different. A spear through an enemy combatant or villager by a Roman legionnaire probably did not impact the operational strategy of a campaign. The complexity of war, particularly counterinsurgency in the digital age, is vastly different.[11] The framework and context for killing enemy combatants are the changing face of warfare. With digitally enabled mission command, leaders are omnipresent while seemingly disconnected from the reality of fighting and tactical decision-making. The interjection of higher echelons into the tactical fight represents a serious challenge to the decision-making of tactical professionals. While killing is only one of many tools used by the military in the pursuit of the nation's goals, because of the added complexity tactical leaders often have to countermand an order of a higher headquarters. Professionals do not enjoy killing the enemy; this activity of the battlefield is a means to fulfilling their professional obligation. The action of killing alone does not win wars; but rather the professional's ability to make decisions and implement dilemmas for the enemy commander does. In the end, that is the military professional's call to fulfillment of duty. Regardless of the circumstances at hand, according to Kant, completion of the mission and fulfillment of the base duty to the citizens of the nation provide an inherent justification.[12]

Breaking the rules is not an indication of indiscipline but rather is a by-product of the operational environment. As any soldier who served in combat can attest, his or her actions in combat are different from actions in training and are difficult to analyze after the event. Service as a military professional presents a difference between ideal situations, academic or training, and the variables dealt with in the real world. Whether it is an ethical dilemma in a garrison environment or the act of imparting violence on the enemy, the professional is expected to be able to navigate these decisions for the best possible outcome of the mission, country, and troops under his authority. "Soldiers make and act on decisions during war. The decision to go to war is political; decisions on the conduct of war are military" in nature.[13] Often military ethics focus on the conduct of military decisions in a conflict deemed unjust or on decisions made in violation of Just War Theory. Theoretical situations fail to consider the variables presented to the military professional that will ultimately require a professional to take a significant personal or career risk.

While strategists and historians have discussed the implication of technology on the battlefield ad nauseam, the implications for the future in the twenty-first and twenty-second centuries are staggering; the human brain of the military professional will be challenged by inputs never seen or imagined before. The ability to conceptualize across multiple domains in tactical and operational situations will require flexibility in thought and organization. The move toward an organization of box checkers and a compliance-driven profession will not allow for this flexibility of thought. This prediction by Israeli expert on mission command, Eyal Ben-Ari, demonstrates why the future will need autonomous professionals now more than ever: "The military organization of the future is likely to be much more 'organic' in nature. Organic organizations are characterized by a more flexible division of labor, decentralization of decision making, low reliance on formal authority and hierarchy and on rules and regulations to coordinate work, and greater reliance on non-restricted, two-way, informal communications and coordination systems."[14]

It is important for the military to embrace a less-risk-averse approach to leadership in operational environments. This mind-set in training and combat operations develops a professional culture from which military leaders can make decisions in more realistic environments, outside of a garrison environment. The autonomous professional often emerges when training, experience, and conscience drive him or her to transcend the limitations of the organizational bureaucracy. Right now, risk aversion protects the entire organization while allowing the burden of any mistake or incident to rest on the shoulders of a lower-level commander.

Risking Careers

Many leaders are faced at some point in their careers with a decision that could put at risk either their future career, or the life of one of their soldiers. Until a point where the organization starts encouraging tactical and operational commanders to accept more risk, military professionals will assume ownership for the risk of their decisions and ultimately any impact on their career. For the autonomous professional, the necessary decision will often ask the decision-maker to place the lives of subordinates over the life of an enemy or third party. A situation could come up where the professional has to risk his or her soldiers against an enemy threat for completion of the mission to protect civilians. This is a burden that occurred often during the wars in Iraq and Afghanistan. Modern military professionals must be willing to accept that burden. The chief of staff of the Army, Gen. Mark Milley, remarked in October 2016 that future conflicts would require a new type of leaders, those who have "the willingness to disobey specific orders to achieve the intended purpose, the willingness to take risks to meet the intent, the acceptance of failure and practice in order to learn from experimentation: these are all going to have to be elevated in the pantheon of leader traits."[15] The US Army will be unable to achieve a force as described by General Milley, if we continue down the path set in place by the organizational conduct of post–Vietnam War force.

An unintended consequence of an all-volunteer force that views the profession as a permanent job and not just a career until the war is over is that decision-making can be impeded by the perceived value of one's career. This can cause risk-averse leaders that choose to play it safe, even in the most mundane of decisions, to propagate throughout the ranks. This trend within the profession can be countered only by dedicated professionals who are rewarded for completing the mission and pushing the limits of their organization. The focus on obedience that was described by Huntington as the basis of military professionalism stresses a dogmatic adherence to the rules and hierarchy of the military.[16] A perceived zero-defect culture and metric-driven micromanagement are the main justifications by surveyed respondents for deceiving the service in various situations in the study *Lying to Ourselves*.[17] The fault of the *Lying to Ourselves* essay is that the individual and the professional ethic take the blame instead of the organization's bureaucracy that generates many of the requirements that are discussed in the text. A self-regulating profession that fails to correct organizational deficiencies will continue to suffer from professional lapses. Even the most ethical professional who acts within a deeply flawed system will be mediocre at best. Obedience should not be the primary judging factor as to the rightness of actions. Good organizations do not make liars of their subordinates. In the military, candor is infrequently accepted as an appropriate feedback mechanism. When candid feedback occurs, it is normally washed over by those saying, "Well, the boss wants . . . ," or "the division wants . . . ," or "We'll see what we can do, but pick your battles, son." All military leaders at some point experience conversations that end with these phrases. Dishonesty in official reports is objectively bad, but is it less bad than losing a war, or failing to meet operational readiness? Judging commanders in combat or operational units that summarily answer requirements while focusing resources on mission accomplishment is subjectively less bad than dishonesty. Tactical leaders who are able to evaluate the enemy, seize the initiative within their commanders' intent, who fully understand the operational and strategic goals of their position, find themselves the victor.

With this discussion in mind, breaking the rules or knowingly violating orders based on this scenario are the tenets of a true military professional.

The authors of *Lying to Ourselves* discussed the phrases "mission accomplishment" and "taking care of soldiers" as euphemisms used to rationalize the dishonesty within the profession. This is counter to the definition of military professionals put forth in this argument. Rather, as the authors of *Lying to Ourselves* suggest, professionals who practice leading truthfully and candidly with senior leaders when able or necessary are shouldering the burden of a true military professional. Being willing to stand on the carpet, before a tribunal, or take a reprimand for pushing the limits of acceptable tactical or administrative behavior is a test of an individual's leadership abilities.

US military history is filled with these types of stories, which are the true bedrock of America's professional military might. As Adm. William Sims put it, "It involves the two wholly essential twin qualities of loyalty and initiative. . . . Loyalty in itself is always indispensable, but initiative without loyalty is dangerous. It is their intelligent and trained cooperation which is the vital characteristic of modern armies."[18] The autonomous professional exercises judgment and initiative under the tenets of loyalty to the mission, nation, and profession.

The weakness in *Lying to Ourselves* is that the essay frames violations as indiscipline and a breakdown of the professional ethic, instead of focusing on how professionals exercise resiliency and their entrusted responsibility to make decisions when confronted with contradictory information or guidance. Leaders in conflicts in the near future might be isolated due to breakdowns in communications created by adversary cyber and electromagnetic activities. In these scenarios, if they follow accepted practices and procedures that could end in failure, the risk of punishment for infractions of policy cannot exceed the consequences of tactical failure. Situations in the post-9/11 era have allowed for scenarios where it is accepted to lose if the rules were followed.

A risk-averse mind-set will fail to capitalize on moments where subordinate unit initiative may win the war. Kant offers a solution to the "dirty hands" of a leader: "All actions that affect the rights of other men are wrong if their maxim [rule] is not consistent with publicity."[19] In this discussion, public acknowledgement of a violation of the rule serves two purposes: transparency for the autonomous professional and reconfirmation of the latitude granted to the professional.

The autonomous professional can function effectively only if candor and trust are reasserted as important values of the profession. Candor requires exposure by a military professional. The military professional that is punished for giving candid feedback or finds candor not a part of his or her organization lacks the ability to influence events when their judgment disagrees with an order or rule. If commanders or the nation are expected to trust their military professionals, then an environment of trust will not exist without candor in communications and relationships among the profession.[20] If it is acknowledged that rules are capable of being broken by the autonomous professional, then sweeping under the rug any evidence of that event would be counter to the basis for an autonomous professional.

Our creeds and ethos support the personal responsibility necessary for an autonomous professional to thrive. The Sixth Declaration of the Code of Conduct for Members of the United States Armed Forces is, "I will never forget that I am an American, fighting for freedom, responsible for my actions, and dedicated to the principles which made my country free."[21] This author believes that the principles of an autonomous professional further the basis that allowed America to build a successful military and country. When confronted with an unworkable problem, these guiding principles present a solution, whether it is revolutionary or evolutionary in its development. Unless the organization is willing to adapt, the autonomous professional must transcend this organizational limitation, because a military that is "expecting audacity among junior leaders in combat while micromanaging in garrison is a recipe for battlefield failure."[22]

Strict obedience to orders and a failure to act autonomously as subordinates can lead to disaster. Consider the Gallipoli Campaign. The operation for the Allies to invade the Gallipoli peninsula in 1915–16 was planned precisely to alter the eastern front and balance of powers in the conflict. A daring amphibious assault in the Dardanelles would relieve pressure on the Russians and cut off the Ottoman forces. On the first day of the invasion, Allied forces hit various beaches with little opposition. Orders were delivered for only individual units to proceed to a point on the beachhead. Under great efforts of discipline, Allied forces sat idle in place while Ottoman forces reinforced their position and prevented a breakout from the beachhead. Subordinate generals and officers failed to seize the initiative and save lives or win the fight. An attack in force in the absence of orders could have turned the tables in this disastrous campaign.

Later, on the western front, subordinate general officers would often push the limits of the orders presented to capitalize on breakthroughs. Due to lessons learned in previous campaigns such as Gallipoli, adjustments in the mission orders presented to Allied commanders by 1917–18 mirrored the flexibility given to German forces on the western front. On Y Beach the British commander faced no Turkish defenders and received no orders for twenty-nine hours after landing.[23] Imagine the different outcome that might have occurred in the campaign if the British commander, in violation of orders not to move past initially planned positions, attacked and potentially saved some of the more than 200,000 Allied soldiers who would later die. Loyalty to the mission and the army could have driven a different result with an autonomous professional opposed to an obedient subordinate commander.

The ability to bend or break rules is not a willful disregard of professional ethical responsibilities, but rather an acknowledgement that there will be moments when events force an impossible situation where a leader will be challenged between obedience and discretion of personal judgment. Leaders that develop quality combat teams will give candid feedback or guidance to a leader making a potentially risky decision, and the leaders' teams will be empowered to do the same.

Conclusion

The idea of violating orders while maintaining one's professional integrity could be viewed as a paradox. Within the US military, orders from headquarters are suggested courses of action based on the information available to the commander at the time of the order. With the shortened decision-making timelines that define combat in the twenty-first century, all too often commanders and staff believe they need to follow orders without initiative, creativity, or judgment. Commanders who are incapable of painting broad intent with allowable solutions to their problem set should not be a part of the mission command structure. Disobeying or applying judgment in a scenario is the reason why we want humans who make decisions based on the facts on the ground and not on preprogrammed inputs like robots. There is a difference in scenarios where soldiers or leaders engage what they believe to be an enemy combatant and make a mistake, versus situations where they knowingly engage noncombatants. As the staff officer whom I replaced in 2010 told me, "FRAGOs [fragmentary orders] from higher aren't orders, but a starting point for negotiations."

A professional military can develop leaders who will protect and grow professionals willing to go all in and risk their selfish desires for the good of the mission and protection of their soldiers. It is possible to violate orders while maintaining good order and discipline. Situational awareness and judgment drive individual actions. Integrity, honor, and selfless service are driving forces that help us make these difficult ethical decisions on the battlefield. The crossover from being a participating member of the military to an autonomous professional occurs when an individual soldier attains enough knowledge and expertise to know when he or she must act autonomously by breaking the rules based on his or her individual judgment.

As stated previously in the Kantian model, if the actions fulfill the outcome of your duty, then those actions are inherently moral. Let the historians debate the significance of military professionals in battle on a given day. If the nation's core values shift and leadership clearly communicates the expectations for outcome of the national objectives, then the military professional is expected to shift accordingly. Failure to consistently communicate this need, as Rebecca Johnson highlights in chapter 6, results in a breakdown of the ability of the profession to conduct its mission and degrades the trust of the nation. Professionals complete the mission, however imperfect, and continue to fight another day. If the bedrock of the military profession is the trust imparted by the civilian population, then the profession must trust its professionals to make decisions and break the rules when necessary if doing so furthers the development of the nation's trust through decisively winning conflicts.

Notes

1. Snider and Matthews, *The Future of the Army Profession*, 361, 365, 367 (quote).
2. For a selection of texts on *jus in bello*, see Harvard's excellent resources: Jennifer Allison, "Program on International Law and Armed Conflict," *Harvard Law School Library*, "Research Guide," last updated 24 May 2017, http://guides.library.harvard.edu/c.php?g=310988&p=2079383.
3. Huntington, "Officership as a Profession," 11.
4. McMahan, *Killing in War*.
5. Center for the Army Profession and Ethic, "What Is the Army Profession?," September 2014, http://cape.army.mil/Army%20Profession/cape-appam-web-sep14.pdf.
6. Liddy, "The Strategic Corporal," 141, 142.
7. Cook, *A Moral Warrior*, 69.
8. Steven Pressfield, *Gates of Fire* (London: Bantam Books, 1998).
9. Walter Swap, Dorothy Leonard, Mimi Shields, and Lisa Abrams, "Using Mentoring and Storytelling to Transfer Knowledge in the Workplace," *Journal of Management Information Systems* 18, no. 1 (2001), 97.
10. David Barno and Nora Bensahel, *The Future of the Army* (Washington, DC: Atlantic Council, 2016): 26.

11. Stanley McChrystal, *Team of Teams* (New York: Penguin, 2015).

12. Sydney Axinn, *A Moral Military* (Philadelphia: Temple University Press, 2009), 147.

13. Axinn, *A Moral Military*, 2.

14. Snider and Matthews, *The Future of the Army Profession*, 386.

15. Gen. Mark Milley, remarks at the Association of the US Army convention, October 2016, https://www.army.mil/article/176231/milley_army_on_cusp_of_profound_ fundamental_change.

16. Huntington, "The Military Mind," 40.

17. Wong and Gerras, *Lying to Ourselves*.

18. Benjamin J. Armstrong, "The Two Most Important Qualities of Followers" [blog], 1 July 2015, http://fromthegreennotebook.com/2015/07/01/the-two-most-import ant-qualities-of-followers/.

19. Axinn, *A Moral Military*, 147

20. Paul Paolozzi, *Closing the Candor Chasm: The Missing Element of Army Professionalism* (Carlisle, PA: Strategic Studies Institute, 2013), 4, 41.

21. Axinn, *A Moral Military*, 51.

22. Barno and Bensahel, *The Future of the Army*, 36.

23. Brett A. Friedman, "The Battle of Gallipoli," *The Strategy Bridge*, https://thestrategy bridge.org/the-bridge/2015/4/24/the-battle-of-gallipoli.

CHAPTER 5

When the Military Profession Isn't

Tony Ingesson

Introduction

Ever since Samuel P. Huntington published his seminal *The Soldier and the State* in 1957, the idea of a military profession has been embraced by military educational institutions worldwide, and particularly by those in the West. However, the concept of the military profession (in the universal sense) is subject to considerable conceptual stretching. In addition, the focus on professionalism in general, and Huntington in particular, obscures the timeless complexity of military decision-making and leadership by reducing it to the status of a profession.

Military leadership demands considerably more than what most traditional professionals have to cope with, due to the fluid nature of strategy, which is essentially political policy, and the need to prevail over an adversary. This does not imply that military service is any less demanding intellectually, or that the ambitions of military organizations are any lower than those of traditional professions. It does mean, however, that the inherent complexity of military decision-making, and its links to policy, needs to be recognized. This is particularly relevant in organizations that strive to adopt frameworks for autonomous decisions by lower-level leaders, such as mission command.

Huntington's Professionals

Let's begin our analysis with Huntington, since he was the one who popularized the concept of military professionalism and its implications. According to Huntington, the three criteria that distinguish a professional are expertise, responsibility, and corporateness.[1]

Expertise refers to a specialized body of knowledge that is furthered through "contact between the academic and practical sides of a profession through journals, conferences, and the circulation of personnel between practice and teaching."[2] In specifying that there should be an academic side, Huntington makes a distinction between the expertise that arises as a result of science and expertise that is based on a craft.

The responsibility criterion refers to the fact that the professional performs a service that is essential to the functioning of society. Huntington states that a professional ceases to be a professional when he refuses to accept this social responsibility. As an example, Huntington mentions a physician who uses his skills for "antisocial purposes."[3] The example does not, however, clarify to whom the physician is responsible first. Is it the rulers of the society or its citizens? If the society in which the physician lives orders him to do something that goes against his own conscience, what would be the antisocial option? Fortunately for the physician, he is part of a profession that is present all over the whole world, and that has a very clear universal ethos, as defined by the Hippocratic oath. The most fundamental aspect is very clear: the physician is responsible toward the patient first. A physician who disregards this principle risks losing his medical license.

While Huntington does not bring it up, we can add another example of a traditional profession: a lawyer. While lawyers might not always have immaculate reputations for assuming social responsibility, especially not in the United States, they too have to submit to a crystal-clear ethos. Their responsibility is toward their clients and the law. While a lawyer can search for loopholes in the law, she cannot break that law. Neither can she betray the trust of a client. If any such transgressions occur, the lawyer risks disbarment.

The last of the three criteria, corporateness, implies that the professional shares a sense of organic unity and sees herself as part of a special group that is separate from lay persons.[4] However, this is a vague criterion. Everyone with any sort of clear specialization, ranging from plumbers to taxi drivers, will arguably see themselves as part of an organic unity and separate themselves from lay persons.

In his definition of the military profession Huntington emphasized that military professionals are experts in "the management of violence." He elaborated by explicitly stating that military officers with different specializations are excluded from the definition of military professionals: "The skills of these experts may be necessary to the achievement of the objectives of the military force. But they are basically auxiliary vocations, having the same relation to the expertise of the officer as the skills of the nurse, chemist, laboratory technician, dietician, pharmacist, and X-ray technician have to the expertise of the doctor."[5]

In large, complex, and specialized military organizations, the distinction becomes difficult to apply. If only officers who are experts in the management of violence are military professionals, then logically that would mean that not only doctors but also for example pilots of unarmed aircraft, sensor operators, technical systems experts, and many other specializations are excluded from the definition of military professionals. Thus, we end up with military organizations that are clearly stratified: those officers directly involved in combat tasks (the professionals), and everyone else (the auxiliary vocations).

Such stratification would be strongly detrimental to the efficiency and esprit de corps of any contemporary military organization. Apart from aspects related to career progression and status, the two categories would not even share the same ethics and level of expertise, according to this definition. Even worse, the two groups would, according to Huntington's definition, not be part of the same organic unity, which would compromise their ability to work together.

Empirically, this definition also leads to problems. How do we, for example, categorize officers who serve in an engineer battalion within an armored brigade? To the extent that they are more concerned with, say, laying bridges or clearing mines, they are more auxiliary than professional, according to Huntington's definition. What if one of them switches to a more combat-oriented assignment? Does she then suddenly become a professional? Or, in the case of the opposite, does she suddenly lose the status of a professional? The increasing prevalence of cyber warfare and other non-kinetic tasks will further complicate this scenario.[6]

Having concluded that there are significant problems with Huntington's definition of a military professional, we next turn to the academic definition of a professional, a definition originally developed by sociologists.

The Definition of a Profession

Huntington's definition of a profession is clearly influenced by the works of sociologist Talcott Parsons, published between the late 1930s and early 1950s.[7] This reveals that Huntington was strongly influenced by the research on professions that was in vogue within sociology at the time. Huntington thus sought to apply the concept of professions used in sociology in a military context. However, the concept of professions is disputed. When *The Soldier and the State* first appeared, a contemporary definition was based on four criteria:

- A high degree of generalized and systematic knowledge;
- Primary orientation to the community interest rather than to individual self-interest;
- A high degree of self-control in behavior through *codes of ethics internalized in the process of work socialization* [my emphasis] and through voluntary associations organized and operated by the work specialists themselves;
- A system of rewards (monetary and honorary) that is primarily a set of symbols of work achievement and thus ends in themselves, not means to some end of individual self-interest.[8]

The issue of ethics is a problem, because while all military organizations have such codes, there is no universal military code of ethics. Military organizations across time and space are very different in this regard. For a doctor or a lawyer, the code of ethics is crystal clear. But what about military organizations? Huntington would argue that the protection of the state and/or its population comes first.[9] In many cases, that is true. But what about armies engaged in opportunistic wars of aggression? Or those persecuting their own populations? They are not morally equivalent to modern military organizations in democratic countries, but they are no less military for doing so, even if their actions are reprehensible. A doctor who kills patients is arguably no doctor, and a lawyer that disregards the law or betrays the trust of a client is no lawyer, but what about a military officer that participates in a war of aggression, or takes part in persecution? That officer is a criminal, for sure, but is he not an officer? The problem is not that military officers fail to rise to the level of traditional professionals, but rather that their vocation is something completely different altogether.

Let's turn to a more modern, frequently quoted, academic definition of a profession:

- It is a full-time, liberal (nonmanual) occupation.
- It establishes a monopoly in the labor market for expert services.
- It attains self-governance or autonomy (i.e., freedom from control by any outsiders, whether the state, clients, lay persons, or others).

- Training is specialized and yet also systematic and scholarly.
- Examinations, diplomas, and titles control entry to the occupation and sanction the monopoly.

Member rewards, both material and symbolic, are tied not only to their occupational competence and workplace ethics but also to contemporaries' belief that their expert services are "of special importance for society and the common weal."[10]

This time there is no mention of codes of ethics. However, a new criterion poses a new problem: freedom from control by any outsiders, which includes the state. A modern Western military organization is normally, and in accordance with basic democratic ideals should be, controlled by the state. Thus, this modern definition also poses a problem for the concept of the military profession. In nondemocratic countries, the military might enjoy more freedom from control, but then a distinct set of issues arises, and therefore nondemocratic countries fall outside the scope of the argument presented here.

Thus, according to the above definition there can be no military profession in the broad sense even though specific military organizations such as the US Army could aspire to create their own professions. Those would, however, be something quite different from the traditional professions, which transcend national borders and have traditions that in most cases date back centuries. Instead of the military profession, it would be the US Army profession, with only tentative links to the military occupations of other eras and nations.

The US Army Profession

The US Army clearly states in the publication *Army Doctrine Reference Publication 1, The Army Profession* that it has embraced the US Army profession. This implies that the US Army profession is a unique vocation, as opposed to the military profession in a universal sense. According to *The Army Profession*, the members of a profession:

- Provide a unique and vital service to society, without which it could not flourish.
- Provide this service by developing and applying expert knowledge.
- Earn the trust of society through ethical, effective and efficient practice.
- Establish and uphold the discipline and standards of their art and science, including the responsibility for professional development and certification.

- Are granted significant autonomy and discretion in the practice of their profession on behalf of society.[11]

The creation of the US Army profession solves the problems inherent in the concept of a universal military profession by creating a specific profession with a clearly defined membership. However, four problems remain: ethics, autonomy, uniqueness, and the basic concept. Next, we will turn to these four problems.

Problem: Ethics

The Army Profession defines what it calls "the [US] Army Ethic" as being "expressed in our moral principles, Army Values, oaths and creeds, laws and regulations, and customs, courtesies, and traditions." Thus, *The Army Profession* makes it quite clear that the US Army ethic is a rather complex construct, which includes a very large number of influences and components. There is no clear, single, overriding core value. It clarifies that the US Constitution and the UCMJ, as well as the US Code of Federal Regulations, serve as the legal and regulatory basis of the Army ethic. The UCMJ and the US Code of Federal Regulations, however, are the result of policy decisions and subject to change over time. This is different compared to legal professionals, because the ethics for US Army professionals are determined by the content of the laws, whereas legal professionals are obliged to uphold the concept of the law itself. Even those who argue that there is such a thing as a professional military ethic acknowledge that it is based on, in addition to the functional imperatives of the profession, national culture as well as international laws and treaties.[12]

The main problem for the Army ethic is that it may not be internally consistent. National cultures inevitably change, and the moral principles of an individual could, for example, clash with laws and regulations. Even lawyers and physicians can run into problems of this sort, but, unlike military leaders, they at least have clearly defined core values to guide them. Thus, if anything, such as individual morals, clashes with these core values, the core values take precedence over the individual morals. For example, a physician is obliged to treat even individuals she thinks are undeserving of life and health. A lawyer, once committed to a client, must defend to the best of his ability even a person he knows is guilty. There is no such clarity for military service members, however.

What happens, for example, when a soldier witnesses an act that would be reprehensible and illegal in her home country, such as sexual abuse, but has standing orders not to intervene, and does not have the legal mandate to act? US troops found themselves in such situations in Haiti in the 1990s and Afghanistan two decades later.[13] If individual moral principles are to take precedence, the military professional that acts to stop abuses can become subject to disciplinary actions. Thus, it seems that the Army ethic is not clear on the hierarchy of the values it encompasses. Which comes first, laws or morals? If it is the latter, where does one draw the line? Is it justifiable to jeopardize an entire mission to save one individual from abuse? If not, how many potential victims are required to make the decision to abandon the mission in favor of protecting the innocent?

In a combat situation, a military service member might face ethical dilemmas of hopeless complexity, to which there are no clear answers. These ethical dilemmas present a problem of far greater magnitude than the problems that physicians and lawyers must contend with in their everyday work.

Problem: Autonomy

The Army Profession also states that a profession is "a trusted, disciplined, and *relatively autonomous* [my emphasis] vocation."[14] However, in any given conflict both the means and the ends tend to be politicized. The fact that military organizations are entrusted with the right to exercise deadly force also means that politicians have strong incentives to limit the autonomy of the military professionals, since the methods employed by the troops may have unwanted political consequences, regardless of whether the goals are achieved.

As a result, in any given operational scenario, political restrictions to the autonomy of the US Army could be applied. In the Vietnam War, the infamous concept of free-fire zones (the correct technical term is "specified strike zone") was used to define a zone in which it was not necessary to obtain clearance from local political leaders before calling in air support or artillery.[15] Thus, in formal terms, troops fighting outside a specified strike zone had to constantly submit to the decisions of not only their own political leaders but also even local ones.

In Afghanistan similar restrictions have been applied, as a result of bilateral political negotiations between the Afghan and US governments.[16] To this is added the issue of national caveats, which allow each coalition nation to determine its own rules of engagement. These national caveats further undermine the concept of a universal military profession by highlighting the differences between how countries deploy military organizations. As in the Vietnam War, these restrictions, in the form of rules of engagement, have even been accused of leading to additional casualties.[17]

These kinds of restrictions might elicit different reactions, but they exist, and they will continue to exist in the future. These restrictions exist because military operations are subject to policy and have immediate and far-reaching political consequences. Thus, military operations can never be fully separated from politics. This symbiotic relationship between military operations and politics distinguishes military service members from traditional professionals. While physicians and other medical professionals are subject to regulations at the collective level, they do not have to submit to micromanagement to the same extent as military leaders. Legal professionals enjoy even stronger protection under the principles of the independent judiciary and the rule of law. In the case of lawyers, as Damaska eloquently put it, "Vigorous promotion of the client's interest is not inhibited by concern that the realization of governmental policy will thereby be obstructed."[18]

Problem: Uniqueness

By defining the US Army profession as something essentially unique, *The Army Profession* solves the problems inherent with the concept of a universal military profession, but creates a new one: What is gained by defining a unique profession? Originally, in the 1930s and 1940s, the British and American sociologists who founded the sociology of professions sought to identify the traits or qualities distinctive to professions. They wanted to establish what separates the professions from "other expert occupations and middle-class occupations."[19]

If the US Army profession is unique, then it cannot claim to belong to the same category as traditional professions, which are usually defined as doctors, lawyers, scientists, and engineers.[20] We have also seen that the Army profession is not based on Huntington's definition, since that would imply a stratification that included only a part of the US Army. What, then, is the purpose of defining the Army as a profession, if it is the only one of its kind, and exists only within a single organization? The use of the word "profession" inevitably leads to association with older concepts, which might be misleading and confusing. Military organizations should, instead of trying to establish similarities to traditional professions, embrace the uniqueness of military service. Those who command should take pride in being military leaders, rather than comparing themselves to traditional professionals.

Problem: The Basic Concept

The final problem with both the military profession and the US Army profession is that the whole concept of professions may be analytically and empirically useless. The tradition of creating lists of criteria that define professions, which was so popular in the 1930s to 1960s, for example, faced serious critique in the 1970s. Research has failed to confirm that the actual behavior of professionals corresponds to the characteristics ascribed to professions, and in fact has often revealed the exact opposite. The second problem is that the lists of characteristics tend to defy theoretical generalization and to be impossible to falsify empirically. For example, some sociologists have questioned why either theoretical knowledge or autonomy should qualify as an essential criterion of professionalism in practice.[21] Even worse, all the criteria of a profession are equally difficult to generalize theoretically and falsify empirically.

A Different Approach

A crucial difference between military leaders and members of the traditional professions is that military leaders implement policy. To quote Clausewitz, "War is a mere continuation of policy by other means."[22] Thus, in this regard, military service is more akin to vocations in the civilian administration, where policy is also implemented, than to traditional, apolitical professions. In this sense, military service members could be similar to the category of public employees Michael Lipsky defined as street-level bureaucrats.[23] Lipsky's definition, based on extensive empirical studies, shows that working within a bureaucracy is significantly more complex, nuanced, and demanding than the definition of a bureaucracy employed by, for example, Don Snider would lead us to believe.[24]

While this label may sound unflattering, it is an analytical concept rather than a normative one. Thus, it is neither below nor above the traditional professions, but rather an alternative view altogether. According to Lipsky, even traditional professionals could be street-level bureaucrats.[25]

Lipsky states that a street-level bureaucrat is a public employee who enjoys a significant degree of autonomy in her decision-making. This autonomy is a necessity, since street-level bureaucrats must cope with goals that often tend to be ambiguous, vague, or conflicting. In addition, street-level bureaucrats rarely have enough resources, and the clients they interact with are more often than not less than enthusiastic about them. The street-level bureaucrats are found in schools, police, and social welfare departments, lower courts, legal services offices, and similar agencies.[26]

The problems that street-level bureaucrats face resemble the military concept of friction, and the policy goals they have to contend with are similar to the complex strategic objectives associated with contemporary counterinsurgency operations and nation-building enterprises. In both cases, autonomy is a solution that helps these decision-makers cope with friction and resistance.

The main problem for street-level bureaucrats and military leaders alike is that the situations they face often are too complicated to reduce to sets of rules and procedures. Traditional professionals usually face technical challenges only in the sense that they have to diagnose the problem and find the most effective solution. Street-level bureaucrats and military leaders, on the other hand, identify not only the problem but also what kind of outcome to strive for. To establish concrete goals, the military leader must interpret strategy, and then translate that into a vision that is applicable on the local level. While a doctor or a lawyer knows what the goal is—either heal the patient or uphold the law—the military leader will often have to ponder what the endgame should look like. Even in a traditional war, where the overall strategic goal might be obvious, there are difficult decisions for military leaders to make. How many troops can be sacrificed to achieve a given set of mission objectives? How many civilian casualties are acceptable? There are no easy answers.

For this reason, it is not possible to regulate in detail the daily activities of a street-level bureaucrat, just as it is impossible to regulate in detail every possible situation a military leader may encounter. Thus, discretion is necessary to provide sufficient flexibility to cope with the complexity of the situations the members of these two categories routinely face. This discretion is like that which a traditional professional enjoys, but unlike the autonomy of a physician or lawyer, this discretion revolves around the achievement of shifting policy goals rather than around the objectives defined by a universal ethos. In a military context this realization is the basis for the implementation of mission command.

It is important to point out that the street-level bureaucracy concept does not imply complete freedom of action. Lipsky argued that rules, directives, and regulations, as well as norms and practices of their respective occupational group, act as restraints. In addition, not all tasks require, or permit, a significant degree of autonomy. For example, Lipsky states that when police officers process gun permit applications, their discretion is limited.[27] In contrast, when these police officers encounter citizens who have committed minor infractions, they can choose whether to invoke the law selectively, often exercising wide discretion, such as letting a speeder off with a warning instead of a ticket.

The Three-Block War Revisited

In his influential article "The Strategic Corporal," Gen. Charles C. Krulak outlined a complex operational scenario in which a corporal found himself forced to make difficult decisions with potentially far-reaching strategic consequences.[28] Although this is a hypothetical rather than empirical scenario, it nevertheless lends itself well to illustrating the argument presented above, since it is a limited but realistic example of situations at the core of the issue.

In Krulak's article, Corporal Hernandez is a squad leader providing security for an international relief organization in a war-torn city in a fictional Central African nation. After two years of internal conflict, followed by the collapse of the government and economy, and finally, famine, the United States intervened by sending troops.[29] A month later the situation seemed to have stabilized, when suddenly one of the previously warring factions, led by a man called Nedeed, starts to congregate near the boundary separating it from its rivals. Shortly thereafter, a crowd comprising an unusually large number of young adult males arrives at the checkpoint where Corporal Hernandez is in charge. They start throwing rocks and chanting anti-US slogans. When Corporal Hernandez, fearing that he is about to lose control over the situation, decides to close the road off completely, the crowd erupts in protest and begins to press forward.

During this development, someone shoots down a helicopter belonging to a nongovernmental organization within sight of the corporal's squad. A squad member sees two survivors emerge from the wreck, as elements from one of the factions rush toward the crash site, presumably with malicious intent.

As if this were not enough, three trucks carrying men from another faction, led by Nedeed's rival Mubasa, armed with automatic weapons and rocket-propelled grenades, appear at the checkpoint and force their way to the gate. The crowd keeps throwing rocks, and one of the corporal's squad members is injured and starts to bleed profusely.

Corporal Hernandez has robust and uncomplicated rules of engagement that state that anyone armed with an automatic weapon is considered hostile, as is anyone who intentionally threatens Marine personnel. Consequently, Corporal Hernandez has the right to use force. However, he decides not to use that option; instead he notifies an Allied unit of the movement of Nedeed's men and the helicopter crash, which prompts them to reinforce their checkpoints. The Allied unit informs Hernandez that it has already sent a team to pick up the survivors of the crash. Shortly thereafter, Marine reinforcements arrive at Hernandez's own checkpoint, which makes Mubasa's men hesitate and withdraw.[30]

Corporal Hernandez is faced with several difficult decisions with potentially far-reaching consequences. First, he must maintain control over the flow through the checkpoint. Second, he must act with consideration to the unfolding situation, in which several different events all demand his attention (Nedeed's men on the move, the crash, the crowd, and the appearance of Mubasa's men), but that he does not himself have enough resources to deal with. Third, he must react to the increasing level of threat to himself and his subordinates.

According to Krulak's interpretation of his own scenario, Corporal Hernandez's decisions had the potential to determine the outcome of the entire mission.[31] This responsibility would not fall on the shoulders of traditional professionals in such an environment, because they do not have to take the strategic impact of their decisions into account. In addition, they do not have to decide when it is justified to use deadly force in the name of the state. The most difficult decision might have been to prioritize among those in need of medical attention. A lawyer, scientist, or engineer would not have to decide whether to fire warning shots while rocks are raining down, causing injuries in a vastly outnumbered squad of a few men, who are trying to maintain order in a chaotic situation.

Policy is a crucial part of each of Corporal Hernandez's three decisions, even if he is not necessarily conscious of the fact. In the first decision, he decides to maintain control even at the risk of escalation, since this reaffirms his own resolve, as well as that of all the US troops in the area. Had he simply backed away, which might have deescalated the situation, the US troops would have been perceived as weak, which would undermine their ability to achieve their strategic goals. His second decision, to inform nearby allies about the helicopter crash and the movement of Nedeed's men, shows that he takes an active responsibility for the strategic situation, including when it concerns his allies instead of fellow Marines. The third decision is to accept the risk of bodily harm to himself and his Marines rather than risk civilian casualties, which shows that he takes into consideration humanitarian principles, as well as the reputation of the US troops and the repercussions these civilian casualties could have on the strategic level. Each of these three decisions, made at the corporal's discretion, could have had far-reaching implications and would thus have shaped future policy. Thus, Corporal Hernandez in the scenario fulfills the key criteria for being a street-level bureaucrat.

However, there are differences, albeit in degree rather than in kind. Corporal Hernandez, along with all other military leaders in similar positions, must face challenges that are far more demanding than those that most, if not all, street-level bureaucrats must contend with. This makes military leaders unique and is why these leaders should emphasize their own affiliation rather than try to compare themselves to others.

Conclusion

There is no such thing as a universal military profession. I have presented four definitions of the concept of a profession; Huntington's version, a 1960s academic version, a more contemporary version, and *The Army Profession*'s version. The four definitions differ from each other, which highlights the inherent problems in the concept itself. In addition, all four definitions are problematic when applied to a military empirical context. While the US Army can claim to have created a profession of its own, this profession has only tentative links to traditional professions. Indeed, in one study conducted in 2000 involving eighty company and field-grade US Army officers, a sizeable number of officers did not consider their vocation to be a profession.[32] However, this is not a critique of the US Army, or those who serve in it. Instead, it should be a source of pride.

First, it is an inevitable fact that military decision-making is constrained and shaped by policy. All other things equal, this makes military decisions more difficult than those of a doctor or a lawyer, since the military professional must scrutinize both the means and the end thoroughly. Thus, the military officer must, on his own, interpret the overarching objective in a complex and ambiguous operational environment, such as the three-block war scenario described by Krulak; this is even more challenging.[33] Add to this the aspect of an adversary that will attempt to predict, obstruct, and counter every decision, and complexity grows exponentially.

Members of traditional professions and military leaders alike should exercise judgment in their decisions, weighing not only the technical dimensions but also ethical considerations. However, unlike traditional professionals, military leaders must apply this process not only when identifying the problem and the means to achieve a solution but also when conceptualizing what that solution might look like in practice.

Being part of a profession may sound more glamorous and respectable than being compared to a street-level bureaucrat, but concealed behind the difference in labels is the fact both require considerable expertise. Thus, it is hardly surprising that military organizations have sought to compare themselves to traditional professions in their pursuit of legitimacy and recognition. However, I argue that military leaders, especially junior ones, have far more in common with street-level bureaucrats than they do with traditional professionals. More senior officers may have moved on from the street level, but nevertheless still must struggle with the same type of challenges. As they advance, they come ever closer to the policy level, and thus must take it into account even more than before. Junior military leaders have more in common with street-level bureaucrats than their senior counterparts, but this difference is related to the nature of the tasks these leaders face, rather than the status they have, or should have. Huntington argued that military organizations should be divided into professional and nonprofessional categories. The street-level bureaucracy perspective, however, does not justify stratification in status outside of the regular rank system. A lieutenant will have different challenges to cope with than a colonel, and although the latter outranks the former, the important thing is the lieutenant is just as much a military leader as the colonel.

By implementing policy under extraordinarily difficult circumstances, military leaders function as an extension of their own political level. This is not a problem, however. In a democracy like the United States, this means that military leaders are more directly linked to the will of the people than any of the traditional professions can ever be.

Being a military officer can require every bit as much specialized knowledge as a doctor or a lawyer, but it also requires something more: an ability to interpret and implement something as fickle and fleeting as policy (in the form of strategy), and, in addition, to prevail over an adversary.

Military officers accomplish all this without the guidance and clarity of purpose a universal ethos provides. Instead, that burden falls on individual judgment and organizational proficiency. That is why every military leader, regardless of rank or position, should take pride in saying, "I'm not just a professional: I am so much more than that. I am a military leader."

Notes

1. Huntington, *The Soldier and the State*, 8.
2. Huntington, 8.
3. Huntington, 9.
4. Huntington, 10.
5. Huntington, 11 (first quote), 12 (second quote).
6. For a more detailed critique of the limits imposed by the focus on the management of violence and how it relates to cyber warfare, see Stavridis, Rokke, and Pierce, "Crafting and Managing Effects."
7. Talcott Parsons, "The Professions and Social Structure (1939)," in *Essays in Sociological Theory* (Glencoe, IL: Free Press, 1954).
8. Bernard Barber, "Some Problems in the Sociology of the Professions," *Daedalus* 92, no. 4 (1963): 672 (quoted list).
9. Huntington, *The Soldier and the State*, 63.
10. Cited in Thomas Brante, "Professions as Science-Based Occupation," *Professions & Professionalism* 1, no. 1 (2011): 5 (quote).
11. US Army, *Army Doctrine Reference Publication No. 1*, 1-1.
12. Tony Pfaff, "Military Ethics in Complex Contingencies," in Snider and Matthews, *The Future of the Army Profession*, 411.
13. For information regarding the mandate and law enforcement in Haiti, see Philippe Girard, "Peacekeeping, Politics, and the 1994 US Intervention in Haiti," *Journal of Conflict Studies* 24, no. 1 (2004), https://journals.lib.unb.ca/index.php/jcs/article/view/290/461. For a more anecdotal story regarding Haiti, see Nathan A. Wike, "What Would We Lose by Winning? The Mission vs. Morality," *The Strategy Bridge*, https://thestrategybridge.org/the-bridge/2015/10/8/what-would-we-lose-by-winning-the-mission-vs-morality. For information regarding the issue of US troops witnessing sexual abuse in Afghanistan, see Joseph Goldstein, "U.S. Soldiers Told to Ignore Sexual Abuse of Boys by Afghan Allies," *New York Times*, 20 September 2015, http://www.nytimes.com/2015/09/21/world/asia/us-soldiers-told-to-ignore-afghan-allies-abuse-of-boys.html.
14. US Army, *Army Doctrine Reference Publication No. 1*, 1-1.
15. US Department of the Army, *Report of the Department of the Army Review of the Preliminary Investigations into the My Lai Incident*, 9-7, https://www.loc.gov/rr/frd/Military_Law/pdf/RDAR-Vol-I.pdf.
16. Rowan Scarborough, "Rules of Engagement Limit the Actions of U.S. Troops and Drones in Afghanistan," *Washington Times*, 26 November 2013, http://www.washingtontimes.com/news/2013/nov/26/rules-of-engagement-bind-us-troops-actions-in-afgh/.

17. Rowan Scarborough, "Shades of Vietnam: Spike in U.S. Troop Deaths Tied to Stricter Rules of Engagement," *Washington Times*, 5 December 2013, http://www.washingtontimes.com/news/2013/dec/5/increase-in-battlefield-deaths-linked-to-new-rules/.

18. Cited in Robert W. Gordon, "The Independence of Lawyers," Faculty Scholarship Series, Paper 1361 (1988), *Yale Law School Legal Repository Service*, http://digitalcommons.law.yale.edu/fss_papers/1361, 10–11.

19. David Sciulli, "Structural and Institutional Invariance in Professions and Professionalism," in *Sociology of Professions: Continental and Anglo-Saxon Traditions*, ed. Lennart G. Svensson and Julia Evetts (Gothenburg, Sweden: Bokförlaget Daidalos, 2015), 39.

20. Sciulli, "Structural and Institutional Invariance," 41.

21. Sciulli, 35, 36.

22. Carl von Clausewitz, *On War* (Ware, UK: Wordsworth, 1997), 22.

23. Michael Lipsky, *Street-Level Bureaucracy: Dilemmas of the Individual in Public Services* (New York: Russell Sage Foundation, 2010).

24. Donald M. Snider, "The U.S. Army as Profession," in Snider and Matthews, *The Future of the Army Profession*, 14.

25. Lipsky, *Street-Level Bureaucracy*, 14.

26. Lipsky, 27–28, xi.

27. Lipsky, 14, 15.

28. Charles C. Krulak, "The Strategic Corporal: Leadership in the Three Block War," *Marines Magazine*, January 1999, http://www.au.af.mil/au/awc/awcgate/usmc/strategic_corporal.htm.

29. Krulak, "The Strategic Corporal."

30. Krulak.

31. Krulak.

32. Gayle L. Watkins and Randi C. Cohen, "In Their Own Words: Army Officers Discuss Their Profession," in Snider and Matthews, *The Future of the Army Profession*, 120–21.

33. Krulak, "The Strategic Corporal."

CHAPTER 6

Ethical Requirements of the Profession
Obligations of the Profession, the Professional, and the Client

Rebecca Johnson

Introduction

While many in uniform equate the concept of professionalism with having short haircuts, staying in shape, and maintaining one's composure in stressful times, military professionals have more-fundamental obligations toward their service, their subordinates, and the public they serve. Each of these commitments holds ethical significance. It is the purpose of this chapter to explore that ethical significance. Since professions exist in relationship with a specific client, the ethical requirements of a profession must be examined relationally. There are the ethical requirements of the profession itself—the expertise, rules, and values that define the standards of the profession—in this instance, the profession of arms. There are the ethical requirements of the professional—the skill, leadership, and character that are needed in those responsible for maintaining the standards of the profession. Finally, there are the ethical requirements of the clients—the guidance, support, and values they need to enable the profession and its professionals to set and uphold those standards.

It might seem strange to examine the profession as distinct from the individual professionals who compose it, but doing so holds value. A profession is an institution that influences behavior in ways its individual members cannot. The profession itself survives the professionals who populate its ranks. Individual members are responsible for maintaining the health and strength of the profession (one cannot conceive of a profession without the existence of competent professionals), but no individual possesses the ability to change the profession itself. In this way, it is useful and important to distinguish between the two when examining ethical responsibility. Individuals have a specific range of ethical decisions for which they could be held responsible. While senior leaders have a significant span of control, which enlarges their range of ethical responsibility, their decisions are bounded by the leaders' tenure and authority. While also bounded by time and authority, institutions—and, by extension, professions—simply have a far greater reach through time and space than individual professionals.

Though often neglected in the study of professional ethics, it is likewise important to examine the ethical requirements of the client. Since the client is on the receiving end of the expertise and service provided by the profession and its professionals, there is a tendency to overlook the client's obligations to the profession and its members. While understandable, this oversight creates a lopsided view of professional relationship. Analysts may be tempted to place too much of the ethical burden on the profession and its members while overlooking the ethical burden of those who receive the profession's service. As can be seen in some of the other chapters of this book, in the context of the profession of arms this undervaluing of the client's responsibility in the civil-military relationship can result in people misdiagnosing a distorted profession–client or professional–client relationship as a lack of professionalism. This chapter will argue that there is a difference between whether the military exists as a profession and whether the relationships that compose that profession are robust.

Examining the ethical requirements of the three elements of the professional relationship reveals some important insights. Fundamentally, when each member of the relationship honors its responsibilities, the professional relationship flourishes. When any member—the profession itself, its members, or the clients—fails to uphold its or their obligations, the professional relationship suffers. In the context of the profession of arms, this can be seen in weakening trust, reduced expertise, and ultimately an erosion of the security provided by the military for the people and state.[1] While others in this volume contend that the military is not a profession, or merely aspires to be a profession, this chapter takes a different approach. When viewed as a three-dimensional relationship based on an agreed combination of expertise, trust, continued improvement, values, and service, one can see that the profession of arms does exist, though elements of the profession-professional, professional-client, and client-profession relationships could all be stronger.

This chapter will examine the proposition that professionalism is best viewed as a tridimensional relationship by looking at each facet of the relationship in turn and then bringing all facets together to evaluate the requirements for maintaining healthy professional relationships. While multiple factors have combined to weaken elements of these relationships, the profession of arms is fundamentally sound and entering a period of profession-professional renewal.

The Ethical Significance of a Profession

It has been established elsewhere, including by others in this book (in chapters 1, 2, and 10, for instance), that the military holds itself to be a profession. Given the generally high level of deference most policymakers and Americans show military leaders' judgment and the unparalleled ways in which Congress and the American people allow the military to self-regulate, this seems to be a reasonable conclusion. If the military is a profession, then logically it possesses certain responsibilities toward the client it serves and the members it trains and regulates. Likewise, the members of the profession—the professionals—have certain responsibilities to the profession itself and the client on whose behalf the professionals leverage their craft. Finally, the client holds obligations in the relationship as well to both the individual professionals who assist and the institution that prepares and supports those individuals. Those obligations and responsibilities hold ethical significance.

Here it is important to differentiate between morals and ethics. The professional relationship includes both moral and ethical responsibilities, but it is useful to understand them distinctly, even if they interact. Briefly, what is moral can be understood as that which strengthens the community.[2] Humans are inherently social beings, and morality is what allows us to flourish together amid all the frustrations and competing interests of communal life. Conversely, that which is immoral can be understood as that which erodes, undermines, or weakens the community.

In one sense ethics is the study of morality; it is the academic discipline many of us learned at school. Its meaning differs when applied to the professions. In this context ethics is understood as that which maintains the standards of the profession or strengthens the profession. Just as morality ensures human flourishing is possible in community, ethics ensure the professional relationships among the profession, the professionals, and the client flourish.

In this way, morality and ethics are conceptually related, but distinct. For example, service members have a moral obligation not to murder, even though they sometimes have an ethical obligation to kill. The military has a moral obligation not to squander the lives of the nations' sons and daughters, though it has an ethical obligation at times to send them to certain death. The American people have a moral obligation to provide sufficient material, social, and political resources to allow the military to do its job, though the people also have an ethical obligation at times to tell their political leaders why they will not provide resources to support one or more particular military campaigns.

Ethical Requirements of the Profession

To evaluate what allows a profession to flourish, we must first understand the basic requirements of the profession and its members. The Army tackled this question back in 2010 under Gen. Martin Dempsey's leadership at Training and Doctrine Command in *The Profession of Arms*.[3] The Army identified five core characteristics of professions, which track with five core traits of professionals (table 6-1).

Table 6-1. Key Attributes of the Profession of Army

THE PROFESSION	THE PROFESSIONAL
Expertise	Skill
Trust	Trust
Development	Leadership
Values	Character
Service	Duty

Source: US Army, *An Army White Paper*, 5.

According to Don Snider, "a profession has as its central organizing feature the production of a unique type of work—expert work—which, by its very nature, the society cannot do for itself. Such work, far from being optional or nice-to-have, is fundamental to life and security and thus essential if the society is to flourish."[4] For the military, this expertise is the disciplined use of violence for a political end; for a doctor, it would be the expert use of medical arts to preserve a patient's health.

Over the years scholars have spent a fair amount of time and mental energy developing the notion of professional military expertise.[5] In his 1957 classic *The Soldier and the State*, Samuel Huntington offers what perhaps is the best known of these conceptualizations. Huntington discusses professional expertise in the context of three functional responsibilities held by the military professional: (1) "a representative function, to represent the claims of military security within the state machinery," (2) "an advisory function, to analyze and to report on the implications of alternative courses of action from the military point of view," and (3) "an executive function, to implement state decisions with respect to military security even if it is a decision which runs violently counter to his military judgment."[6] While service members develop and demonstrate these facets of expertise in different ways as they mature in the profession, society expects the military to represent its judgments accurately concerning the disciplined use of violence for political ends, advise its leaders thoughtfully on the feasibility of violence to reach desired political results, and to then execute society's decisions effectively.

Since society lacks the military's expert ability to leverage disciplined violence for a political end, it largely trusts the military to define the standards for expertise, and subsequently holds the military accountable for the consequences for failing to demonstrate it. In the case of the US military, the client whose trust must be maintained is literally the US Constitution, though we most often think of the spirit of the Constitution as embodied by the American people. Service members take their oath to support and defend the Constitution, and not a political leader or party. Richard Swain identifies different facets of the trust relationship the military must maintain with the American people:

> The American people trust the Armed Forces with the armed defense of their nation. They trust military leaders with the lives of their spouses, their sons and daughters. They trust the Armed Forces to husband the resources they supply to provide for their defense. They trust military professionals to behave with legal and moral restraint when acting on their behalf and make known their displeasure when they stray. The American people trust the military forces to do their best to secure U.S. interests when ordered by their President, to be accountable to law, and not to threaten their lives and welfare when stationed among them.[7]

As long as the military maintains the public's trust by fulfilling each of its three functional responsibilities to represent, advise, and execute, the client (here seen as the American people, not its literal client, the Constitution) allows the profession to determine the rules and procedures by which it will operate. The professional is the expert, after all, and knows how best to employ her craft.

To build and maintain expertise, professions put a high premium on the development of individuals. Not just anyone can join a profession. Only those who demonstrate sufficient skill and potential for continued growth are allowed in, and each profession has some semblance of a credentialing process to evaluate that skill and potential (that, again, is largely self-regulated without overly invasive input from the client). Basic training, Officer Candidate School, and the Basic School are illustrations in the military context. Law school and the bar exam are illustrations in the legal context. Since expertise is perishable and must be maintained, professions also require continuing efforts to develop their members. These can be technical promotion requirements, annual fitness tests, rifle qualifications, and professional military educational requirements.

To ensure the profession remains focused on its client, this development of expertise must be tied to foundational values that benefit and resonate with the client. "Honor, courage, commitment" are the Marine Corps' values that support the mandates of the US Constitution and resonate with the American people. Without these values, the professional may be tempted to prioritize expertise over the client and undertake so-called expert actions that harm the client more than they help.

The final piece of glue that binds a profession to its client is the characteristic of service. Businesses exist to provide profit. Bureaucracies exist to provide efficiency. Professions exist to provide service to the client.[8] In chapter 2 of this volume, Jo Brick describes this type of service in terms of a fiduciary relationship between the profession and the American people. The client places trust in the professional's expertise because that expertise is used for the client's benefit. If the profession or its members were to stop serving the client and instead focus on serving themselves or chasing profit, they would cease to be a profession or professionals. Mercenaries or private security contractors are not professionals; security contracting is not a profession. Both groups possess the same skills as service members—often they have been service members before transitioning into contracting as veterans—but their activities are no longer understood as serving a client, but rather as servicing a contract for financial gain.

The most significant illustration of this commitment to service, and a stark distinction between service members and contractors, is the military's "unlimited liability," or "the acceptance of the risk of serious harm or of death, true service before self."[9] While it is common to focus on the giving end of disciplined violence, the true service element of the profession of arms comes on the receiving end. The military sacrifices its own members—sometimes in shockingly large numbers and against its own better judgment—in service to its client. Clearly security contractors die in combat zones as well, but they accept that danger to receive the financial reward that compensates for the level of risk. Service members receive combat pay, but that is often not what motivates individuals to join the military to begin with, to seek deployments once in uniform, or to drive their actions when deployed.

Ultimately, the profession itself is responsible for serving and maintaining the trust of its client by developing and demonstrating its expertise consistently and effectively in a manner consistent with its client's values. For the profession of arms, this means that the military is ethically responsible for ensuring that successive generations of professionals are capable of effectively applying violence in a disciplined manner for a political end in a manner that is consistent with American values.

Ethical Requirements of the Professional

If those are the ethical requirements of professions generally, and the profession of arms specifically, it follows that individual service members must fulfill certain responsibilities to maintain the standards of the profession. These responsibilities are seen in relationship; while the profession possesses ethical responsibilities to both its members and its client, so too does the professional possess ethical responsibilities to its institution and to the client he serves.

Service members have an ethical responsibility to maintain and develop their skill. To enter the profession, the minimum standard is tactical proficiency. To progress as professionals, the goal must be tactical excellence. Innovation—tactical, doctrinal, and strategic—is essential to maintaining and developing professional excellence in a complex, rapidly changing environment. In chapter 4 Mike Denny is right when he notes that professionals know when to break the rules. Why? Because expertise requires judgment, and sometimes that judgment tells the professional that the textbook answer will not work in a given set of circumstances. The professional accepts the consequences of bucking doctrine, tradition, or culture, and contributes to the profession by doing what his knowledge and experience tell him is right.

Service members have an ethical responsibility to maintain trust with the American people. One might immediately jump to Abu Ghraib, the desecration of corpses, or other battlefield crimes to illustrate this point, but arguably the services' seemingly lackadaisical attempts to eliminate sexual assault in the ranks is more telling. Congress was willing to allow the UCMJ to adjudicate potential breaches of combat ethics and the law of armed conflict, but it is considering removing UCMJ authority from commanders in sexual assault cases. While this is unlikely to happen, the National Defense Authorization Act 2015 calls for removing the statute of limitations on sexual assault prosecutions as well as a mandatory dishonorable discharge for certain sex offense convictions because the American people have lost confidence in the services' ability to prevent and punish sexual assaults on their own.[10] Trust, once lost, takes time to rebuild. It is every military professional's responsibility to maintain that trust in the first place and repair it where necessary. That is, unless the profession is willing to lose the significant latitude it currently holds for self-regulation.

Professionals have an ethical responsibility to develop those junior to them. This responsibility can become particularly challenging in times of protracted conflict when leadership development can take a backseat to mission accomplishment. Mentors will talk to service members about the importance of broadening opportunities and key developmental assignments, but the past decade and more of war has bred some leaders to focus on execution of tasks at the expense of cultivating subordinates' skill and judgment. Leaders must fight the temptation to micromanage and crush failure (failure being an essential element of innovating in response to an increasingly complex environment and enemy). Micromanaging and the zero-defects mentality make perfect sense for an individual in the short term, but they are disastrous to the profession over time. Leaders have the responsibility to allow subordinates to practice, fail, and grow without fear of negative consequences. Subordinates have the responsibility to show initiative and sometimes even to fail in order to grow.

Service members have an ethical responsibility to uphold American values while leveraging their expertise. There has been a lot of talk lately about the civil-military divide. Recently, James Fallows argued that the civil-military relationship has frayed in the United States due to the public's "reverent but disengaged attitude toward the military."[11] While Fallows certainly spurred a vigorous debate with his column, he high-lights the challenge of upholding a nation's values when the natural ties that would transmit those values have weakened.[12] While it is easy (and fair) to blame Americans for failing in their civic responsibility to know about the wars their country wages on their behalf, it is the professional's responsibility to consistently go back to the well to ensure his decisions and actions resonate with the nation he serves. In those moments when what is "right" contradicts what is tactically effective, efficient, or prac-tical, the professional must search for a way to leverage his expertise in the lethal use of force in a manner that upholds American values. If he ignores American values in the pursuit of lethality, he might be a very effective killer, but he is not a professional ably serving his client.

Service members have an ethical obligation to serve. This seems obvious, but the current uproar over retirement, education, and medical benefits highlights that segments of our military place a monetary value on their time in uniform. To be clear—I fully support service members receiving the benefits they were promised when they entered service. This is part of the nation maintaining the military's trust in its client. Still, a profession exists to serve someone other than the professionals. Leaders who recognize and value a commitment to service in their units and sub-ordinates make an important investment in the health of the profession of arms.

There has been a vigorous debate concerning the point at which a ser-vice member ought to be considered a professional, and therefore respon-sible for these professional requirements. Historically, enlisted service members were not considered professionals. This fact has been justified using two reasons. The first relates to the process needed to screen pro-fessionals into the profession. Because enlistees traditionally have served for a shorter length of time than officers and NCOs, they were less likely to develop and internalize the level of skill, depth of leadership, charac-ter, and commitment to service as those who spent longer being formed by the profession. The second argument relates to a functional division some analysts make between a professional and a practitioner. For some analysts, a defining element of professional expertise is novelty. A pro-fessional can apply her skills to new, unfamiliar situations for the client's benefit. A surgeon looking at a patient on the table and instinctively knowing which procedure is best able to save his life is an example of the sort of problem-solving ability some attribute to professionals. Junior enlisted service members are trained to perform rote tasks (shoot, move, and communicate) in response to certain defined criteria and on order. They do not problem solve in the way expected of professionals, according to this argument, and so should not be given the title of professional.

While these arguments may have held some merit in the context of a conscription military, neither seems terribly persuasive in light of the performance of even the most junior enlisted service members in the post-9/11 world. There is no question that it takes time to socialize a service member into the standards of a profession, and individuals are permitted to participate in the activities of the profession for a period before earning full acceptance into its ranks. Likewise, there is no question that many of the tasks service members perform are repetitive and lack any real need for complex problem solving. Still, in the current all-volunteer force it is harder to make the persuasive argument that enlisted service members should be excluded from the ranks of military professionals than it is to argue convincingly that enlisted service members have earned both the title and responsibilities of being military professionals.

Ethical Requirements of the Client

While the profession is responsible for setting its standards based on its institutional and collective expertise, the professional is responsible for maintaining those standards in herself and in those she leads. The client is responsible for enabling both the profession and the professional to fulfill their fiduciary responsibilities. Just as the profession and professionals have ethical responsibilities concerning expertise, trust, continued improvement, values, and service, so does the client. Without the client's trust, the profession would not have the authority to self-regulate. Without the client's material support, the professional would not have the resources needed to develop his and his subordinates' skill. Without sufficient communication concerning the client's values, the profession and its members could apply violence in situations and ways that undermine the public good.

The most basic ethical obligation the client possesses is to provide sufficient political guidance to direct and constrain the disciplined application of violence for a political end. The client identifies the political end—communicated through the country's political leaders—and communicates its expectations concerning what constitutes the disciplined application of violence. While some argue that a US action like fire-bombing sixty-seven Japanese cities in World War II was immoral, by the standards communicated by the American public through its political leaders at the time, it was not undisciplined. It was also consistent with and seen to be the course of action most likely to achieve the desired political end—Japan's total defeat.[13] Because political ends and the appropriate definition of the term "disciplined" change over time, the client must maintain open channels of communication with the profession and its members. This communication happens through those the American people elect to represent them and through civilian oversight at the Department of Defense.[14]

The unifying obligation across all dimensions of the professional relationship is trust. Just as the profession and its members must maintain trust with the American people, so too must the American people maintain trust with the profession and its members. Service members trust that the American people will not send them to fight unjust or unnecessary wars. They trust the American people to champion their representatives to provide sufficient financial and political resources to enable them to achieve political ends using disciplined violence. They trust the American people to honor their service by providing for the soldiers and families of those who are injured or killed in the line of duty.

The past fifteen years have been a challenging time for this element of the professional relationship. As more is known about Iraq's weapons of mass destruction programs, some in uniform have begun to question the value of Operation Iraqi Freedom. As Islamic militants have destroyed the fragile peace that existed when US troops formally withdrew from Iraq in 2011, some service members have grown even less trusting of the strength of American political will for protracted conflict. Those familiar with Clausewitz know that the public is the element of the trinity that contains the country's passion.[15] Still, the public has an ethical obligation to marshal that passion in a way that guides and constrains policymakers' decisions regarding the military's resort to force. When the country allows itself to be swept up in fear or excitement, it fails to uphold its end of the relationship.

Tied to trust is the client's responsibility to support the profession and its members financially, socially, and politically. Ian Bryan makes the connection clearly when he writes, "Society's trust is always at stake, modulating the resources and autonomy delegated to those in uniform."[16] While the American people may withhold resources and authority if its trust has been violated, the professional relationship also demands that the American people have a responsibility to provide both while its trust is maintained. Public opinion demonstrates that America's trust in its military is significant. A June 2014 Gallup Poll indicates that 74 percent of Americans have a "great deal/quite a lot" of confidence in the military, compared to 30 percent of Americans who felt the same about the Supreme Court, 29 percent who felt that way about the president, and 7 percent who feel that way about Congress. What is even more telling is that public confidence in the military has increased by more than 30 percent since the Vietnam War, while confidence in courts, the presidency, and Congress has declined over that same period.[17] This certainly does not mean the American people should give the military a blank check. It does mean the public must adequately fund the military to accomplish the missions and maintain the members it demands.

Equally important to the professional relationship is the client's clear and consistent articulation of the core values it expects the profession to maintain. Without this communication, the professional will be challenged to fulfill his duty. According to Ian Bryan, "An officer's conception of the military's role must begin with understanding society's values and how those values are expressed in the form and philosophy of a government that supplies and legitimates the officer's work."[18] Without that connection, the soldier risks becoming like the mercenary or the contractor—killing for money, and not for purpose.

From time to time it happens that the public's values evolve in a way that seemingly conflict with the profession's expertise. Congress' repeal of so-called Don't Ask, Don't Tell to allow openly homosexual service members to join the profession's ranks and the push by Congress to integrate women into combat roles illustrate how the American commitment to equal rights shapes the guidance it provides the profession and its members. The fact that the actual execution of these directives has been far less dramatic than the rhetoric surrounding either decision suggests that on this issue individual service members' and American society's values might have more in common with each other than either does with the military's institutional values. Either way, the key here is for the American people to communicate their core values clearly and consistently so that the military and its members can adjust their professional judgment and actions accordingly.

Finally, the client has an obligation to remain committed to those who serve it. The profession is oriented by service to the client and is called to fulfill its duty to the country. The country is bound in return to honor its commitment to the profession and its professionals. This commitment is seen most clearly in how the country cares for its wounded warriors and Gold Star families.[19] It is not just the political and financial support the American people provide for America's troops but also the social support they provide service members and their families that demonstrate the nation's commitment to the professional relationship. There is no question that this commitment is stronger today that at any time in recent memory, but with 22 veteran suicides a day, a Veterans Affairs system that is so broken veterans must wait months for treatment, and more than 50,000 veterans homeless on any given night, it is clear the American people have work to do in honoring their commitment to the military and its members.[20]

Conclusion

Incorporating the role of the client in the professional relationship provides a clearer picture of the health of the profession and its members, as well as a clearer understanding for the strengths and weaknesses of each member of the relationship. While many have seen a weakening of the civil-military relationship over the past two decades, understanding the client's role in setting appropriate constraints, providing necessary support, articulating clear values, and remaining committed to the profession and the professionals who serve them provides insight into why trust may be frayed.

Table 6-2. Key Attributes of the Professional Relationship

THE PROFESSION	THE PROFESSIONAL	THE CLIENT
Expertise	Skill	Constraints
Trust	Trust	Trust
Development	Leadership	Support
Values	Character	Values
Service	Duty	Commitment

Source: US Army, *An Army White Paper*, 5; and author calculations.

Table 6-2 provides a more robust conceptualization of the profession of arms. As the nation continues to send service members to increasingly complex and intractable conflicts abroad at the same time the nation's financial realities force strong cuts in personnel, training, and equipment, the profession itself, its members, and those it serves will confront some stark choices. Those working in military professionalism—in any element of this relationship—would do well to approach those choices in terms of how well they fulfill these key attributes. Doing so will strengthen the foundation on which the profession of arms stands and enable the military, its members, and the American people to confront the nation's national security threats with a more unified front.

Notes

1. Ian Bryan, "Know Yourself Before the Enemy: Military Professionalism's Civil Foundation," *Joint Force Quarterly* 62 (2011): 33.
2. While there are numerous definitions of morality and what is moral, the discussion at the *Stanford Encyclopedia of Philosophy* offers a thoughtful and robust look at the term (http://plato.stanford.edu/entries/morality-definition/). I offer a hybrid of the descriptive and normative definitions offered in that resource. Moral actions strengthen the community because they are a communally agreed code (descriptive) and they strengthen the community because they are the actions the community agrees are most beneficial (normative).
3. US Army, *An Army White Paper: The Profession of Arms* (West Point, NY: Center for the Army Profession and Ethic, 2010).
4. Don M. Snider, *Dissent and Strategic Leadership of the Military Professions* (Carlisle, PA: Strategic Studies Institute, 2008), 11.
5. The landmark examinations of this topic are Huntington, *The Soldier and the State*; Janowitz, *Professional Soldier*; and Snider and Mathews, *The Future of the Army Profession*.
6. Huntington, *The Soldier and the State*, 72–73 (including quotes).
7. Richard Swain, *The Obligations of Military Professionalism: Service Unsullied by Partisanship* (Washington, DC: National Defense University, 2010), 4–6, 7 (quote).
8. Snider, *Dissent and Strategic Leadership*, 9–12.
9. Swain, *Obligations of Military Professionalism*, 6 (including quotes).
10. David Vergun, "Legislation Changes UCMJ for Victims of Sexual Assault," 7 January 2015, http://www.army.mil/article/140807/Legislation_changes_UCMJ_for_victims_of_sexual_assault/.
11. James Fallows, "The Tragedy of the American Military," *The Atlantic*, January/February 2015, https://www.theatlantic.com/magazine/archive/2015/01/the-tragedy-of-the-american-military/383516/.
12. For the best rebuttal of Fallows' claims, see Sebastian Junger, "What's the Matter with the American Military?" *The Atlantic*, 23 February 2015, http://www.the

atlantic.com/international/archive/2015/02/whats-the-matter-with-the-american-military/385735/. For another take on the importance of a strong civil-military relationship, see Peter Feaver and Richard Kohn, *Soldiers and Civilian: The Civil–Military Gap and American National Security* (Cambridge: MIT Press, 2001).

13. Henry Lewis Stimson, "The Decision to Use the Bomb," *Harper's Magazine*, February 1947, 97–107.

14. Richard Kohn, "Tarnished Brass: Is the U.S. Military Profession in Decline?," *World Affairs* 171, no. 4 (Spring 2009), 73–83.

15. Carl von Clausewitz, *On War,* trans. Michael Howard and Peter Paret (Princeton, NJ: Princeton University Press, 1976), book 1, chapter 1.

16. Ian Bryan, "Know Yourself Before the Enemy: Military Professionalism's Civil Foundation," *Joint Force Quarterly* 62 (3rd qtr. 2011), 36.

17. Gallup, *Confidence in Institutions,* http://www.gallup.com/poll/1597/confidence-institutions.aspx.

18. Bryan, "Know Yourself," 33.

19. A Gold Star family is a family who has lost a member in military service to the country.

20. Janet Kemp and Robert Bosarte, *Suicide Data Report 2012* (Washington, DC: Department of Veterans Affairs, 2012); Scott Bronstein, "It's Not Over: Veterans Waiting Months for Appointment," CNN, 14 March 2015, http://www.cnn.com/2015/03/13/us/va-investigation-los-angeles/; US Department of Housing and Urban Development, *The 2013 Annual Homeless Assessment Report (AHAR) to Congress* (Washington, DC: Department of Housing and Urban Development, 2013).

PART II

CHAPTER 7

The Rise, Fall, and Early Reawakening of US Naval Professionalism

William M. Beasley Jr.

We are told the naval officer of today is a fighting engineer and this mockery of truth has been accepted by the profession. On this pernicious theory, naval education now concerns itself with the engine room and the battery alone. There it stops. Naval education now concerns itself with the training of arms and legs only. It takes no thought of brains.

Stephen B. Luce, 1911

Introduction

Seafaring is a technical enterprise. Since early humans first took to the sea they required some form of technical knowledge to build the craft that carried them. As these early mariners ventured away from coastal waters, shipbuilding became far more complex to withstand the towering swells and heavy rolls of the open ocean. Building ships of war compounded the importance of technology: suddenly the sea was not the sailor's only enemy. From the development of the oared galleys that ruled the surface of the Mediterranean to the nuclear-powered submarines that prowl the ocean depths today, technology, the art of seafaring, and technicism—training in technical skills—have played a critical role in designing, operating, and fighting ships at sea. However, technology alone is not decisive and can often prove distracting unless it is coordinated with a proper understanding of wider national security objectives.

Effectively wielding the art of maritime power requires broad analytical knowledge of several interrelated subjects. Operating a ship efficiently and employing maritime power strategically are altogether different. The former depends on training, a process of learning to perform certain functions that, ideally, can be perfected over time. As maritime historian Clark Reynolds has instructed, throughout history "any individual was—and is—capable of learning the art of seamanship, with adequate training, exposure to and experience on the water."[1] The art of maritime strategy, on the other hand, encompasses a much broader sphere. Geopolitics, history, international relations, sociology, economics, and diplomacy are all critical interrelated subjects that officers must study to grasp a proper understanding of maritime power: the use of sea-based forces and diplomatic skill to guard maritime resources and secure freedom of transportation and of communication, and a stable international system to facilitate trade and economic prosperity. Mastering these areas and their interrelation cannot rest on technical training alone but requires the officer to think broadly and educate the mind over years of analytical practice.

Throughout its history, the US Navy has struggled to maintain a healthy balance between mastering the technical jurisdictions of seafaring and the higher art of maritime thought, a body of knowledge crucial to its professional existence. During the late nineteenth century a generation of reform-minded naval officers led by Stephen B. Luce set the Navy on course toward harmonizing these skills, which professionalized the service through thoughtful debate, advocacy for their positions, and the creation of the Naval War College (NWC), which became the intellectual heart of the Navy. In an era of technological innovation, Luce and his reform-minded Young Turks emphasized the interconnected role the study of history, analytical planning, and war gaming played—alongside technical training—in learning to think about the broader application of sea power and its relation to national security objectives. The process solidified naval identity around a professional body of abstract knowledge that naval officers studied and employed to diagnose security problems, advise their civilian clients, and perform operations with unmolested autonomy, thereby professionalizing the naval service.

After World War II a return to technicism fractured Navy identity and undermined the serious study of maritime strategy in the officer corps. Spending more time at sea, naval officers devoted their time to operations and technological training in their respective platform communities, spending little time thinking about maritime power in a broader context. Because of this intellectual atrophy and tighter civilian control, civilians performed the majority of the nation's strategic thinking and no longer relied on the advice of naval officers to formulate national strategy, resulting in a deprofessionalization of the service and a diminished appreciation for sea power within the wider national security framework. The

US Navy remains the most powerful naval force in the world today, but it can no longer claim professional status because the study of sea power and maritime strategy are no longer central to its officers' mind-set, nor do these subjects fall within the Navy's exclusive jurisdictional control. Sailors have become mere cogs in a bureaucratic machine; instruments of strategic policy made by civilians, with little input from a professional body of officers. Yet there are rumblings of an intellectual renaissance, especially among younger officers, who are beginning to think seriously about the wider application of maritime power again. If they are to revive naval professionalism, they cannot wait on policy changes but must look to themselves, using the past as a guide, to rediscover the healthy balance between technical training and the higher art of maritime power.

Professions, Professional Development, and the US Navy

Not all vocations are professions. While certain groups claim unique skills and perform those skills efficiently, this does not mean they are professions. Yet defining professions and how they develop has proven difficult because the very term "profession" is a social construct that changes over time.[2] Undeterred by this historical critique, sociologists now tend to employ a loose definition, based on the work of Andrew Abbott, defining professions as occupations that use an abstract system of knowledge to diagnose and treat problems deemed essential to society.[3]

How these occupational groups form or develop remains more controversial. The formal process of professionalization, which identifies a strict storyline of events that must occur to gain professional status, has been attacked because it fails to account for diverse development and professional competition.[4] Yet there is still much to appreciate in the formal approach, especially among modern professions in the United States. While professionalization might not be the result of a strict structural process, common mile-markers are decipherable, which different occupational groups will reach at different times aimed at developing professional knowledge and ensuring its efficient application.

Thus, while any definition is a potential intellectual land mine, for present purposes the professionalization of an occupation will be defined as the emergence of a vocational group that develops a systemic body of abstract knowledge—requiring extensive study and training at a postgraduate institution—and earns a reputation for performing analytical skills that clients rely on to diagnose problems, provide advice, and carry out work. As group identity solidifies and matures, a professional body is often formed that coordinates admission requirements and education standards and formulates policy for professional direction.[5]

Yet it is ultimately the client, not the worker, who awards the title of professional by determining whether an occupational group is performing effectively.[6] Professional status is by no means permanent and can be lost if group identity is fractured, enabling jurisdictional infighting, or if members allow their reputational knowledge or skills to atrophy. In such cases, the client tends to lose confidence and will either seek service elsewhere (allowing a different occupational group to perform the former's thinking for it), order work carried out under tighter bureaucratic control, or simply perform the task on her own.[7] Therefore the development of professional knowledge and skills plus their healthy maintenance are crucial to a profession's emergence and survival.

In 1957 Samuel Huntington published *The Soldier and the State*, the vanguard study of the military as a profession.[8] His triad of expertise, responsibility (the performance of an essential service), and corporate identity remains an impressive description of professional character. Huntington's study has its faults, but its recognition that professionalism is inextricably linked to strenuous education and critical thinking, enshrined and guarded by a common cultural identity to ensure operational effectiveness, remains unblemished.[9] This chapter builds on Huntington's ideas because many currently underappreciate them.

This chapter departs from Huntington's study in several ways, however. First, it examines the US Navy as a separate profession. The branches of the US armed forces do not share a common corporate identity. They patrol separate jurisdictions of work, often battling over roles and missions; possess different histories, customs, and traditions; and are governed by their own bureaucratic departments. Second, Huntington's conception of military expertise, the management of violence, is overly simplistic. Since its inception, the Navy has primarily existed to maintain a stable, rule-based international system to protect the free flow of commerce and maritime resources. In carrying out this mission, its jurisdictional duties have had far more to do with diplomacy and peacekeeping than with the application of force. Finally, as Don Snider notes, perhaps Huntington's gravest shortcoming is his implication that once professional recognition is gained, it is permanent, which is simply untrue. Professions exist in competitive environments, battling one another for jurisdictional control over areas of work.

As time passes, many vocations lose their professional status for the reasons previously discussed or cease to exist all together.[10] Fortunately for Americans, the US Navy has suffered from the former, not the latter.

Most vocations generally acknowledged as modern professions came of age in the United States in the last decades of the nineteenth century. The older professions of law and medicine and newer fields like social work laid the foundation for their modern forms by moving away from an apprenticeship system of education toward professionalized schooling that imparted analytical methodologies alongside hands-on skills. In the 1880s no professional group had achieved full professional status, but scientific discoveries in the medical field, standardized education in law and medicine, and the founding of the American Bar Association had doctors and attorneys on their way.[11]

The same could be said for the Navy's officer corps in the 1880s, since the US Naval Academy, founded in 1845, with its entrance exam and standardized curriculum, provided a formal system of selection and training. However, the Navy still lacked a specialized, theoretical body of knowledge and tended to focus on what Huntington referred to as technicism, the concentration of training in technical skills, rather than on educating the mind in the art of maritime power.[12] Additionally, its corporate identity remained fractured. With few ships to sail, officers dedicated their careers to mastering skills within one of the Navy's autonomous bureaus that built ships, researched gunnery and ordinance, provided resources, and handled administration with little coordination. This dedication emphasized technicism and prevented the emergence of a united professional body.[13]

Sailing in Shoal Waters

Most of these difficulties stemmed from technology. Prior to steam-powered propulsion, advances in naval technology occurred slowly. Galley warfare remained unchanged for thousands of years while naval technology and tactics were also relatively static during the Age of Sail. This snail-paced evolution reversed course in the mid-nineteenth century. Suddenly, vessels long subservient to wind, wood, and smoothbore cannon were replaced with fleets that employed a complicated system of self-propelled ships driven by steam-powered screws. Advances in ballistics, heavy armor, exploding shells, rifled gun barrels, and self-propelled torpedoes made fleet design a guessing game that demanded specialized expertise. While the bureaus hoped to master these developments, lack of coordination led to poor results and pulled officers away from understanding the broader purpose of navies.[14]

Traditional American values also set up hurdles. The descendants of minutemen and privateers were suspicious of a professional officer corps leading a permanent standing army and viewed large blue-water fleets as an overly expensive tool that could unnecessarily entangle the United States in European affairs. Americans were citizen soldiers who defended liberty in time of emergency and returned home after the threat had passed. They desired no Napoleons or Nelsons and held permanent soldiers and sailors in low regard.[15] Blinded by Manifest Destiny, most Americans remained ignorant that their increasing economic strength and political integrity depended on maritime trade, open sea-lanes, and a stable international system.

Congressional legislation reflected these values. While the US fleet exploded in numbers during the Civil War, Capitol Hill starved the Navy of funding after the surrender at Appomattox and most vessels were either sold off or left to rot.[16] Legislators also maintained a linear promotion system that ensured the officer corps would remain small.[17] The number of young recruits swelled during the Civil War and promotion was swift, but for midshipmen graduating after the war, this linear system created a lieutenant logjam. With fewer ships to sail, officers remained lieutenants into their fifties. Faced with few prospects of promotion, the pay raise that came with it, and lucrative private sector jobs, junior officers with connections tended to retire. Others lost themselves in the Navy bureaus and either served their time or attempted to master individual technologies. They thought little of broader reform.[18]

But others did. Christened by historians as the Young Turks after a group of constitutional reformists in the Ottoman Empire carrying the same name, this intellectually gifted group of younger officers—including James Soley, William S. Sims, and Bradley Fiske—and their older allies navigated the Navy through its perfect storm by taking advantage of political, social, and cultural changes that encouraged naval development and a professional officer corps.[19] Influenced by German military reforms, these officers founded and developed the NWC, which created a systemic body of abstract knowledge and ensured it became central to the American naval officer's professional outlook. They also pushed for administrative reforms that unified service identity and created a single body of officers that coordinated policy and planning, managed technological innovation, and advised civilian superiors, who put their recommendations into practice. Finding a healthy balance between technicism and the higher art of naval warfare, their efforts professionalized the service.[20]

"O Captain! My Captain!"

Many men aided the Navy's professionalization, but Stephen Bleeker Luce captained them. Luce did not professionalize the Navy, but he did provide the tools for that to happen. Entering the service in the Age of Sail, Luce believed in training the mind toward professional responsibilities through self-education, an idea he developed on his first cruise.[21] While on duty, Luce learned the technical side of his trade but used his spare time to read broadly in literature and history.[22] This reading, combined with his exposure to foreign cultures, taught him much about humanity and conflict and calcified his conviction that naval officers required a broad professional education to learn the duties of command, never losing sight of the importance history played as a map of human interaction.[23] He became heavily influenced by German military reforms, especially the Prussian staff college and its general staff, both of which placed a heavy emphasis on military history to guide strategic planning.

Worried about the Navy's trend toward technicism after the Civil War, Luce embarked on a quest to emulate the professionalization of the German military. He hoped to pull officers away from specialization by creating a professional body of knowledge for naval officers, a college where it could be taught, and a navy general staff to coordinate naval policy and strategy. Due to the revolution in naval technology, no concrete concepts of naval theory existed anywhere in the world, much less a methodology for their study. Luce's approach for training minds in the science of naval warfare budded during the Civil War. As he later recalled, "It dawned upon me that there were certain fundamental principles underlying military operations—principles of general application whether the operations were conducted on land or at sea."[24] Luce believed these principles could be used to guide the practice of naval operations. The key to distilling them lay in the study of naval affairs as a whole, rather than the study of technical subjects that dominated the Navy's intellectual analysis.

Luce divided his science of naval warfare into four interrelated subjects: statesmanship (or the art of diplomacy), strategy, tactics, and logistics.[25] At the time, naval education omitted these subjects from its curriculum, so Luce insisted the Navy needed to create a postgraduate school to remedy this deficiency. "As extraordinary as it may appear," he wrote the Navy Secretary, "the naval officer whose principal business is to fight is not taught the higher branches of his profession. . . . But with the recent revolution in naval warfare comes a demand for a higher order in the conduct of naval operation."[26] Unfortunately no books had been written to guide thinking in these areas either. Therefore, Luce developed a methodology that he hoped would lay the foundation for a professional body of thought by leading officers into "a philosophic study of naval history" so they could uncover the general principles that governed naval affairs through comparative historical research, essentially reasoning by analogy.[27]

History's Higher Order

Luce's emphasis on naval history as the key to establishing professional theory occurred within a larger intellectual movement.[28] From 1873 through the interwar period, officers sought to understand the broader aspects of maritime power, many looking to history as a guide. Prompted by John Knox Laughton, a British historian and close associate of Luce, these scholars opened archives and studied naval documents to review the past conduct of competing nations to understand all the historical factors that influenced maritime strategy, essentially putting Luce's method into practice. This historical school of thinkers argued that maritime powers must be prepared to exercise all forms of naval power as well as diplomatic and legal means to fully exploit the economic superiority maritime power provided. The work they produced popularized and improved naval history, but its main aim was to advance, if not outright create a professional body of knowledge for understanding the theory and practice of naval operations.[29]

This historical school of naval thought began on the western side of the Atlantic in 1873 with the founding of the United States Naval Institute. The group first met in the physics and chemistry building at the Naval Academy and discussed a variety of topics including naval history, strategy, policy, and technological modernization. Commodore Foxhall Parker, a firm believer in historical study to enlighten strategic analysis, lectured on the Battle of Lepanto, a 1571 engagement involving oar-propelled galleys, vessels that were unrestricted by wind, in an effort to guide thinking about steam-powered fleets that had the same advantage.

The group began to publish a collection of essays later christened U.S. Naval Institute *Proceedings*.[30] The Institute's founding eventually demonstrated an emerging corporate identity and the need to establish a professional journal to exchange ideas and advance the Navy's corporate knowledge.[31]

Younger officers also contributed to the rise of the historical school. Robert Solely, a staff officer at the Naval Academy, placed a heavier emphasis on the study of naval history at Annapolis. Solely added lectures on naval history to historical survey classes and established an independent course that required a tactical familiarity with fourteen famous naval battles from 494 BC to the present. In 1882 Solely became librarian of the Navy Department and served as superintendent of the Naval War Records Office, which he organized. To improve naval scholarship, he reorganized the library's seven-thousand-volume collection, which dated back to 1800, and acquired as many books and original documents on naval affairs as possible to advance naval theory. Solely's own work used these original documents to challenge previous studies of naval history and to demonstrate the critical role played by the Navy in national security affairs.[32]

Soley developed into one of the first Young Turks, supporting Luce's drive for reform and serving as the instruments for implementing those changes. Though most remained devoted to technology in their early years, Luce and his comparative approach converted others while they remained junior officers, many turning to *Proceedings* to aid the development of maritime theory. In 1882 William G. David, citing Luce directly, examined the ancient maritime states of Venice, as well as the Spanish, Dutch, and British empires, to explain the decay of America's merchant marine.[33] He concluded that the rise and fall of these powers illustrated that maritime trade depended on three factors: a favorable geographic position, industrious shipbuilding, and a strong navy to protect vital sea-lanes.[34] Other Turks placed less emphasis on history but still focused on strategy, tactics, and technology, demonstrating a balanced intellectual interest in Luce's higher order of thinking before it became institutionalized.[35]

The historical school and the advance of naval professionalism took its most important step in 1884, when Luce, over stiff opposition from many in the Navy, founded the NWC at Newport, Rhode Island. To put his methodological approach into practice Luce recruited Alfred Thayer Mahan, who had recently worked with Solely on a history of the Navy in the Civil War, to serve as professor of naval warfare.[36] After a year of research, Mahan lectured on the strategic principles taught by the Royal Navy during the Age of Sail. In 1890 Mahan, with Luce's help, published his lectures as *The Influence of Sea Power upon History, 1660–1783* with Little Brown and Company, one of the oldest and most influential publishing houses in America.[37] Mahan's book and his tidal wave of sea power writing that followed aided the Turks' own drive for intellectual reform, many having written similar arguments that had gone unread because their publications failed to reach the mainstream audience of Little Brown and Company.

The cornerstone of Mahanian thought examined sea power in a political and social context, elucidating its geopolitical advantages for nations willing—and able—to practice it. He highlighted the value that command of the sea granted certain states by accentuating the economic benefits of overseas markets through trade. Nations prepared to defend their commercial shipping and sea-lanes with sufficient naval power, supported by overseas bases, held a powerful advantage over coastal states that could not because it left them open to blockade in wartime and diplomatic coercion in peacetime.[38] Much of Mahan's writing emphasized the importance of battle between concentrated fleets where the outcome, he argued, depended on capital shipping and an offensive-minded spirit. But his main thesis placed maritime power in a broader context by highlighting the economic and security benefits derived from the global trading network that undergirded so much of the world's peace and prosperity.[39] While his historical accuracy was questionable and his concepts not necessarily original, Mahan's thinking did represent the first effective attempt by an American to address grand strategy in a serious academic context and laid the foundation for a professional body of naval thought.[40]

Newport and the General Board: Finding the Weather-Gauge

With a foundation of professional knowledge laid and a methodology for its impartation in place, the NWC now needed minds for enlightenment to balance the analytical education it provided with the technicism of the Navy's bureau system. Unfortunately, it won few converts in its early years, at least within the Navy. Most naval officers believed in sea power as a concept but saw little value in listening to lectures on the Age of Sail during an era dominated by steam propulsion. Civilians were another matter. Theodore Roosevelt, a close associate of Luce and then Mahan, was a firm believer in Newport, as were most of the Secretaries of the

Navy, who increasingly relied on the NWC for advice on strategic planning during war scares with Britain and Spain.[41]

In the 1890s Henry C. Taylor, an officer close with Luce and Mahan, added an annual war problem to the NWC course. The war scenario required students to plan operations based on original historical research, to draw charts and defensive positions, and to draft sample orders, which trained officers in staff work, critical for effective planning.[42] At Taylor's direction, NWC began to research and draft plans in 1894 for the coming conflict with Spain. Early in the process, Taylor confided to Luce that the Secretary of the Navy, the Navy's chief client at the time, "is now . . . using me and the College as General Staff and me as the Chief of same with considerable powers."[43] Because of the planning, Secretary John D. Long and his assistant Theodore Roosevelt had concrete strategic plans in place and the fleet positioned to execute them when hostilities commenced.[44]

Despite these developments, the NWC's value still went unappreciated by most officers. This finally changed under the leadership of William S. Sims. Initially devoted to gunnery and a Newport skeptic, after he attended NWC and witnessed the advantages it provided to officers serving in World War I, Sims strove to make it the most important institution in the Navy, even if it meant a smaller fleet.[45] While he stressed the importance of professional reading and writing, his tenure focused on operations and tactics. As a result, war gaming took center stage. Refined by William McCarty Little during the Taylor years, gaming provided a laboratory for students to test strategic planning, operational concepts, and the new technologies that emerged at almost no cost. During the interwar years, students examined submarine warfare, amphibious assaults, and naval aviation, leading Sims to conclude "the battleship is dead" before most aircraft carriers even existed.[46]

For the most part, Sims' reforms remained permanent. The NWC became a test lab for operational and tactical concepts and an institution designed to instill officers with a sense of mission and a strict process of analytical decision-making.[47] Although he served only two years, he produced a fraternity of naval officers schooled in operational and tactical analysis who ensured Newport played a prominent role in promotion and prevented officers, one wrote, from "becoming administrators rather than leaders."[48] In 1919 only 50 percent of the Navy's admirals had attended Newport; by 1941 the number reached 99 percent.[49] The Navy's

acceptance of professional education as critical to an officer's development went a long way to completing the professionalization process, but
the Navy still lacked a body of officers that could guide overall naval policy, rein in the bureau chiefs, and put Luce's science of naval warfare into
practice. In short, it lacked a general staff, an institution for which Luce
had lobbied for years.

Luce would eventually get his wish but would not live to witness its
maturation. Impressed with the advice he received from several ad hoc
Navy War Boards before and during the Spanish-American War and
pressured by Taylor and other officers unhappy with the Navy's uneven
performance against Spain—mostly due to lack of coordination by the
bureau chiefs—Secretary Long established the General Board. Initially
an experimental body charged with war planning, the Board eventually
coordinated all matters of naval policy and strategy. This broad mission
required the Board to manage the Navy's bureau system, guide war planning, and create policy for every level of warfare. Faced with so many
tasks, the Board's development finally forced the Navy to find the professional balance between technicism and the art of naval power it had
always lacked.[50]

The Board's interwar membership and methodology reflected this
reality. In 1915, due to Young Turk lobbying led by Bradley Fiske, Congress created the Office of the Chief of Naval Operations (CNO), which
granted the Navy operational control of the fleet, a dramatic development in professional autonomy. The CNO sat on the Board with the president of the NWC, commandant of the Marine Corps, director of naval
intelligence, and other officers appointed to represent the Secretary of
the Navy, most of whom had attended the NWC. The Board encouraged
cooperation throughout the Navy. It coordinated fleet design with the
bureau chiefs after sufficient testing and analysis had occurred on Newport's game boards. Operational concepts were developed, first through
war gaming and then by CNO fleet exercises. The Board developed technical and tactical issues by holding hearings, which solicited testimony
from Navy, Army, and civilian experts alike. After the Board believed a
concept or policy had been tested and studied sufficiently, it debated the
issue with the Secretary of the Navy and issued a recommendation, but
never without thorough analysis. As historian John Kuehn concluded,
"Over time . . . advice from the General Board on a particular topic was
considered the institutional 'party line' for the entire Navy."[51]

The General Board's coordination among Newport, the CNO, and the bureaus transformed the Navy into a modern fleet, fought and commanded by a professional officer corps schooled in the technical arts of seamanship as well as the art of war. Luce, Mahan, and their Young Turks bestowed much on the officers who fought World War II, including an offensive-minded ethos and a uniform professional identity as the guarantor of American greatness, which prepared the Navy well for the conflict.[52] Civilians still controlled the service, but they relied on the professional advice of officers to diagnose problems, formulate solutions, and carry out operations once directed by their civilian clients. However, while World War II seemed the ultimate vindication of Mahan's vision and the Navy's professional prowess, the Navy's oversimplification of Mahan's wider theories, the historical analysis that yielded them, and a growing reliance on technology together welled beneath the surface and ultimately doomed naval professionalism as a hot war turned cold.

The Price of Command: The Ebbing Tide

During World War II, the Navy had become the most powerful naval force in existence. Yet, in planning to execute the basic strategy officers sketched out as early as the 1890s and modified over a half century to defeat the Axis powers, they had forgotten how to think about the application of maritime operations in a broader context. Officers had become so focused on Mahan's writings regarding offensive battle that they neglected to reexamine the social and political factors that underpinned his larger geopolitical analysis of maritime power as the contemporary strategic environment evolved.[53] The failure to exercise these skills left the Navy bereft of strategic thinkers who could reexamine and diagnose how maritime power might be leveraged in the postwar world to fend off new threats to open-market stability, which eventually proved critical to Western Europe's reconstruction and containment but went unobserved by naval officers.[54]

The Navy revealed its superficial strategic skills almost as soon as the war ended during the debates over unification of the armed services. Arleigh Burke, in charge of the Navy's testimony during a set of hearings derisively dubbed the "Revolt of the Admirals," held to examine the Navy's postwar roles and missions, later admitted, "People in the navy did not know very much about strategy. . . . That's why we did not have any organization to lay out the Navy's case or defend ourselves. . . . We suffered from a lack of knowledge within the Navy of what a navy was all about. . . . [This] was an ingrained attitude, and it had terrible consequences."[55] J. C. Wylie's contemporary analysis confirmed what Burke could only reveal in hindsight: the Navy did not possess a clear understanding of sea power and maritime strategy.[56] Naval officers seemed to think their performance during the war spoke for itself, vindicating sea power and the Navy's professional reputation. However, as the United States began its long standoff against a new continental adversary, several naval officers realized they had been overly optimistic. "Our understanding and our exposition of the indispensable character of our profession and the undiminished and vital nature of Sea Power," wrote Richard Conolly to the CNO in 1951, "have been dangerously superficial and elementary."[57]

While all three of these officers attempted to revive strategic thought through historical study, the nuclear age caused a rapid deprofessionalization of the service as technicism reasserted itself within the officer corps and strategic thought. This retreat from history to technical issues resulted largely from nuclear weapons and the birth of modern deterrence theory. Pioneered by Bernard Brodie, deterrence argued that the purpose of military force was no longer to win wars but rather to avert them.[58] Many early deterrence theorists, dominated by civilians like Herman Kahn and Hedley Bull, believed, much like early NWC critics in the Navy, that nuclear weapons had rendered history irrelevant to military affairs. They embraced a material school of strategy, which argued that overwhelming military firepower aided by advanced technology—material strength—could deter total war and thus should be the sole focus of a nation's defense needs.[59] Certainly not a new theoretical school, it dominated the postwar strategic thinking of civilians and officers and arguably still holds sway.[60]

The rise of the civilian strategists and their eventual control of the Pentagon magnified the material focus and seized jurisdictional control of strategic planning. The postwar years witnessed a waterfall of civilian publications on deterrence, which employed ahistorical methodologies like quantitative analysis and game theory that overwhelmed military thought. As a result, the military outsourced much of its strategic research and war gaming to civilian think tanks like the RAND Corporation, instead of the service colleges, which further diluted strategic thinking inside the military and demoted service-college interaction with planning.[61] Robert McNamara's civilian whiz kids intensified this demilitarization of strategic thought by introducing systems analysis directly into military planning when McNamara became secretary of defense, bringing his civilian strategists with him.[62]

McNamara's tight bureaucratic control of decision-making and planning furthered the deprofessionalization process by undermining the influence of the Navy's general staff–equivalent, leading many to conclude civilians were making the Navy's decisions for it.[63] During the 1950s the CNO still wielded full operational control of the service, assessed the strategic environment, and managed long-term planning. But when McNamara entered the Pentagon, Congress had deprived the CNO of operational control, and he ended up reporting to the Office of the Secretary of Defense, which had final say on all the Navy's decisions, curtailing its professional autonomy.[64] During the days of the General Board, the Secretary of the Navy relied heavily on its guidance but this did not occur within the Office of the Secretary of Defense. Civilians now made policy, and the Navy simply served as a bureaucratic sea-based instrument for implementing strategic decisions made by its former clients. This proved disastrous in the Vietnam War, a limited war controlled by RAND theorists impervious to naval advice. Sailors steamed off North Vietnam, whose coast and harbors went un-blockaded and unmined despite Navy protests, bombed their civilian-selected targets, and watched as they were rebuilt or replaced within a matter of days.

Inside the Navy the chief culprit for the Navy's return to technicism was Hyman G. Rickover. Following the launch of Sputnik, Rickover believed America's technical knowledge trailed the Soviets' and argued that the Navy needed to emphasize technical education and training at the expense of liberal arts. He demanded deeper emphasis on specialized expertise in individual platforms—surface, subsurface, or aviation—which shattered Luce's advice that commanding officers needed to think about the Navy as a whole, rather than focus on its individual parts. The Bureau of Naval Personnel endorsed Rickover's recommendations and eventually required officers to obtain a technical subspecialty. This demanded additional technical training and embedded numerous subcultures within the Navy, each with its own language, operating doctrine, personnel priorities, and even its own professional associations, further adulterating professional identity and service culture.[65] Training requirements, which continued to grow, created career paths dominated by technicism where officers focused on their own community issues.[66] These changes contrasted starkly with "the cross-pollination of ideas and experiences" that characterized the platform communities of the pre–Cold War Navy where submariners served aboard surface vessels, surface-warfare officers served as the chiefs of staff for aviators, and vice versa.[67]

The Navy's emphasis on operational experience further diluted broad professional knowledge. During the interwar period, the promotion system began to place a heavier emphasis on operational experience, but the fleet spent far fewer days at sea. Officers rotated between shore and sea-based billets, which included a stint at Newport. By contrast, the postwar fleet remained deployed forward and on virtual war footing throughout the Cold War, where it remains to this day. This forced officers to spend far more time at sea, especially as junior officers. "Operations," according to Peter Haynes, "became the lens through which [the Navy's] officers viewed the world, the defining element of [the Navy's] narrow and empirically based worldview."[68]

Running Aground

Because of these policy shifts and the NWC's increasingly narrow focus on operations, professional military education, which is the foundation of professional development, simply collapsed. The few postwar officers the Navy sent to Newport, glad to take a break from long deployments, viewed these assignments as an opportunity to play golf rather than engage in serious research on strategic problems.[69] The teaching methodologies emphasized by Luce and Mahan had also been abandoned. The chair of naval history remained vacant since Mahan left the position in 1894, allowing the advancement of maritime theory to languish. While the presidencies of Raymond Spruance and Richard Connelly attempted to revive strategic theory and maritime history, their reforms proved short lived.[70] The curriculum eventually abandoned thesis-writing, historical case studies, and heavy required reading in history, strategic theory, and economics for lectures on contemporary international relations, systems analysis, and foreign policy that failed to challenge or engage the students. Officers claimed they learned more from listening to each other than from their lecturers.[71]

Predictably, with few officers studying subjects that required analytical thought and the weighing of evidence, the importance and quality of their professional writing, which had been a staple of the interwar Navy, also declined. In 1946 Raymond Spruance created the *Naval War College Review* for naval officers to share their views on sea power, but by the

1970s so few officers submitted quality articles that the *Review* was forced to recruit civilian academics for submissions to simply survive.[72] Submissions to *Proceedings* by junior and mid-grade officers also dropped, which harmed the Navy's ability to communicate and discuss ideas.[73] With operational experience and training now controlling advancement and constant forward deployments, the long relay of officers from Luce to Sims to Ernest King, Chester Nimitz, and Spruance, who viewed Newport as the intellectual heart of the Navy and frequently submitted pieces to *Proceedings*, failed to pass the torch to their postwar brethren. Luce's strategic thinkers had become Rickover's managerial technocrats.

Following the Vietnam War, the profession's balance between technicism and warfare-centric analysis seemed to revive. In 1972, Stansfield Turner transformed the NWC into a serious graduate program. Turner recruited some of the brightest civilian minds to the faculty to teach a rigorous, progressive curriculum.[74] In his opening address Turner informed the new students they were not being challenged intellectually, lamented the outsourcing of strategic thinking to civilians, and warned that military officers must be able to hold their own "with the best of the civilian strategists or we will abdicate control over our profession."[75] To improve the situation, he returned the NWC to Luce's original vision of self-education that redeployed the historical school of strategic thought, exemplified by his reintroduction of Thucydides' *The Peloponnesian War* to the curriculum.[76] Designed to teach officers *how* to think instead of *what* to think, the course jettisoned passive lectures for seminars, rigorous reading, and historical case studies to illustrate recurring issues in strategy and tactics.[77]

Alongside the quality of professional naval education, its priority also improved. In the 1980s Secretary of the Navy John Lehman, a firm believer that history should guide strategy, built on Turner's reforms with lucrative fellowships that attracted the most active scholars in military history to Newport, while CNO James Watkins insisted the Navy's brightest minds would attend NWC as part of his overall emphasis on maritime strategy.[78] Their support aided the ongoing intellectual renaissance within the Navy, evidenced by Watkins' release of *The Maritime Strategy*, created by a well-educated group of officers that served in the Navy's Strategy and Policy Division between tours, and the vigorous debates concerning it in *Proceedings* and the *Naval War College Review*.[79]

But these years proved exceptions. Serious support for professional education ended with Watkins and Lehman; while *The Maritime Strategy* certainly proved a breath of fresh air, it remained mired in the same battle-centric thinking of the interwar period, which left the Navy ill-prepared to deal with the unknown threats of the post–Cold War years. Even after legislative reforms required service-college attendance, a 2008 study taken twenty years later revealed that 80 percent of the Navy's flag officers had not attended a service college.[80] To this day, orders to Newport are viewed by some as a risk to their careers; while most NWC civilian faculty members remain the best in the professional military education system, their curricula are dictated from above, producing mixed academic performance.[81]

Due to its technical and training-centric ethos, the Navy frowns on the study of history, especially among the Naval Reserve Officer Training Corps, which, as Luce and Mahan proved, forms the very foundation on which a strategic education is built.[82] Navy fitness reports discourage officers from obtaining advanced degrees at civilian institutions, which are far more effective programs for educating officers because their programs last longer and are far more demanding.[83] Williamson Murray offers a dire assessment of military education: "It . . . largely remains an arena that the services merely tolerate; for the most part, it neither challenges the students nor employs first-class intellectuals from within or outside of the military."[84] Lacking a graduate-level education in strategic analysis, ignorant of historical knowledge, and for the most part controlled by civilians who have neither asked for nor relied on the officers to provide strategic guidance, the Navy's strategy skills have simply atrophied and left the Navy reliant on civilians to formulate strategic policy, instead of the other way around.

These signs of deprofessionalization are worrying. The United States is a maritime power—a fact dictated by its geopolitical position—but its postwar leaders have largely failed to appreciate how to apply the deft strategic power-balancing diplomacy required of maritime powers to avoid strategic overreach. American statesmen's obsession with technology has allowed "technological means . . . to wag the strategic dog."[85] With continued unrest in the Middle East, Europe, and Western Pacific, demands for naval power are increasing while defense budgets, Navy retention rates, and combat strength decline.[86] These realities suggest the return of the same difficulties faced by Luce and his Young Turks: a shrinking fleet, a broken promotion and retention system, poor strategic thinking, over-reliance on technology, a must-do culture that fails to question top-down command, and a variety of communities concerned with their own technical problems instead of the overall health of the Navy. The deaths of seventeen sailors in collisions at sea due to systemic failures of basic seamanship skills and the lack of a questioning operational and readiness culture are symptomatic of a profession that is losing its grip on basic professional skills.[87]

Conclusion

In fairness, the declining state of naval professionalism cannot be laid solely at the feet of naval officers; congressional reforms must also shoulder blame.[88] The Navy is also making improvements.[89] In addition, Congress has indicated a willingness to revisit the Goldwater-Nichols Act, which many rightly blame for their professional ills.[90] But to reverse the signs of deprofessionalism and provide guidance for reform, a new generation of naval officers must rediscover a broader understanding of sea power. The revival must start with education and Luce must be the guide: "If we are to learn this highest, noblest branch of our profession at all, we must be our own teachers."[91] Some of the most prominent naval theorists, all of the historical school, including Mahan, Julian Corbett, Herbert Richmond, Henry Eccles, and J. C. Wylie, produced timeless theoretical work with little or no academic training; they studied and read history prodigiously to master the art of naval warfare.

But "art is a jealous mistress; most of all so is the art of war," warned Luce.[92] This is why James Mattis has cautioned that history must not only be read, but also studied.[93] Analyzing history is a key component in developing naval thought, unsaddling dogma, and appreciating the benefits and limitations of maritime power because it does not divorce the human element from conflict, reining in unbridled theory and guesswork by providing a roadmap for decision-making. As Thucydides has long reminded his readers, the nature of war remains unaltered. Yet the character of war and societies that wage it can change rapidly, leading students who search for historical rules by neglecting to read broadly, widely, and deeply to account for context to catastrophic conclusions.[94] Accordingly, officers of all stripes should follow the advice of Mattis and engage in the study of history as early as possible in their careers.

The study and acquisition of professional knowledge are not spectator sports. They depend on engagement with others and the ability to think and write as well as read. Roger Misso and Chris O'Keefe have challenged the Navy's junior officers to engage in professional writing and debate, indicating a new generation of Young Turks could be on the rise. Scott Cheney-Peter's founding of the Center for International Maritime Security is an inspiring example of individual initiative to create a platform for younger officers and civilians to debate and share ideas on maritime history, strategy, and technology, some of which have entered the fleet.[95] Other online publications like the *USNI Blog, The Strategy Bridge, War on the Rocks*, and more formal publications like *Proceedings* and *Naval War College Review*, combined with social media, provide excellent forums to share arguments and debate ideas.[96]

Ultimately, though, the Navy must do some serious soul-searching about its technical, platform-centric mind-set. To resolidify professional identify, the General Board and the cross-community coordination it provided might offer helpful guidance. The Navy should also think seriously about reincorporating the NWC into its planning process. Creating a strategist career path that incorporates officers from every community and educates them accordingly, bolstering the Navy's emphasis on policy and strategy, and continually updating their strategic concepts to coordinate ways, ends, and means should also be considered despite recent setbacks.[97] However, these changes will all prove fruitless if naval officers do not have a balanced understanding of what maritime power is and how it has been leveraged effectively, which circles back to historical education.

Let us hope that a new generation of officers can reverse course. These sailors will face stormy seas in the form of fierce resistance from entrenched policies and ideas that they must navigate with caution, but to preserve naval professionalism and American sea power, the civilians of the United States need their Young Turks at general quarters. For, as Mahan warned, it is once again true that "a vague feeling of contempt for the past, supposed to be obsolete, combines with natural indolence to blind men even to those permanent strategic lessons which lie close to the surface of naval history."[98] To revive naval professionalism, this contempt for the past cannot remain afloat.

Notes

1. Clark G. Reynolds, *Command of the Sea: The History and Strategy of Maritime Empires* (New York: William Morrow, 1974), 18.
2. James Burk, "Expertise, Jurisdiction, and Legitimacy of the Military Profession," in Snider and Matthews, *The Future of the Army Profession*, 41.

3. Andrew Abbott, *The System of Professions: An Essay on the Division of Expert Labor* (Chicago: University of Chicago Press, 1988).

4. According to the formal approach pioneered by Harold Wilensky, the storyline of events unfolds as follows: the founding of a training school, followed by a university school, a local association, national association, legal recognition through state licensing laws, and the development of an ethics code. See Harold L. Wilensky, "The Professionalization of Everyone?," *American Journal of Sociology* 70 (1964): 137–58; Abbott, *The System of Professions*, 9–20.

5. This definition represents a hybrid approach. While it incorporates Abbott's theories regarding abstract knowledge, diagnosis, and treatment, it also includes group identity and professional regulation as major elements, which Abbott tends to downplay or takes for granted due to his focus on work and professional competition. Professional regulation and direction includes the self-policing of ethical conduct, but the traversing of the ethical minefield by the US Navy is beyond the scope of this chapter, so I will not examine it here. However, as many of the other writers in this study point out, ethics is critical to professionalism, and while its regulation has certainly improved since a culture of dueling, brutal Naval Academy hazing, and other unethical conduct ruled the service, one could easily make the argument that its regulation, as in most professions, has always proven difficult, evidenced most recently by the Fat Leonard scandal. For a small taste of Fat Leonard, see Craig Whitlock, "'Fat Leonard' Scandal Swells; Three More Navy Figures Charged," *Washington Post*, 27 May 2016, https://www.washingtonpost.com/world/national-security/fat-leonard-scandal-swells-three-more-navy-figures-charged/2016/05/27/2e1d7b0e-2442-11e6-aa84-42391ba52c91_story.html?utm_term=.f6a5b53e5e3a.

6. Don M. Snider, "Professionalism and the Volunteer Military: Will Army 2025 Be a Military Profession?," *Parameters* 45, no. 4 (Winter 2015–16): 41.

7. The field of law is beginning to witness such a loss as infamous tort litigation; rampant unethical conduct has injured the profession's reputation while high legal fees have prompted several online companies to provide standard legal documents, such as prenuptial agreements, operating agreements for limited liability companies, and even legal research, available to the general public without the retention of legal counsel. Many who find these documents challenged in court, however, discover that proper legal guidance on the front end is far cheaper than the litigation and liability costs imposed on them when their documents are judged unenforceable. Engineers, pharmacists, and teachers are also witnessing deprofessionalization.

8. Huntington, *The Soldier and the State*.

9. Williamson Murray, "Professionalism and Professional Military Education in the Twenty-first Century," in *American Civil–Military Relations: The Soldier and the State in a New Era*, ed. Suzanne C. Nielsen and Don M. Snider (Washington DC: Johns Hopkins University Press, 2009), 134.

10. Snider, "Professionalism and the Volunteer Military," 41–42.

11. Ronald Spector, *Professors of War: The Naval War College and the Development of the Naval Profession* (Honolulu, HI: University Press of the Pacific, 1977), 3–4, 152.

12. Huntington, *The Soldier and the State*, as cited in Joan Johnson-Freese, *Educating America's Military* (New York: Routledge Taylor and Francis Group), Kindle edition, locations 2548–49.

13. Spector, *Professors of War*, 3–4.

14. Spector, 4–5, 65–69; John B. Hattendorf, "Luce's Idea of the Naval War College," in *Naval History and Maritime Strategy: Collected Essays* (Malabar, FL: Kriegar, 2000), 19–20.

15. Spector, *Professors of War*, 7.

16. The United States emerged from the war as one country, but the national debt had exploded. With the Southern states essentially decimated, Congress rightly focused on Reconstruction and could not afford to spend funds on a modern navy during an age of such revolutionary change, even if it had wanted to. Naval evolution was so fast during the period that ships whose service lives tended to last forty years now counted their modern lives in years instead of decades. A modern blue-water fleet also required coaling stations, which the United States could not afford to acquire or maintain. Accordingly, the US Navy returned to vessels of wind and wood, which could still show the flag overseas, and kept a small fleet of ironclads afloat for costal defense. On post–Civil War naval policy see Allen R. Millett, Peter Maslowski, and William B. Feis, *For the Common Defense: A Military History of the United States, 1607–2012*, 3rd ed. (New York: Common Press, 2012), Kindle edition, chap. 8, locations 4430–46.

17. As long as an officer remained alive, he would eventually be promoted to admiral. However, an ensign or any other rank could not be promoted until a superior officer vacated a spot.

18. Peter Karsten, *The Naval Aristocracy: The Golden Age of Annapolis and the Emergence of Modern American Navalism* (Annapolis, MD: Naval Institute Press, 1972), 277–86; Spector, *Professors of War*, 10.

19. The closing of the West, the growth of large corporations that produced goods for export and sought international credit, the discovery of rich mineral deposits, a rising population, and a desire to continue Manifest Destiny into the Pacific and the Caribbean all combined to produce the environment that enabled the rise of the modern US Navy. John D. Hayes and John B. Hattendorf, eds., *The Writings of Stephen B. Luce* (Newport, RI: Naval War College Press, 1975), 2.

20. Spector, *Professors of War*, 10–11.

21. Luce sailed the Mediterranean with a history of ancient Greece given to him by a friend. The book's inscription provides a Rosetta Stone for the mind that fathered modern naval professionalism and, with its emphasis on self-education, professional development, and the importance of history to the naval mind, provides a shibboleth for its maintenance: "With this little volume my Dear Luce, you can teach yourself the history of one of the most important epochs of the world—when learning was in its infancy—and when education was the monopoly of a class. In giving it to you, I am animated by a sincere wish for your welfare, and with a sincere desire to contribute my all in order to improve you. It would be gratifying to see you an officer in every sense of the word, and to accomplish this end, you must exercise your energy. With a view of leading your mind to a sense of its duties, this book has been presented to you." Luce kept the little volume with him throughout his life and put the inscription's teaching to work immediately. Hayes and Hattendorf, *The Writings of Stephen B. Luce*, 5.

22. As he sailed around the world in the ebbing tide of the Age of Sail, Luce filled his journal with references to Milton's *Paradise Lost*, the works of Charles Dickens and Shakespeare, George Grote's twelve-volume *History of Greece*, as well as literature by Byron, Mommsen, and James Fenimore Cooper and poetry by the sailor-poet Falconer. Hayes and Hattendorf, *The Writings of Stephen B. Luce*, 6.

23. Hayes and Hattendorf, *The Writings of Stephen B. Luce*, 5–6.

24. As quoted in Spector, *Professors of War*, 17.

25. Statesmanship stood atop all the others because it was far more important for naval officers to understand the deterrent value and limitations of naval power to accomplish national security objectives in peacetime as well as war and its broader relationship to overall security policy. Hattendorf, "Luce's Idea of the Naval War College," 20.

26. As quoted in John Hattendorf, "History and Technological Change," in *Naval History and Maritime Strategy*, 8.

27. Stephen B. Luce, "War Schools," U.S. Naval Institute *Proceedings* 9 (1883): 656.

28. This methodology paralleled a growing view among historians of the time who believed humanity was governed by a set of laws and that the proper duty of the historian was to discover these laws for the betterment of society, rather than record facts in the proper order, the consensus view among historians of the time. Spector, *Professors of War*, 18.

29. Reynolds, *Command of the Sea*, 10–11, 413–16.

30. Benjamin F. Armstrong, ed., *21st Century Mahan: Sound Military Conclusions for the Modern Era* (Annapolis, MD: Naval Institute Press, 2013), 79. True to form, Luce christened the inaugural issue in 1874 with an article that called for educational reform for the merchant marine. Stephen B. Luce, "The Manning of Our Navy and Mercantile Marine," *Proceedings* 1 (1874): 17–37.

31. Spector, *Professors of War*, 4; Hattendorf, "History and Technological Change: The Study of History in the U.S. Navy, 1873–1890," in *Naval History and Maritime Strategy*, 2.

32. Hattendorf, "History and Technological Change," 2, 5–6.

33. On the ruinous commerce raiding campaign waged by the Confederate Navy that drove American-flagged merchant shipping from the sea, see George W. Dalzell, *The Flight from the Flag: The Continuing Effect of the Civil War upon the American Carrying Trade* (Chapel Hill: University of North Carolina Press, 1940).

34. William G. David, "Our Merchant Marine: The Cause of Its Decline, and the Means to be Taken for its Revival," *Proceedings* 8 (1882), 155–56; as cited in Karsten, *The Naval Aristocracy*, 306. Many Turks wrote similar pieces for *Proceedings* as part of one of the Naval Institute's essay contests; see J. D. Kelley, "Our Merchant Marine: The Cause of Its Decline, and the Means to Be Taken for Its Revival," *Proceedings* 8 (1882): 3–34; C. J. Calkins, "Our Merchant Marine: The Cause of Its Decline, and the Means to Be Taken for Its Revival," *Proceedings* 8 (1882): 35–73; Richard Wainwright, "Our Merchant Marine: The Cause of Its Decline, and the Means to Be Taken for Its Revival," *Proceedings* 8 (1882): 121–49.

35. See W. I. Chambers, "The Reconstruction and Increase of the Navy," *Proceedings* 11 (1885): 3–50.

36. Solely joined the faculty to teach international law, which eventually blossomed into one of the NWC's most successful departments. Other permanent faculty and guest

speakers addressed students on naval tactics, logistics, war gaming, gunnery, military strategy, and naval history. However, the lectures were not the primary purpose of NWC. Luce designed the curriculum around his steadfast belief in self-study and perceived the college as more of an institute than a school; attendance for lectures was not mandatory. Spector, *Professors of War*, 32. Luce explained, "The value of lectures on professional subjects must not be underrated. They are indispensable. But it is one of the principles of the Science of Education that throughout youth and in maturity the process in the acquisition of knowledge shall be one of self-instruction. Knowledge which the student has himself acquired, a problem which he has himself solved, becomes by virtue of the conquest much more thoroughly his own than it could otherwise be." Stephen B. Luce, "The U.S. Naval War College (concluded)," *Proceedings* 36, no. 3 (1910): 695. As Casper F. Goodrich instructed a handful of early students, "This is not a school and you are not scholars. What you will learn and take away with you depends on you." As quoted in Spector, *Professors of War*, 32.

37. Mahan published *The Influence of Sea Power upon the French Revolution and Empire, 1793–1812* (London: Sampson Low, Marston, 1892) on the heels of *The Influence of Sea Power upon History, 1660–1783* (New York: Little Brown and Company, 1890). Mahan had failed to find a publisher on his own and Little Brown was already famous for publishing such influential classics as Peter Gibbon's *Decline and Fall of the Roman Empire*, *The Letters of John Adams*, and Louisa May Alcott's *Little Women*. Hayes and Hattendorf, *The Writings of Stephen B. Luce*, 99. Theodore Roosevelt penned an anonymous review for the *Atlantic Monthly* calling the book "the best and most important . . . book on naval history which has been produced on either side of the water in many a long year" (*Atlantic Monthly*, April 1890).

38. For Mahan, Great Britain's rise to hegemony illustrated that to exercise sea power effectively a nation needed to possess a geographic position that enabled it to defend itself and project power without large contingents of soldiers. Maritime powers also needed sufficient access to the oceans, deep-water ports, extensive seaboards, and a population inclined toward commercial pursuits governed by individuals willing and able to exercise sea power. Mahan, *The Influence of Sea Power*, 29–58.

39. Geoffrey Till, *Sea Power: A Guide for the Twenty-First Century*, 3rd ed. (New York: Routledge, 2013), Kindle edition, Locations 2049–173.

40. Julian Corbett and Herbert Richmond later refined Mahan's thinking based on their own historical research, creating the classic strategic theory of command of the sea.

41. Naval History and Heritage Command, Documentary Histories, Spanish-American War, Pre-War Planning, "Introductory Essay," http://www.history.navy.mil/research/publications/documentary-histories/united-states-navy-s/pre-war-planning.html.

42. Spector, *Professors of War*, 72–82. Taylor published the war problem in *Proceedings* and distributed copies to educators and journalists to improve the school's image and challenge the naval minds not in attendance.

43. Capt. Henry C. Taylor to Rear Adm. Stephen B. Luce, 22 January 1896, DLC-MSS, Stephen B. Luce Papers, as quoted in Naval History and Heritage Command, "Introductory Essay."

44. This efficient prewar planning contrasted starkly with the Army, whose train cars of troops destined for their departure points in Florida remained backed up to Charleston.

45. Huntington, *The Soldier and the State*; Janowitz, *The Professional Soldier*; Hackett, *The Profession of Arms*.

46. Michael Vlahos, *The Blue Sword: The Naval War College and the American Mission, 1919–1941* (Newport, RI: Naval War College Press 1980), 63–75; Murray, "Professionalism and Professional Military Education," 141; as quoted in Benjamin F. Armstrong, ed., *21st century Sims: Innovation, Education and Leadership for the Modern Era* (Annapolis, MD: Naval Institute Press, 2015), Kindle edition, Location 247.

47. Dudley Knox played a critical role at Newport during the interwar years as guest lecturer, imparting students with a geopolitical ideology and sense of mission based on Mahanian precepts. Knox visited Newport throughout the early 1930s to deliver lectures on American grand strategy that were purely maritime. His lecture titled "National Strategy" emphasized the maritime advantages America's geographic position as a world island provided. Sandwiched between Atlantic and Pacific markets, the United States could be the center of the world's commerce, provided sufficient naval power existed to protect its sea-lanes. See Vlahos, *The Blue Sword*.

48. As quoted in Vlahos, *The Blue Sword*, 91. After World War II Chester Nimitz claimed "the classes were so thorough that after the start of WWII nothing in the Pacific was strange or unexpected," due to the research produced at Newport. As quoted in Vlahos, *The Blue Sword*, 119.

49. Vlahos, *The Blue Sword*, 91–93.

50. John T. Kuehn, *Agents of Innovation: The General Board and the Design of the Fleet that Defeated the Japanese Navy* (Annapolis, MD: Naval Institute Press, 2008), Kindle edition, Locations 496–514.

51. Kuehn, *Agents of Innovation*, Location 547–58; 513–14 (quote).

52. Peter Haynes, *Toward a New Maritime Strategy: American Naval Thinking in the Post–Cold War Era* (Annapolis, MD: Naval Institute Press, 2015), Kindle edition, Location 375.

53. Henry Stimson's analysis of the Navy captures the problem quite succinctly. As he recalled, "The peculiar psychology of the Navy Department . . . frequently seemed to retire from the realm of logic into a dim religious world in which Neptune was God, Mahan his prophet, and the United States Navy the only true church." Henry L. Stimson and McGeorge Bundy, *On Active Service in Peace and War* (New York: Harper and Brothers, 1947), 506.

54. George Kennan, the chief architect of containment, envisioned a series of limited wars that would apply pressure to the Soviet Union over time until a bankrupted economy eroded Soviet power from within. To fight these limited actions, Kennan argued that the military would need a conventional force of highly mobile divisions that, when deployed, could exercise local air and sea control anywhere around the world. See George F. Kennan, *Memoirs: 1925–1950* (Boston: Little, Brown and Company, 1967), 311–12. His strategic research also relied on the work of Alfred Thayer Mahan during his teaching preparation at the National War College. John Lewis Gaddis, *George F. Kennan: An American Life* (New York: Penguin Press, 2011), 233.

55. As quoted in George Baer, *One Hundred Years of Sea Power: The U.S. Navy, 1890–1990* (Stanford, CA: Stanford University Press, 1993), 278.

56. "Naval participants in the unification hearings displayed a considerable degree of confusion, internal contradiction, and lack of originality whenever they spoke about strategic meanings of sea power. Navy professional journals show a striking reluctance to discuss controversial strategic problems. The Navy, it would seem, has been unable to successfully educate the American people in the imperatives of modern naval strategy and largely because the Navy has no clear concept of just what its strategic necessities are." As quoted in John Hattendorf, *Sailors and Scholars: The Centennial History of the U.S. Naval War College* (Newport: Naval War College Press, 1984), 201.

57. Adm. Richard L. Conolly, USN, letter to Chief of Naval Operations Adm. Forrest P. Sherman, USN, 1 May 1951, as quoted in Haynes, *Toward a New Maritime Strategy*, Location 391–93

58. Bernard Brodie, "War in the Atomic Age," in Bernard Brodie, ed., *The Absolute Weapon: Atomic Power and World Order* (New York: Harcourt, Brace and Company, 1946), 76.

59. Reynolds, *Command of the Sea*, 10–12, 548–49.

60. The material school had influenced many officers in the Royal and Imperial German Navies during Britain's naval race with Germany prior to World War I, especially Alfred von Tirpitz and John Jellicoe. Arthur Radford's demand for a carrier role in the atomic blitz and Arleigh Burke's decision to move forward with the Polaris program, a submarine-launched nuclear missile, exemplified these views. However, Burke's strategic thinking was far more mature than Radford's. Realizing he knew little about strategy after the Admiral's Revolt, Burke embarked on a campaign of self-education, focusing primarily on the study of history and international relations to improve his strategic knowledge. Accordingly, Burke's thinking bridged both material and historical schools.

61. On civilian strategists and their methodology, see Russell F. Weigley, *The American Way of War: A History of United States Military Strategy and Policy* (Bloomington: Indiana University Press, 1973) 399–440; Lawrence Freedman, *Strategy: A History* (New York: Oxford University Press) 146–77; Herman Kahn, *On Thermonuclear War* (Princeton, NJ: Princeton University Press, 1961); Lawrence Freedman, *The Evolution of Nuclear Strategy*, 3rd ed. (London: Palgrave, 2005).

62. For the McNamara Pentagon, war and planning were simply a matter of numbers, which flew in the face of thousands of years of human conflict, ignoring the Clausewitzian concept of friction.

63. Edward L. Katzenbach, "The Demotion of Professionalism at the War Colleges," *Proceedings* 91 (March 1965), 34.

64. Haynes, *Toward a New Maritime Strategy*, Location 568–74; Baer, *One Hundred Years*, 370–80.

65. Adm. James Stavridis and Capt. Mark Hagerott, "The Heart of an Officer: Joint, Interagency, and International Operations and Navy Career Development," *Naval War College Review* 62, no. 2 (Spring 2009): 31–32; Christopher D. Hayes, "Developing the Navy's Operational Leaders: A Critical Look," *Naval War College Review* 61, no. 3 (Summer 2008): 88; Haynes, *Toward a New Maritime Strategy*, Location 476. Hattendorf, *Sailors and Scholars*, 257–62. Stavridis and Hagerott point out that

Rickover's emphasis on individual platforms and technology was probably warranted due to the advanced and dangerous environment of nuclear reactors, but Rickover's influence on technology-focused education and training cast a long shadow that continues to haunt naval education and the Navy's professional status. On Rickover's education views, see Hyman G. Rickover, *Education and Freedom* (New York: E. P. Dutton, 1959).

66. Aviators and surface warfare officers, for example, opposed Arleigh Burke's decision to move forward with Polaris because it meant less money for naval aviation and surface combatants. Many submariners, including Rickover, also objected, believing the program too expensive. Baer, *One Hundred Years*, 353–59.

67. Haynes, *Toward a New Maritime Strategy*, Locations 479–82.

68. Haynes, Locations 347–51.

69. Murray, "Professionalism and Professional Military Education," 141–42.

70. Their tenures produced research by Henry Eccles on naval logistics, studies by the World War II Battle Evaluations Group, and the School for Advanced Study in Strategy and Sea Power run by J. C. Wylie, which maintained the historical school's approach and were of incalculable value. Hattendorf, *Sailors and Scholars*, 186–88, 189–91, 201–4.

71. Hattendorf, *Sailors and Scholars*, 234–36, 244–48, 276–80; Katzenbach, "The Demotion of Professionalism," 34–41.

72. The *Review* also suffered because it remained classified until 1964. Hattendorf, *Sailors and Scholars*, 197–98.

73. According to one junior officer, many flag officers and senior leaders view individuals who submit articles to the Naval Institute or other publishers outside the Navy that advocate serious reform as outsiders. Roger Misso, "Sea Power and Fortitude," *Proceedings* 141 (April 2015).

74. Hattendorf, *Sailors and Scholars*, 276–95.

75. Stansfield Turner, "Challenge! A New Approach to Professional Education at the Naval War College," *Naval War College Review* (November–December 1972): 3.

76. Turner introduced Thucydides while the Vietnam conflict and student protests surrounding American involvement still raged. When one professor's seminar discussed the Athenians' Sicilian expedition, without mentioning Vietnam, several students openly wept. John Lewis Gaddis, "George Kennan and American Grand Strategy During the Cold War" (evening lecture delivered at the Naval War College, Newport, RI, 3 October 2011).

77. Turner, "Challenge!," 2–9; Hattendorf, *Sailors and Scholars*, 276–95.

78. Williamson Murray, "Grading the War Colleges," *National Interest* 6 (Winter 1986/87): 15.

79. The Office of the Chief of Naval Operations distributed classified versions of the document and released a declassified version in a special issue of *Proceedings*. On the development and evolution of the Maritime Strategy see Hattendorf, "The Evolution of the U.S. Navy's 'Maritime Strategy,' 1977–1987," in *Naval History and Maritime Strategy*, 201–28.

80. Hayes, "Developing the Navy's Operational Leaders," 95. See also David M. Rodney, Christine H. Fox, Samuel D. Kleinman, Michael J. Moskowitz, and Mary E. Lauer,

Report: Developing an Education Strategy for URL Officers, CRM D0017231.A2/Final (Alexandria, VA: Center for Naval Analyses, March 2008).

81. On the naval officer corps' resistance to professional education see Milan Vego, "There's No Place Like Newport," Proceedings 136, no. 2 (February 2010); on assessing professional military education, see Johnson-Freese, Educating America's Military.

82. Only 15 percent of the Navy's scholarship offers are reserved for NROTC Navy-track midshipmen who plan to major in nontechnical subjects. In fairness, midshipmen are allowed to change their major without disenrollment, provided the change is approved and the NROTC program goal is a graduating class with 65 percent technical majors upon commissioning. However, the policy still acts as a major deterrent to prospective midshipmen interested in studying liberal arts. For current Navy policy on academic majors see NROTC Training Selection Policy, NSTC Instruction 1533.3A, http://www.netc.navy.mil/nstc/NSTC_Directives/NSTC_Instructions/NSTC%201533.3A%20-%20NROTC%20Academic%20Major%20Selection%20Policy%20(CH-1).pdf.

83. Rodney et al., Developing an Education Strategy, 56–57. In 2016, the Navy introduced a number of initiatives that could allow its officers to obtain advanced degrees from civilian institutions. However, these programs seem geared toward degrees in business and administration, rather than advanced degrees in history or strategic studies. See Department of the Navy Talent Management Initiatives, N1 Handout FINAL—N1, available at http://navylive.dodlive.mil/files/2015/05/N1-Handout-FINAL.pdf. On the problems facing the study of military history in American universities, see John Lynn, "The Embattled Future of Academic Military History," Journal of Military History 61, no. 4 (1997): 777–89; Lynn, "Breaching the Walls of Academe: The Purposes, Problems and Prospects of Military History," Academic Questions 21.1 (2008): 18–36. David Petraeus learned about the academic rigor of civilian institutions to his dismay after receiving a D on his first test at Princeton, having finished at the top of his class at the US Army Command and Staff College. David Petraeus, "Beyond the Cloister: Civilian Graduate Programs Broaden a Soldier's Horizons," American Interest, 2 July 2007, http://www.the-american-interest.com/2007/07/01/beyond-the-cloister/.

84. Murray, "Professionalism and Professional Military Education," 143. Murray seems to exclude the Naval War College faculty from this criticism.

85. Michael I. Handel, Masters of War: Classical Strategic Thought, 3rd ed. (Portland, OR: Frank Cass, 2001), 271.

86. On retention problems see Guy M. Snodgrass, "Keep a Weather Eye on the Horizon: A Navy Officer Retention Study," Naval War College Review 67, no. 4 (Autumn, 2014): 64–92.

87. On 17 June 2017 the guided-missile destroyer USS Fitzgerald collided with the the Philippine-flagged container ship Motor Vessel ACX CRYSTAL near the approaches to Tokyo Wan. The collision resulted in the death of seven US sailors due to impact with Fitzgerald's berthing compartments, located below the waterline of the ship. Two months later, on 21 August 2017 another guided-missile destroyer, USS John S. McCain, collided with the the Liberian-flagged oil and chemical container ship Motor Vessel ALNIC MC in the Straits of Singapore. This collision killed

ten US sailors due to the same reason. The Navy deemed both collisions avoidable. See Adm. John M. Richardson, "Memorandum for Distribution," (Washington, DC: OPNAV: October 23, 2017), https://s3.amazonaws.com/CHINFO/USS+Fitzger ald+and+USS+John+S+McCain+Collision+Reports.pdf. Two other vessels in the 7th Fleet also collided with other ships in 2017 but no one was killed. On Navy culture, see Michael Bayer and Gary Roughead, "Strategic Readiness Review: 2017" (Washington, DC: OPNAV: December 11, 2017) https://www.documentcloud.org/documents/4328654-U-S-Navy-Strategic-Readiness-Review-Dec-11-2017.html.

88. As Peter Haynes deftly points out about the most recent reform, the Goldwater-Nichols Act, "Goldwater-Nichols . . . shaped an understanding of strategy such that the White House, the secretary of defense, and the chairman of the Joint Chiefs of Staff determined the ends, the geographic combatant commanders determined the ways, and the CNO and OPNAV focused on the means." Haynes, *Toward a New Maritime Strategy*, Locations 5065–67.

89. OPNAV's release of "A Cooperative Strategy for 21st Century Sea Power" demonstrated that officers are able to examine maritime power in a broader context, but its recent replacement places far more emphasis on war fighting and downgraded its predecessor's focus on the protection of open-market connectivity. Compare Adm. Gary Roughead, Gen. James T. Conway, and Adm. Thad Allen, *A Cooperative Strategy for 21st Century Seapower* (Washington, DC: OPNAV, October 2007) to Adm. Jonathan W. Greenert, Gen. Joseph F. Dunford Jr., and Adm. Paul F. Zukunft, *A Cooperative Strategy for 21st Century Seapower: Forward, Engaged, Ready* (Washington, DC: OPNAV, March 2015); B. J. Armstrong, "The Brutal Realities of Naval Strategy," review of *Toward a New Maritime Strategy: American Naval Thinking in the Post–Cold War Era*, by Peter D. Haynes, War on the Rocks, 29 July 2015, http://warontherocks.com/2015/07/the-brutal-realities-of-naval-strategy/. Additionally, the Navy's release of its memo on the USS *Fitzgerald* and USS *McCain* collisions and the recent Strategic Readiness Review indicate that the service is taking a hard look at its professional shortcomings. See Adm. John M. Richardson, *Memorandum for Distribution* (Washington, DC: OPNAV, 23 October 2017) https://www.scribd.com/document/363215306/navy-collision-report-for-uss-fitzgerald-and-uss-john-s-mccain-collisions; *Strategic Readiness Review: 2017* (Washington, DC: OPNAV, 11 December 2017) https://www.documentcloud.org/documents/4328654-U-S-Navy-Strategic-Readiness-Review-Dec-11-2017.html. Whether their recommendations are put into effect is a different story.

90. Joe Gould, "HASC and SASC Chairs Want Goldwater-Nichols Review," *Defense News*, 20 October 2015, https://www.defensenews.com/2015/10/20/hasc-and-sasc-chairs-want-goldwater-nichols-review/. It now seems these reforms, if made, will do little to heal the many problems associated with jointness culture. However, it should not be forgotten that Goldwater-Nichols resulted from the services' ineffective conduct during the invasion of Grenada in 1983. Simply another case of the client losing confidence and restricting service autonomy through tighter bureaucratic control.

91. Stephen Bleecker Luce, "On the Study of Naval Warfare as a Science," in *The Writings of Stephen B. Luce*, edited by John D. Hayes and John B. Hattendorf (Newport: Naval War College Press, 1975), 65. Luce designed the NWC as an institution of

personal study where strategic problems could be researched and debated. Faculty expected officers to research and produce work independently and lectures formed a small part of their education, typical of modern-day graduate work.

92. As quoted in Hayes and Hattendorf, *The Writings of Stephen B. Luce*, 44.

93. Williamson Murray, "Introduction," in *The Past as Prologue: The Importance of History to the Military Profession*, ed. Williamson Murray (Cambridge, UK: Cambridge University Press), 9.

94. Hattendorf, "Luce's Idea of the Naval War College"; John B. Hattendorf, *Maritime History: The Eighteenth Century and the Classic Age of Sail* (New York: Krieger Pub Co, 1997), 270; Michael Howard, "The Use and Abuse of Military History," reprinted in *Parameters* 11, no.1 (1981): 13.

95. Scott Cheney-Peters, personal correspondence with the author, 3 July 2015.

96. However, CNO John Richardson's recent order not to discuss operational capabilities could prove a gag order, deterring many officers from writing.

97. James A. Russell, James J. Wirtz, Donald Abenheim, Thomas Durrell Young, and Diana Wueger, *Naval Strategy Development in the 21st Century*, Project #FY14-N3/N5-0001 (Monterey, CA: Naval Postgraduate School, June 2015), 35–36.

98. Mahan, *The Influence of Sea Power upon History*, 11.

CHAPTER 8

An Educated Military
Professional Education and the Profession of Arms

Simon Anglim

Introduction

Education is vital to twenty-first-century professional militaries, and likely to become more so, given the challenges they face.[1] Education is related to but different from training; we must clarify this difference before we can continue: Training is, of course, the basis of any armed force: to fulfill their role, forces must shape the skills and attitudes of their members, especially recruits but also those in mid-career, with clearly defined aims and immediate, practical application. For instance, training must convert recruits who cannot fire rifles, drive tanks, or fly aircraft into trained personnel who can do these things with set minimum levels of proficiency. Likewise, officer training aims at instilling minimum levels of competence. At the tactical level, platoon and company commanders are trained to fight and to lead soldiers under fire; at the operational level, staff officers are trained to plan procedures and manage logistics, among other things. Training, therefore, is fundamental, clear-cut, and skills based.

A professional military, however, needs programs of personal development in areas beyond basic training requirements: it must instill knowledge, intellectual skills, and, most important, the ability for members to think about the world and the military's place in it in an independent, informed, and logical manner. Personal development at this level goes beyond training and is more accurately referred to as education. Of course, in the military as in most environments, training and education overlap: training courses for potential officers at West Point or Sandhurst, or courses for middle-ranking officers at staff colleges, contain a strong element of education, while the British Army's former education for promotion courses for senior NCOs included identifiable training, albeit in fields that require some application of intellect, such as management and administration.

Whereas training aims at building, maintaining, and improving work-related skills, and training in the military also aims at preparing personnel physically and psychologically for combat, education instills knowledge. Not just knowledge for its own sake, either—not just filling a student's brain with facts or figures but expanding her understanding of the world in hope of steering her decision-making along routes that achieve more good than harm for herself and others. Thus, most professions have a degree of ethical education as part of their induction process, the aim being to enable people to think about why they do things beyond just how they do them, and how and why their actions might impact others.

Samuel Huntington can be disputed on many things, but he was right in arguing that a key component of any profession is awareness that it is, in fact, a profession, a group with specialist knowledge differentiating it from others, and that this specialization gives members status within society, balanced by a duty of service to that society. Professionals should never forget that their relationship with society is subject to circumstances of history, politics, culture, and economics, meaning in turn that technical expertise and specialist education must combine with a degree of liberal and ethical education, so that professionals understand their place in the world and how their actions might affect it.[2] A profession's importance to a functioning society means that its knowledge must be preserved so it can be passed on to future generations of professionals. Another difference between education and training is that the latter hinges on demonstration, imitation, and practice rather than on any theoretical corpus.

The Historical Context

Education has been a key feature of modern professional militaries since the nineteenth century. The rudiments of professional structures were visible in many European armies, and the embryonic US Army, by 1800. However, up to the 1790s armies were a long way from Huntington's ideal model. Before then the feudal aristocracy, which is the landowning classes, held a virtual monopoly over officership in European armies, and officers received little education for their role, reflecting a belief that leadership was innate in those of a certain social breeding. Military education before 1800 can be divided into two types. The first was schools for the preliminary military education and officer training of boys of noble birth, such as Frederick the Great's appropriately named Ritter Akademie. Technical training establishments for artillery and engineer officers make up the second category. Perhaps the most famous among them is the Royal Military Academy at Woolwich, founded in 1741 to provide mathematical and technical education for future officers of the Royal Artillery and Royal Engineers, and the US Military Academy at West Point, founded in 1794 as a technical school for engineers and gunners.

Foundations of Professionalism

The emergence of modern professional militaries and the education systems to go with them was one small expression of the main defining social trends of the seventeenth and eighteenth centuries, which were rooted in the growth of economies based on industrial production in cities. The political power of the old landed aristocracy waned sharply because of this, and the industrialization of society brought the emergence of the professions, a new middle class of educated specialists who served the new industrial economy and society as managers, teachers, lawyers, doctors, and scientists. The nationalist and liberal revolutions provided the political context in which population growth and the Industrial Revolution allowed states to mobilize armies on a scale previously unthinkable and enabled armies to develop a class of professional commanders to organize and lead them. Indeed, the key role of the military profession over the next two hundred years was to provide a core of commanders for mass armed forces of citizen soldiers formed from a combination of conscription and short-service wartime volunteers.

Napoleon showed what this profession should do, and in turn shaped ideas about why and how the profession should be educated. Under the Napoleonic system, armies that previously marched and fought as single bodies were divided into separate corps, advancing on broad fronts before closing in on the enemy. The movement of these corps was coordinated via a bureaucratic staff who drew up maps, issued orders, and made sure each corps had enough supplies to get where it needed to go and could fight when it got there; this staff needed to be trained and educated to the level of technical expertise needed to accomplish this. Many of Napoleon's victories prior to 1809 can be attributed to his staff organization, and his enemies adopted their own versions of the Napoleonic staff and command system in response to his successes against them.

After 1815 industrialization allowed states to perfect the Napoleonic system of warfare, and the new professional middle class was better adapted to take many positions in what became an increasingly technical and technological endeavor. From 1850 to 1875 advanced technical establishments, staff colleges, were created to train officers for higher levels of command and staff work. A leading figure in this was Napoleon's former general Gouvion St. Cyr, who was allowed to continue serving after Waterloo, and who was appointed French War Minister twice. St. Cyr established a coherent system of officer education based on the premise that all officer entry should be from the ranks or by competition from one of France's two military schools, the Ecole Polytechnique, founded 1794 to train artillery and engineer officers, and L'école spéciale militaire, Grande école d'enseignement supérieur at Fontainebleau, founded in 1803 on Napoleon's orders and moved to Saint-Cyr in 1808.

Across the Channel, the Royal Military College for infantry, cavalry, and staff officers of the British Army was founded by General John Le Marchant at High Wycombe in 1802 and moved to Sandhurst in 1812; attendance at the Royal Military College or Royal Military Academy for all officer candidates of the British Army was compulsory from 1879. However, the global leader in the development of military education was Prussia, where class restrictions on entry to the officer corps were abolished in 1808 and officially sanctioned educational requirements, strictly enforced, meant that all Prussian officers were kept to a uniform, high standard. Under General Helmuth von Moltke, its head from 1857, the Prussian General Staff became the model for all others. Moltke's staff officers were not just technologists, but also were trained experts in war making, who monitored and advised commanders, ensuring conformity with officially prescribed tactical doctrine.

New Professionals

The rise of professional military education was in reaction to the profound changes in war and society that took place courtesy of the French and Industrial Revolutions, the development of mass armed forces, and the growing technical nature of warfare. The form and development of military education in the twenty-first century must reflect contemporary developments. To begin, Western nations at least are moving away from the idea of the conscripted or volunteer citizen-soldier to that of the long-serving military professional, conscription in most Western countries, and many Eastern ones, being either abolished or permanently suspended since 1989.

Armed services made up of long-service professionals can be trained far longer and more thoroughly than the conscripts in a mass armed force, leading to two further developments. First, forces are professional at all levels. When Huntington wrote *The Soldier and the State* in the 1950s, the only real career professionals who could be identified as such were officers, and generally only those above a certain rank or filling specific positions. There were forces that had NCOs and senior soldiers with many professional characteristics, like the British Army, the US Marine Corps, and the French Foreign Legion, but they tended to be rare and the exception. Today all ranks above lance corporal need serious professional qualifications to do the jobs required of them, along with a strong sense of themselves as professionals.

This leads to the second point: professional militaries now exhibit high levels of specialization and division of labor. These extant forces often rely on technology to compensate for their relatively smaller size, which means that instead of the old mass army model, where the bulk of forces consisted of infantry, artillery, or armor, combat arms now tend to be in the minority, with specialists outnumbering combat formations.

The change in the internal structuring of armed forces has coincided with evolution in ideas about the purpose of the military. The prevalent view in the age of mass armies and total war was that armed forces existed to protect the state from existential threats. Now, it seems armies exist to project the power of the state overseas to protect its political and economic interests. Some states might also take responsibility for protecting others from suffering created by natural or manmade disasters sufficiently seriously to want their forces to make liberal/humanitarian interventions. So, the background to military education in the West in the twenty-first century is one of smaller, highly professional forces developing and preserving the capability to intervene globally.

Why Military Education Is Different

It is the education military professionals receive, the why they do a thing, that glues together the different schemes of training they pass through into a coherent whole. Members of the military are professionals in applying deadly force on behalf of their government in pursuit of that government's policy aims. The more professional the military, the more seriously it should take this role, the more efficient it will be, and the better the chances of achieving those policies.

The military differs from other professions in several other ways, thereby affecting the educational programs the military needs and how they are delivered. First is the career structure of military forces. All soldiers, sailors, and airmen start from the bottom of a rigidly hierarchical structure with a promotion system intended to move talent upward, so that the young people recruited by the forces are developed from within to become the leaders of tomorrow. Officers and soldiers progress through a series of appointments, each presenting new mental demands, requiring some adjustment of attitude, and demanding development in diverse areas ranging from the theoretical background to different types of warfare to technical and trade training. Moreover, some military employments require skills, such as foreign languages, not covered by basic military training, thus requiring a higher level of individual instruction than the standard training process can allow for. Alongside this, to get the best out of their charges, officers and NCOs require education in the art and science of management as well as in the right way to lead troops under fire. Despite the sentiments expressed in recruiting literature and in many a Sovereign's Parade Speech at Sandhurst, no professional force expects commanders to get by on natural flair alone.

The second major way in which the military differs from civilian professions in its approach to education stems from the unlimited liability it imposes on its members. In stark contrast with any other profession, the military can require its members to be in situations where they must kill or be killed. Military professionals must, therefore, have the greatest possible degree of understanding of their reasons for doing the job and the commitment it entails, and of what motivates those they operate with and against. Put starkly, they must understand why they must apply deadly force where, when, and in the way they do. The third difference is the very high level of responsibility that the military places on leaders, putting them in charge of what are literally life-or-death decisions. Unconstrained by economic factors, the military officer must appreciate his responsibilities to his colleagues, his soldiers, his superiors, and, most important of all, to his country, the people he serves, and the way of life he protects. All war is explicitly political, and so every action by any member of the armed forces in the performance of any military operation will have political intent and implications. This leads to a key reason

why education is so important for militaries now, and why that education
needs to be crafted especially for the kind of situations they are likely to
face on the ground.

Narrative and the Profession

Some otherwise very well-trained militaries have been found wanting
in political awareness, particularly in the complex scenarios that have
emerged in twenty-first century warfare. Thanks to their training and
experience, most individual officers and NCOs will know a good solution to a problem when they see one, but militaries collectively can
sometimes give the impression of institutional autism, as the slowness of
the US and British militaries to adapt to the situation in Iraq in 2003–4
indicates. Several recent books on Afghanistan, particularly those by
Emile Simpson and Frank Ledwidge, present the idea of competing narratives, or the notion that there can be an accepted idea of what a war
is about, why it is happening, who the good guys are, who the bad guys
are, who is going to win, and how. However, other people in that same
war could have radically different views on all these same things, possibly including your friends as well as your enemies. Such narratives can
be the backbone of combat motivation and morale for the troops and
for public support for military action, in the areas of operations and the
domestic constituency, in the case of intervening forces. Yet, a reading
of Simpson's and Ledwidge's books shows many have tried to impose an
inappropriate narrative on what has happened in Afghanistan and Iraq
recently. The old Maoist model of revolutionary warfare being imposed
on the Taliban and Daesh, these entities being portrayed as a single, all
pervasive insurgency carried out by evil people, hard-core religious fanat-
ics intent on imposing a totalitarian theocracy on those protected by the
West.[3] The reality is a complicated patchwork of tribal, family, and criminal networks, all pursuing their own aims, which can stem from ideology, commercial interests, or simply turf. These personal alliances might
be fighting viciously one month and allied with each other the next.
These alliances tend to be far more influential than state governments
across large parts of Africa, the Middle East, and Asia. Yet Ledwidge,
in particular, cites numerous examples of the kind of embarrassing and
occasionally self-defeating things that happen when supposedly professional militaries do not appreciate the complex and unpredictable environments created by these informal networks.[4] This failure to adapt is of

particular concern, and indeed, rather paradoxical, given that interventions into genuinely multicultural, multitribal, and multilingual societies of the sort found in the Middle East, Africa, and across much of Asia are exactly the scenario for which most Western professional armed forces claim to train and structure themselves today.

It is therefore doubly essential that service personnel receive historical, political, and cultural education about the people they are working with and against. If, at the very least, forces develop a good, accurate understanding of why the enemy sees the world the way he does, then those forces are some way along the road to defeating or at least neutralizing him. If they understand the culture and worldview of the people among whom they operate, particularly during interventions and insurgencies, it will help immensely in gaining local confidence and cooperation and improving efficiency in areas like intelligence gathering. Moreover, the importance of narrative means that, on one level, a basic understanding of the part the modern media play in shaping the narrative is vital, particularly in an age where satellite and cable television and social media mean that anyone in a war zone with a mobile phone is a potential war correspondent whose stories can reach vast audiences within hours.

On one level, therefore, all military personnel should have at least basic education in what the media does and the level of its importance in the modern world. On another level, having a positive narrative of the war you happen to be fighting, and a positive narrative that is accepted by most of the public, is vital. Indeed, wars of choice such as the United States and its allies have fought recently can be won or lost on the narrative. One need only refer back to Clausewitz's trilogy of forces; it is the will of the public that decides how far the war will and can be pursued, and that depends entirely on which narrative of the war it accepts.[5] The narrative presented to the Western public about Iraq and Afghanistan was that NATO troops were engaged in a liberating, liberalizing mission, but that narrative would be easier to sell if everybody on the ground behaved accordingly. Best, therefore, to avoid stories such as those of Sergeant Blackman and the perpetrators of the Abu Ghraib atrocities—idiotic to allow the electronic recording of their crimes, but even more idiotic to commit those crimes in the first place, recorded or not.

Explaining the Why: Ethics

It follows that on one level the art of crafting narratives and understanding how they are developed and employed needs to be studied and taught to service people at all levels. On a more fundamental level, ethics and soldiers' virtues should form a key part of any military education scheme, and for more than just cosmetic reasons. Not only does an uncompromising code of conduct underlie any profession, but also, combined with the political intent behind their actions, that code is a strong ethical underpinning that differentiates the military from a band of armed thugs. As to what this framework should be, for clarity we defer to the model laid out by David Fisher, who before his academic career was required to engage with moral dilemmas practically as a senior civil servant with the British Ministry of Defence. Fisher argued that the main virtues the military must cultivate are courage, practical wisdom, and a keen sense of justice: of these, justice is the one virtue that can be taught most obviously in a classroom.[6] Justice is an interesting concept that can be described as doing the right thing because that is what you are conditioned to do. It might be argued that a real moral dilemma—indeed, most real-world moral dilemmas—involves choosing the lesser of two evils. Such decisions are complicated further by the speed and chaos of the modern battlefield, where warriors sometimes have to make decisions on the basis of rapidly evolving information under conditions where military personnel, their peers, and subordinates might be in deadly danger.

Nevertheless, military professionals can be educated that there are some things that are morally unacceptable because they are illegal under domestic or international law or the general concept of *jus in bello* and that true military professionals do not forget this even if the enemy does. A good working knowledge of the Geneva and Hague Conventions is a good place to start. Educators of military members must make clear to the recruit or officer cadet that such international agreements are not just things to be recited in promotion examinations, but rather a code that shapes the military profession and one that members of the armed forces are expected to live by. This is where practical wisdom or common sense becomes important. Practical wisdom is the ability to look at a situation, weigh up the options for dealing with it, assess potential costs and benefits to all those involved, then come to the option that solves the situation most effectively and at least cost to all those involved. To some extent, practical wisdom is a function of personality, sharpened by experience and maturity; it is perhaps the most vital attribute of anyone in a position of leadership. Fisher cited the example of the US Marine Corps officer in Vietnam who came across one of his Marines, "enraged by the death of his comrades," about to shoot a Vietnamese civilian woman. The officer simply said, calmly but firmly, "Marines don't do that," and the Marine snapped out of his rage and lowered his weapon. "Where an appeal to the just war principles would have failed, an appeal to the military virtues embodied in the Marine's own code of honor worked. Marines do not kill innocent women. Marines are not murderers but just warriors."[7] Like courage and loyalty, practical wisdom and a sense of justice can be developed, in particular by presenting military trainees with historical examples of virtuous or evil behavior in war and incorporating frequent problem-solving exercises involving an ethical element into programs of military training and education.

Doctrine and the Profession

Another vital component of the argument in support of military education is why each armed force goes about its business in the way it does. The word "doctrine" can be defined as principles to be taught, and so refers explicitly to education. The concept of doctrine started in religion and was transferred to politics, and then to the military. It denotes any attempt to create a coherent, systematic way of doing things, usually taking the form of an officially endorsed set of recommended actions for any given situation. Doctrine is the "why" for most military people and is more of the glue tying all professions' training, organization, and acquisition policy together into a coherent whole that works better than the sum of its parts. Education is particularly important to the US and British militaries because of their attitude to doctrine. A general philosophy in both forces is that doctrine should not be too prescriptive, but rather a set of guidelines that can and must be adapted to whatever situation it comes up against. US and British military doctrine hinges (in theory) on the concept of mission command: fundamentally, give a commander an objective, a time to achieve it by, and then trust him to get on with it without too much supervision, adapting to the situation as he sees fit. Mission command requires all commanders to have sufficient intellectual breadth to appreciate the overall mission of the entire force, how they fit into it, and the impact, for better or worse, of certain actions on the enemy. It is important, therefore, that commanders have some knowledge of the evolution of strategic theory and military history. Understanding strategic theory is important because it answers another set of "why" questions; Why is there a particular arm of service, called on by its political masters to perform specific tasks, and why does each service go about them in the way it does? Just as important, might there be better ways of doing these things the professional should know about? A truly professional officer, of any service, should be asking these questions constantly to help his service adapt and evolve not only day to day on the ground but also decade to decade as history throws new shocks at it.

Military history is vital as well. History is accumulated vicarious experience, allowing decision-makers today to learn from what others did before. Serious, instructive history is about the study of change and process over time, which is another way of explaining how and why things happen now in the way that they do. History also provides guidelines for what professional militaries might be doing now—history does not repeat itself, but it does occasionally rhyme. While a good knowledge of military history probably will not teach explicit lessons for today's armed forces, if understood properly such knowledge will send important messages. The first and most important of these messages is, "Nothing starts with us." Truly unprecedented situations are rare, contrary to what many claimed in the aftermath of the attacks of 9/11. Others have dealt successfully with similar situations in the past. While studying history might not provide specific answers, it can direct professionals toward which questions need to be answered.[8]

Consequently, officers' education in military history should cover defeats and fiascos as much as it does successes, if not more so. A study of events that lead to defeat usually teaches more than triumphalist celebration of success of the sort that followed Operation Desert Storm, a celebration that shaped perceptions of how operations in Iraq and Afghanistan ten years later would play out. There is also something more visceral about military history, perhaps one reason why the British Army places such great stock on recording regimental histories and why the US Marine Corps makes knowledge of Corps history a requirement for all its recruits and officer candidates. History reminds people they are part of something bigger and older than they are, in which those going before have set standards of conduct and behavior that today's people are expected to keep up. It also shows people that others have faced apparently impossible challenges in the past and overcame them. For any profession, including the military, history both serves an inspirational purpose and teaches humility.

Jointness and Interagency Cooperation

The final argument in support of military education is linked explicitly with the intervention-based missions and organizations that modern Western forces train for. Twenty-first-century military interventions
combine jointness with the comprehensive approach, a country's armed
forces acting in cooperation with each other and the forces of allies, be
they local or part of broader international coalitions. It is now presumed
that civilian agencies will be involved at all levels of a conflict as well,
particularly in humanitarian interventions and counterinsurgencies. The
comprehensive approach is controversial, but a professional force must
adapt to it. Its application necessitates some understanding and appreciation of how other agencies work, and in many cases, how the armed
forces of allies work. As to the latter, coalition operations, under tight
political control, are now the norm, and senior officers find themselves
operating alongside officers from allied countries who sometimes have
greater firsthand knowledge of a situation than they do, and civil servants, senior police officers, and civilian intelligence personnel of their
own country and others, who are all highly qualified professionals themselves. For senior military officers to play their part effectively at this
level and to retain their credibility with colleagues, they must develop
awareness of the complexities of defense and political issues, international history, and regional security as well as some sensitivity to the cultural mores of other groups.

The growth of jointness means that, in future, knowledge of advanced
and integrated warfare, and even strategy, might have to stretch down to
junior levels. In the British Army this process begins at Sandhurst and
continues via Joint Services Command and Staff College to the Royal
College of Defence Studies. At an individual level, the language courses
provided at the Defence School of Languages, Beaconsfield, include
strong elements of the subject nation's culture, society, and politics.
Such a broad, humanities-based education does not just involve understanding these other nations and agencies now, but also involves learning something of their past, giving insight into what they are capable of
and prepared to do, with the aim of improving the planning process and
cooperation on the ground. It also seeks to reduce the chance of cultural
clashes, particularly between the military and civilian agencies that might
have widely divergent reasons for why something is happening and what
they are going to do about it.

Conclusion

Western forces are facing a complicated and sometimes rather awkward operational environment in the twenty-first century, the main scenario for which most militaries train being intervention in areas geographically and culturally far from home. All service people, be they airmen, sailors, soldiers, or marines, are going to need the breadth of knowledge, vision, and understanding to do their jobs in this environment. They will need a degree of cultural understanding, because culture shapes everything from the political aims of allies and enemies down to their organization for achieving this, and the way in which a professional military navigates this environment. Awareness of the way in which effective performance has been produced in the past will give service people a greater understanding of how to perform effectively now or at least avoid poor or counterproductive performance in the future. Combined with an understanding of the social and historical context of the military as a profession, this awareness, developed through education, will allow the military at all levels to ask itself and others the right questions to produce the right answers. Education is vital to the twenty-first-century militaries, and likely to become more so, given the challenges they face.

Notes

1. The author would like to thank Col. David Benest, Prof. Christopher Dandeker, the late Dr. David Fisher, Col. John Hughes-Wilson, Frank Ledwidge, William F. Owen, and Emile Simpson for their ideas, inspiration, and support.
2. Huntington, *The Soldier and the State*, 10, 16–18.
3. Daesh is the Arabic language acronym for the Islamic State group, or ISIS.
4. Frank Ledwidge, *Losing Small Wars: British Military Failure in Iraq and Afghanistan* (New Haven, CT: Yale University Press, 2011), esp. 62–71; Emile Simpson, *War from the Ground Up: Twenty-First Century Combat as Politics* (London: Hurst, 2012), 3–4, 15–24, 31–39.
5. Carl von Clausewitz, *On War*, trans. Michael Howard and Peter Paret (London: Everyman, 1993), 83–85, 101, 158–59.
6. David Fisher, *Morality and War: Can War be Just in the Twenty-First Century?* (Oxford: Oxford University Press, 2011), 108–33.
7. Fisher, *Morality and War*, 128–29 (including quotes).
8. As argued by General James Mattis, former Supreme Allied Commander, Europe in an interview in *Military History* (July 2015): 14–15.

CHAPTER 9

Mentoring for a Military Professional Identity

Raymond A. Kimball

Introduction

Professions, by definition, require professionals: individuals who embrace the identity of the profession to further its aims and work within its constraints. Much of this book is devoted to defining what the military profession is and, conversely, what it is not. By extension, that debate carries over into what and who military professionals are. This chapter, however, seeks to sidestep much of that debate and look instead at a proven mechanism for professional identity creation: workplace mentoring. In this view, how someone becomes a professional is at least as important as who becomes one. In this chapter, I will discuss the scholarly research on workplace mentoring and related fields to argue for a methodology of professional identity formation. Moreover, I will highlight problems and issues for workplace mentoring arising from unique elements of military culture.

The association of mentoring with military professional identity is not new. The origin of the term comes from Greek mythology: Odysseus assigned Mentor to tutor his son, Telemachus. Athena, the Greek goddess of war and wisdom, often assumed Mentor's form to further Telemachus' instruction in the arts of war and strategy.[1] A 2010 study of formal and informal military mentoring found that it played a significant role in identifying and promoting talent, but noted that systemic studies of military mentoring prevalence and outcomes were few and far between.[2] This point cannot be emphasized enough: despite the importance of mentoring to military leader development, there has been almost no in-depth study of how mentoring functions on an individual level for service members. Part of the challenge in this area is the widely varying service cultures as well as the significant differences in roles and expectations between officers and enlisted personnel. I next discuss the current literature on workplace mentoring, including the functions, norms, and processes of mentoring, from a civilian perspective, with proposed insights for the literature's implications in a military context.

Definition, Actual Relationships, and Functions

What is workplace mentoring and how does it work?

Workplace mentoring must first be distinguished from youth mentoring and classroom mentoring; while the latter two fields are important and worthy of study, they do not directly impact the formation of professional identity.[3] Mentoring studies have used multiple definitions, but most scholars agree that mentoring relationships are dynamic learning partnerships, asymmetric yet reciprocal. A commonly used definition of mentoring comes from *The Blackwell Handbook of Mentoring:* "[Mentoring is] a relationship between a less experienced individual (the protégé) and a more experienced person (the mentor) where the purpose is the personal and professional growth of the protégé."[4] Formal and informal mentoring are further differentiated by the role of external agencies in initiating the formation of the mentoring pair. In formal mentoring, an outside party such as an organizational construct creates the match between mentor and protégé. Informal mentoring is driven solely by relationship initiation between the two individuals themselves. I prefer the term "protégé" over the commonly used "mentee," since the latter implies that the less experienced person is solely receiving guidance and wisdom, potentially as a replacement for the mentor. In reality, the relationship is much more complex, with mentoring engagements being opportunities for reflection and growth on the part of both parties.

Every mentoring relationship is unique, but there are broad commonalities that recur in and shape the mentoring process. Most mentoring relationships can be charted through four phases: initiation, cultivation, separation, and redefinition.[5] The transition from one phase to another is driven by a combination of individual developmental changes and concerns as well as organizational contexts, including any transfers or promotions. Therefore, the amount of time spent in each phase varies widely among pairings; still, the overall consistency of these steps within mentoring relationships warrants their inclusion here.

The initiation phase comprises the steps both parties take to avidly pursue the relationship with high expectations for its outcomes. The cultivation phase begins when the mentor and protégé settle into a sustainable rhythm as they get a better sense of one another's needs and capabilities. The separation phase marks the point at which changes in either the protégé's organizational role or personal development begin to pull the mentoring dyad apart. As the mentoring pair separates, the redefinition phase sees their relationship either end or continue as a less intense association.

The impacts of a mentoring relationship on an individual's personal growth and development are normally referred to as mentoring functions, which fall into three broad categories.[6] The first category—career functions—involve the exchange of ideas that helps the protégé better understand the functions of the organization and his role in it. Popular conceptions of mentoring primarily focus on a mentor's public sponsorship of the protégé through patronage. Equally important, though less visible, is the mentor's coaching of the protégé by suggesting ways and means for accomplishing critical workplace tasks. Of equal importance to career functions is the second category—psychosocial functions—where the mentor helps affirm a protégé's personal sense of competence and identity. In this respect, the mentor is less of a workplace figure and more of a close friend or family member. The final mentoring function is role modeling, in which the mentor deliberately sets an example for the protégé to incorporate into his own professional identity. Each mentoring relationship has a varying emphasis on the different functions driven by the needs of the mentoring pair, their interpersonal skills, and the organizational context in which they operate.

Becoming a Mentor or Protégé and Reasons for Doing So

The reasons for becoming a mentor or protégé are complex and vary widely; we can largely group those reasons into categories of personal development and organizational process. Studies have consistently found that a previous positive experience as a protégé makes an individual much more likely to serve as a mentor.[7] Another characteristic highly predictive of success as a mentor is a desire to serve and benefit others.[8] In one study mentors indicated a consistent desire to build a competent workforce and a gratification in seeing others succeed.[9] For their part, potential protégés who are perceived as having a strong desire to learn and high emotional stability are more likely to make matches with mentors.[10] The single greatest predictor of protégés successfully matching with mentors is similarity of the protégé to the mentor, which raises potential concerns of groupthink and stagnation.[11]

Organizational elements that promote or hinder mentoring pairs are connected to the perception of mentoring as a means of advancement.

One model posits that mentoring can be understood as a trigger for career exploration, with mentors and protégés alike using the relationship to explore work roles and levels of learning.[12] In this model, the stages of a mentoring relationship are tied to career cycles, with the most intense mentoring engagements taking place as a mentor or protégé is confronted with new work challenges. There is some evidence that mentoring provides extrinsic and intrinsic career rewards to mentors by helping them avoid stagnation in their work roles.[13] Organizational conditions that encourage mentoring include the presence of and access to a clear hierarchy, a defined reward system within the organization itself, and cultural norms that can be fully comprehended only by the acquisition of tacit knowledge.[14] Organizational factors that inhibit mentoring primarily center on time and work demands that prohibit mentors and protégés from taking time to engage with one another and reflect on the relationship.[15] Individuals seen as rising stars within the organization are much more likely to be accepted as protégés than others.[16] Finally, the majority–minority dynamics in an organization can greatly impact the development and maintenance of mentoring processes due to the similarity dynamics described in the previous paragraph.[17]

Benefits of Mentoring

Similar to the reasons for becoming a mentor or protégé, the benefits of a mentoring relationship can largely be grouped into personal and organizational outcomes. Most studies consistently show better career outcomes, including compensation, promotion, and satisfaction among workers in a mentoring relationship.[18] The specific personal outcomes from a mentoring relationship appear to vary based on the functional focus of the relationship itself. Mentoring pairs who focus mostly on career functions appear to reap great objective outcomes such as promotion and compensation, while mentoring relationships that emphasize psychosocial mentoring produce greater job satisfaction for mentor and protégé alike. Much of this emphasis, in turn, appears to be driven by the personal learning styles of both the mentor and the protégé.[19]

One intriguing finding is that the actual presence of a mentor appears to play a larger role in objective outcomes than the degree of mentoring experienced. In other words, the frequency of mentoring engagements is far less important than the existence of the relationship itself.[20] The organizational benefits of mentoring are largely centered on the mechanism of socialization, the process through which an individual adjusts to her role in an organization. Six content areas heavily drive socialization: performance proficiency, people, politics, language, organizational goals and values, and history.[21] A 2007 study of socialization outcomes found a significant impact of mentoring on all six content areas, driven both through career and psychosocial functions.[22] An earlier study chose to examine mentoring's impact on organizational commitment and found that protégés had higher levels of affective commitment (greater engagement in the organization) and continuance commitment (longevity within the organization) than non-protégés.[23] The same study assessed that protégés with mentors who were also their supervisors showed greater levels of affective commitment than protégés with nonsupervisory mentors. Because the researchers of that study were unable to directly and separately attribute the greater affective commitment to mentoring to higher supervisor engagement, they cautioned against mandatory mentor assignments.

The reasons for and benefits of mentoring help us to understand why mentoring is so attractive for the creation of a military professional identity. Military teams are potent fusions of individual capabilities and cohesive organizations, and the best leaders constantly find ways to strike the balance between those two. The high stakes and constant upheaval associated with military life leave members desperately seeking a way to better make sense of their potential roles in the larger whole. This imperative is consistent with the mastery of abstract knowledge as a factor of professional identity and an imperative for those serving within the profession.[24] There is a compelling argument that such sense making should be the sole responsibility of the military chain of command rather than being left to the chance formation of mentoring relationships. However, the hard reality of military organizations as large bureaucracies, with the imperative to move individuals according to career timelines, virtually guarantees that not all service members will have leaders in their chain of command capable of connecting with them on an individual level.

Mentoring and Identity Formation

The previous section clearly demonstrates the potential power of mentoring in enhancing a workplace experience but does not specifically speak to the formation of a workplace or professional identity. To better understand that process, we must first understand the ideas of identity formation through social learning. Lave and Wenger first tackled this concept with their idea of legitimate peripheral participation, defined as how new members of a profession secure legitimate access to the profession.[25] They stressed that the technology of a practice or profession requires an understanding of both the use of the profession's tools and how the heritage of the profession developed and flourished. They noted that the process of displacement and growth in the practice means that the profession itself is always in flux. Wenger later went on to conclude that the creation and sustainment of identity within a practice or profession is fundamentally time-based, nonlinear, and defined by the interaction of multiple timelines.[26] This conception of identity formation is critical to workplace mentoring, because it allows for both the differing shape of mentoring relationships and their widely varying timelines.

Although much of the work on legitimate peripheral participation is commonly associated with the formation and maintenance of communities of practice, Wenger himself did not impose this limitation. Instead, Wenger emphasized the primacy of social learning spaces, areas that blended the formal emphasis on profession with informal engagements on personal issues.[27] In a social learning space, participants use engagement, imagination, and alignment to both define their identities and to seek the assistance of others in doing so. The shared profession among members of a social learning space creates natural boundaries between those who are and are not engaged in professional practice. These boundaries, in turn, create differing identity imperatives for individuals and organizations. Individuals in social learning spaces seek the communities where they most naturally fit and negotiate their membership in those communities over time. Effective organizations foster individual participation in those communities while recognizing the organizations' limited control over them. In a military context, social learning spaces can be perceived as problematic precisely because they seemingly emphasize the individual over the collective. However, once we understand that the goal of such a space is the formation of a professional identity, we can return a balance between individual and team to this approach. A recent study of informal learning practices found a strong linkage between these ideas of professional identity formation and mentoring, but mentoring processes alone are not enough to understand how mentoring engagements form professional identities.[28] That requires exploration of other subsets of informal learning, including experiential learning, storified learning, and cognitive apprenticeship.

Experiential Learning

The idea of experiential learning emerged from the work of David Kolb, who posited that learning emerges from a continuous cycle of concrete experience, reflection, abstraction, and creation of new experiential opportunities.[29] This simple but powerful observation opened the door to new thinking about how people maximize their own learning potential and draw wisdom from the experiences of others. Subsequent research divided most learning experiences into two categories: inside-out learning, where learners reflect on their own experiences for learning; and outside-in learning, where external forces act on learners and shape their learning opportunities.[30] Both categories of learning can contain characteristics of experiential learning, but the reflective process inherent in inside-out learning makes it a better mechanism for experiential learning. Experiential learning cannot simply be understood as an exchange of knowledge between two people but must include an examination of the learning environment itself. Baker emphasized the concept of a receptive space as one that empowers multiple perspectives and supportive contexts for conversations. Receptive spaces support experiential learning by empowering participants to listen to different voices, value the cognitive and emotional dimensions of learning, and maintain a moderate pace of engagement to allow for reflection.[31] Experiential learning also embraces peer learning by envisioning networked learning relationships among teachers, students, and other agents.[32]

Mentoring, at its core, is an experiential learning activity. The cycle of experiential learning is manifested in ongoing engagements between mentor and protégé that expose each of them to new ideas and new experiences. Those ideas and experiences, in turn, drive reflection and a desire to answer new questions about one another. Mentoring can be considered both inside-out learning (by focusing on the engagements of the mentoring dyad) as well as outside-in learning (by drawing in the outside forces coming to bear on both the mentor and protégé). Mentoring does not take place in a vacuum, but instead requires a space that is protective and receptive of mentoring engagements. Finally, including peers as a source of learning opens the question of peer mentoring and how it can play a role in professional development.

Storified Learning

A close companion to experiential learning is storified learning, where authentic stories serve as the transmitters of wisdom and opportunities for reflection. Storified learning is different from conventional storytelling, which focuses on idealized attributes of protagonists and antagonists. As Schank puts it, "The stories of heroes are more for copying than adapting."[33] Instead, storified learning uses stories to draw people together for a more meaningful exchange of ideas. Tacit knowledge flows more readily between individuals when it is related in the form of a story, since the story gets the listener to live an idea instead of merely comprehending it.[34] Authentic storytelling is by no means easy: it requires the speaker to make himself vulnerable and the listener to set aside judgments in order to better comprehend the speaker's experience. The payoff is immense, because storytelling builds on the underlying cognitive mechanisms of availability, elaboration, and episodic memory to build new schema for learning.[35] By using the common humanity inherent in stories, storified learning creates new opportunities for learning one engagement at a time.[36]

Professional development through mentoring draws heavily on the precepts of storified learning. One person sharing stories of an organization's past glories or failures with another does not constitute a mentoring dyad. Only when mentors and protégés alike share stories with each other is a mentoring relationship truly established. Authenticity is a vital component of trust, which in turn drives the impact of the mentoring relationship. A speaker may be able to fabricate her stories when speaking to a group, but the intimacy inherent in a mentoring relationship will soon expose fraudulent narratives. In many respects, storified learning explains why mentoring can be difficult for many people. Mentors and protégés are supremely open to one another through their shared ideas and experiences, and some individuals simply cannot make themselves that vulnerable in a professional setting.

Cognitive Apprenticeship

Cognitive apprenticeship, a third component of informal learning, is the final aspect of completing an understanding of mentoring as a source for professional identity formation. Cognitive apprenticeship emerged in the late 1980s with a focus on teaching the processes that experts in a field use to handle complex tasks, with a focus on cognitive and metacognitive skills instead of physical practices.[37] It emphasizes individualized modeling, coaching, self-articulation, self-reflection, and exploration of the learner's chosen field rather than simply executing a set of steps on a checklist. Cognitive apprenticeship identifies those tasks that are salient to the professional engagement between student and practitioner but are not readily apparent to those outside the profession.[38] The practitioner uses collective problem solving to put the student in multiple roles, experiencing ineffective strategies and misconceptions as they refine their individual and collaborative work skills. Cognitive apprenticeship does not treat a new professional entrant as a vessel to be filled but rather draws on the student's own life experiences to build new learning constructs that ease the transition into the profession.[39] This approach best equips the newest members of a profession to prepare for their entry into an unfamiliar environment that will challenge their preconceptions and prejudices.

When a mentoring relationship focuses on the protégé's professional identity, it can be considered a form of cognitive apprenticeship. As previously noted, career-related elements constitute a significant portion of a mentoring relationship and how the protégé develops within the profession. The emphasis on those aspects of the profession that are unique to the job help the mentor and protégé build a bond that can withstand human frailty. For instance, balancing subordinate welfare with mission accomplishment is a constant challenge to military professionals, with no single agreed solution and many ways to fail. Mutual sharing of shortfalls in this area can help both members build a strong, enduring connection. Mentoring is not the mere transfer of knowledge from mentor to protégé in the shortest time possible, but rather is an exchange of ideas and insights. By acknowledging who the protégé is at the start of the relationship, mentoring helps to build on the protégé's own views and beliefs instead of starting from scratch. At the same time, such an approach acknowledges that the mentor may have things to learn from the protégé, either directly or through reflection. Therefore, mentoring via the lens of cognitive apprenticeship allows both members of the mentoring dyad to grow and benefit from the relationship.

Problems

The power of the processes in the preceding paragraphs begs the question: Why isn't professional mentoring more prevalent in the military? Why is it so hard to make and maintain a mentoring match that sustains both parties? For example, the most recent study of US Army leaders found that four in ten soldiers report that they have no mentor.[40] Mentoring engagements themselves remain largely hidden from view: individuals rarely refer to another individual as "my mentor" or "my protégé." Besides the friction that comes from working within the human domain, there are some elements of military culture that work against the successful initiation and support of mentoring pairs. The following will outline the scholarly literature examining those elements of culture in mentoring relationships and then discuss how they manifest in military environments.

Formal vs. Informal Mentoring

Although most mentoring literature argues for an emphasis on informal mentoring as being more effective and sustainable, this is by no means a settled argument. One researcher argues that since mentoring is such a powerful tool for individual development, organizations must deliberately create and structure mentoring opportunities to avoid duplication of effort or leaving people behind. This concept uses the metaphor of an organization's human resources department as an air traffic controller, getting mentoring relationships under way while avoiding conflict over limited resources.[41] This argument gains weight when taking into account the propensity of high performers to be mentored with greater frequency than low performers, even though the low performers would arguably benefit more from mentoring.

A large-scale review of literature on formal mentoring programs concluded that formal mentoring has great promise but also significant potential for dysfunction due to incorrect matches and potential breaches of trust.[42] Formal mentoring programs that stress the involvement of both the mentor and protégé in a matching process are far more likely to succeed than programs that simply make matches with no regard to individual preference. In general, formal mentoring programs prosper when they mimic successful aspects of informal practice such as network formation and peer engagement.

Military culture manifests many of the tensions between the legality of formal mentoring systems and the flexibility of informal mentoring relationships. Military personnel systems emphasize fairness and giving all members of the system equal chances at career-enhancing opportunities. The equal opportunity approach is both mandated by congressional statute and is ingrained in a culture that must grow its own leaders in order to sustain itself. This desire for fairness therefore manifests in a push to mandate mentoring engagements and ensure that all service members have a fair opportunity to benefit from mentors and protégés. However, the same systems that carry extensive information about an individual's career and evaluations contain almost no usable insights on that same individual's developmental wants and needs. Therefore, the desire of the military profession to share widely the benefits of mentoring grinds up against the shoals of uncertainty and doubt about who is ready for mentoring, and when. This friction is a manifestation of what Snider described as an inherent tension between the professional and bureaucratic aspects of a military force.[43]

This tension between formal and informal mentoring manifests itself at the micro level as well as the macro level. Leaders in military units are expected to develop their subordinates as professionals but might not feel comfortable with the level of empathy required to establish a true mentoring relationship. That potential discomfort is why the difference among counseling, coaching, and mentoring is so important. Counseling is directive guidance given by a leader to a subordinate to correct perceived shortfalls or identify areas of improvement. Coaching, by contrast, can be conducted by someone outside of the chain of command to improve performance in a function or group of skills. Both of these relationships can be involuntary, as opposed to the explicitly voluntary nature of mentoring. The best leaders are willing to share some of the leader development authorities with others through coaching and counseling to help their subordinates perform at a higher level. A leader might never serve as a mentor to a subordinate or might only do so after time has passed and trust has been established. Informal mentoring allows the best chance of subordinates making the connection they truly seek, whether it is with their boss, someone else's boss, or a peer.

Peer Mentoring

Another cultural aspect of the military that both enhances and limits mentoring potential is the role of peers. Peer mentoring is an accepted field of study in mentoring literature. Some of the first scholarly work on mentoring established a typology of peer mentors, including informational (short-term focused), collegial (long-term focused), and special (psychosocially focused).[44] The flatter organizations get, the more important peer mentoring becomes in sustaining the kind of skills professionals need to remain credible in their duties.[45] This conception of mentoring does not crowd out the traditional conception of a mentor as someone higher up in an organization, but accommodates the reality of how professionals work and learn. Peer mentors fulfill multiple functions, including passing on observations on conduct and sustaining more-directive roles with protégés to expose them to new ideas and techniques.[46] Peer mentoring is therefore part of a larger network of developmental opportunities that professionals can tap into throughout their career.

For its part, military culture simultaneously empowers peer mentoring and presents obstacles to it. Because so many peers have similar jobs and roles early on, they are encouraged to share ideas and techniques with one another to make their units better. In doing so, they facilitate the use of double-loop learning, the integration of multiple perspectives into professional development.[47] The emergence of the CompanyCommand.army .mil and PlatoonLeader.army.mil online professional forums in the early 2000s is perhaps the broadest example of this, but many units and posts have formal and informal mechanisms to encourage knowledge sharing among peers.[48] However, the peer who provides great insights into the nuances of a particular position is the same peer competing for promotions, choice assignments, and career-enhancing schools. This inherent competition potentially undermines trust among peers and creates barriers to meaningful mentoring relationships.

Because of this tension among peers, it is fair to question whether true peer mentoring can exist in the military. A study of mentoring among Army officers found significant divides in opinion on this topic, with several officers claiming that the tensions of competition and the similarity of peer experiences make true peer mentoring impossible. Others countered that such a relationship can exist when it focuses on professional practices like professional writing and small unit leadership.[49] The diversity of backgrounds among military leaders is a significant factor in this phenomenon: officers may be peers by rank but have significant differences in age and experience by virtue of prior enlisted service or civilian work. Peer mentoring within the military is perhaps best typified by the idea of mutuality, or a view of mentoring that posits the role of mentor and protégé flipping back and forth depending on the specific practice being discussed.[50] This significant diversion from the perception of traditional mentoring may make it less likely for military professionals to consider mentoring as a viable source of personal development.

Computer-Mediated Communications Mentoring

The spread of information technology has opened new opportunities for mentoring via computer-mediated communications while raising questions about how effective this method of mentoring is. Mentoring research differentiates three categories of this subset of mentoring: relationships conducted solely via electronic means, relationships with most engagements on electronic means supplemented by face-to-face contact, and traditional mentoring engagements augmented or extended with electronic interactions.[51] Computer-mediated communications mentoring potentially increases the availability of mentors and decreases social bias in mentoring. It also provides greater flexibility in scheduling and implementing mentoring sessions, possibly even allowing interaction with multiple mentors at once.[52] Computer-mediated communications mentoring is not a panacea. For instance, role-modeling functions are potentially much harder to carry out via electronic means. Other concerns include the greater potential for miscommunication in computer-mediated communications and significant threats to personal privacy.[53]

In an era where every service member has an official email account and most have a social media presence of some sort, computer-mediated communications mentoring would seem to be a foregone conclusion. Because of the elevated level of personnel turnover in military organizations, computer-mediated communications mentoring offers a means of sustaining mentoring contacts long after both individuals have left their original units. Computer-mediated communications mentoring also offers individuals in low-density or highly specialized career fields an opportunity to engage more-senior people in that same field who might be geographically distant. All these elements support the potential expansion of military professional focus beyond the management of violence to the achievement of effects.[54] The primary strike against computer-mediated communications mentoring is a military culture that sees time spent on email or social media as a distraction from the pressing tasks of the day. As a result, official email is closely monitored and social media sites are often blocked on official networks.

Cross-Gender Mentoring

Finally, gender-based considerations have a significant impact on mentoring relationships, especially the formation of cross-gender mentoring dyads. A study of corporate mentoring in the United States found that even though women were more likely than men to have a mentor, a far larger percentage of women than men saw a lack of mentoring as a barrier to advancement.[55] Well-intentioned efforts to ignore gender in mentoring relationships can often lead to stereotypical gender roles and increased tension that undermines the work relationship. One significant challenge is that much of the same intimacy and trust that underpins a mentoring relationship also exists in a romantic relationship.[56] It is therefore essential that cross-gender mentoring relationships establish clear internal and external bounds to prevent the former from blurring into the latter. This issue also contributes to fears about cross-gender mentoring relationships, as participants seek to avoid any perception of sexual harassment.[57] More research is needed into how cross-gender mentoring relationships differ in content and form from same-gender relationships, and whether computer-mediated communications mentoring is a help or hindrance to cross-gender mentoring.[58]

Gender dynamics in military organizations are complex, fluid, and often as much about tacit norms as explicit standards. A perception of fewer career opportunities for women due to their exclusion from direct combat roles has led to a decades-long push to open those same roles to women. Cross-gender mentoring will have to be a part of that effort to effectively communicate organizational norms and standards. Because women make up only 16.2 percent of the armed services, there is no way for women to get the kind of broad development they need without cross-gender mentoring.[59] Standing in the way of this trend is the persistent issue of sexual harassment and sexual assault in the military. The corrosive impact of sexual harassment and sexual assault on unit cohesion is equally felt in its degradation of the trust essential for effective mentoring. Both military women and men might shy away from mentoring to avoid situations that could leave them vulnerable to acts of sexual harassment and sexual assault, or to avoid perceptions of the same.

The discussion here of cross-gender mentoring also begs the question: Do similar dynamics exist for cross-ethnic mentoring? Again, the lack of significant in-depth research on grass roots military mentoring inhibits our understanding. One key difference is that differences in gender lead to very real differences in military standards, ranging from physical fitness to service dress to living quarters. There are valid cultural and physical reasons for these differences, but we cannot ignore that they exist and have an impact on the individual's identity as a military professional. With respect to ethnicity, the US military has gone to great lengths since 1948 to eliminate any sort of professional distinction on ethnicity, with the result that the services are far closer to national averages in this area than they are with respect to gender. Therefore, it is entirely possible that the barriers to cross-ethnic mentoring in the military are not as high as the barriers to cross-gender mentoring, but that question will have to await further study.

Conclusion

The military professional who has made it this far through the narrative is no doubt crying out for some clear, concise guidance on how to best support military mentoring for a professional identity. The single most powerful means of advancing mentoring is to talk about it, publicly and frequently. The more military leaders openly discuss their mentoring experiences, both as a protégé and as a mentor, the more mentoring becomes a demystified and commonly accepted practice. Military professionals feel no compunction about discussing coaching or counseling that changed their lives, but mentoring experiences remain shrouded due to their inherent intimacy. Such open discussion should not undermine that intimacy or betray the trusts of a mentoring relationship. A greater frequency of commentary about mentoring will impart the idea of multiple modes of mentoring and the need to shape those engagements to the unique needs of the protégé and mentor.

Military organizations can best promote mentoring by creating mentoring spaces rather than matching mentoring faces. This chapter has already discussed how military human resources systems lack the fidelity to make mentoring matches. Even though tactical-level units allow for greater engagements between individuals, the numbers of people involved still work against a detailed understanding of an individual's developmental needs. The task of the organization, then, is to build and support receptive spaces that showcase individual strengths, allowing protégés to seek out potential mentors in needed areas. These receptive spaces can take many forms: one manifestation that has fallen out of favor is the after-work social gathering to discuss topics of professional interests. These gatherings might appear to be boisterous revelry to outsiders, but they perform a vital function of allowing unit members to share ideas and begin to open up to one another.

Finally, mentoring should not stand alone for the formation of a professional identity. Not every service member is mentally and emotionally ready for mentoring at every stage of his or her career. As previously noted, counseling and coaching are equally important for the creation and sustainment of a professional. Both counseling and coaching are set apart from mentoring by the depth of engagement and the length of the relationship, though mentoring could well have the deepest and longest-lasting impact on a service member's professional development. Any long-term development of a professional identity must incorporate all three.

In chapter 6 in this volume, Rebecca Johnson lists the ethical requirements necessary for the military to maintain its professional identity. Mentoring is intimately tied to three of those requirements: (1) professionals
maintain and develop expertise, (2) professionals develop those junior
to them, and (3) professionals uphold American values while leveraging professional expertise. This chapter has offered a better understanding
of how mentoring works and how it can be used to develop professional
identity on a large scale.

Notes

1. Belle R. Ragins and Kathy E. Kram, "The Roots and Meaning of Mentoring," in *The Handbook of Mentoring at Work: Theory, Research, and Practice*, ed. Belle R. Ragins and Kathy E. Kram (Los Angeles: SAGE, 2007).
2. W. Brad Johnson and Gene R. Andersen, "Formal Mentoring in the U.S. Military: Research Evidence, Lingering Questions, and Recommendations," *Naval War College Review* 63, no. 2 (2010).
3. Unless otherwise noted, the use of the term "mentoring" in this chapter refers to workplace mentoring.
4. Lillian T. Eby, Jean E. Rhodes, and Tammy D. Allen, "Definition and Evolution of Mentoring," in *The Blackwell Handbook of Mentoring: A Multiple Perspectives Approach*, ed. Tammy D. Allen and Lillian T. Eby (Malden, MA: Wiley-Blackwell, 2010), 16 (quote).
5. Kathy E. Kram, *Mentoring at Work: Developmental Relationships in Organizational Life* (Glenview, IL: Scott, Foresman, 1988).
6. Kram, *Mentoring at Work*.
7. Tammy D. Allen, "Mentoring Relationships from the Perspective of the Mentor," in Ragins and Kram, *The Handbook of Mentoring at Work*; Tammy D. Allen, Mark L. Poteet, and Susan M. Burroughs, "The Mentor's Perspective: A Qualitative Inquiry and Future Research Agenda," *Journal of Vocational Behavior* 51, no. 1 (1997).
8. Tammy D. Allen and Lillian T. Eby, "Relationship Effectiveness for Mentors: Factors Associated with Learning and Quality," *Journal of Management* 29, no. 4 (2003).
9. Allen, Poteet, and Burroughs, "The Mentor's Perspective."
10. Allen, "Mentoring Relationships"; Thomas W. Dougherty, Daniel B. Turban, and Dana L. Haggard, "Naturally Occurring Mentoring Relationships Involving Work-place Employees," in Allen and Eby, *The Blackwell Handbook of Mentoring*.
11. Allen and Eby, "Relationship Effectiveness for Mentors."
12. Douglas T. Hall and Dawn E. Chandler, "Career Cycles and Mentoring," in Ragins and Kram, *The Handbook of Mentoring at Work*.
13. Allen, "Mentoring Relationships."
14. Dougherty, Turban, and Haggard, "Naturally Occurring Mentoring Relationships."
15. Allen, Poteet, and Burroughs, "The Mentor's Perspective."
16. Ragins and Kram, "The Roots and Meaning of Mentoring."

17. Belle R. Ragins, "Diversified Mentoring Relationships in Organizations: A Power Perspective," *Academy of Management Review* 22, no. 2 (1997).
18. Tammy D. Allen, Lillian T. Eby, Mark L. Poteet, and Elizabeth Lentz, "Career Benefits Associated with Mentoring for Protégés: A Meta-Analysis," *Journal of Applied Psychology* 89, no. 1 (2004).
19. Melenie J. Lankau and Terri A. Scandura, "An Investigation of Personal Learning in Mentoring Relationships: Content, Antecedents, and Consequences," *Academy of Management Journal* 45, no. 4 (2002).
20. Allen et al., "Career Benefits."
21. Georgia T. Chao, Anne M. O'Leary-Kelly, Samantha Wolf, Howard J. Klein, and Philip D. Gardner, "Organizational Socialization: Its Content and Consequences," *Journal of Applied Psychology* 79, no. 5 (1994): 740.
22. Georgia T. Chao, "Mentoring and Organizational Socialization: Networks for Work Adjustment," in Ragins and Kram, *The Handbook of Mentoring at Work*.
23. Stephanie C. Payne and Ann H. Huffman, "A Longitudinal Examination of the Influence of Mentoring on Organizational Commitment and Turnover," *Academy of Management Journal* 48, no. 1 (2005).
24. Burk, "Expertise, Jurisdiction, and Legitimacy of the Military Profession," in Snider and Matthews, *The Future of the Army Profession*.
25. Jean Lave and Etienne Wenger, *Situated Learning: Legitimate Peripheral Participation* (New York: Cambridge University Press, 1991), 92.
26. Etienne Wenger, *Social Learning Capability: Four Essays on Innovation and Learning in Social Systems* (Lisbon, Portugal: MTSS/GEP & EQUAL, 2009), 2.
27. Etienne Wenger, "Communities of Practice and Social Learning Systems," *Organization* 7, no. 2 (2000).
28. John R. Mattox, "Measuring the Effectiveness of Informal Learning Methodologies," *T+D* 66, no. 2 (2012).
29. David A. Kolb, *Experiential Learning: Experience as the Source of Learning and Development* (Englewood Cliffs, NJ: Prentice-Hall, 1984).
30. Alice Y. Kolb, "The Evolution of a Conversational Learning Space," in *Conversational Learning: An Experiential Approach to Knowledge Creation*, ed. Ann C. Baker, Patricia J. Jensen, and David A. Kolb (Westport, CT: Quorum Books, 2002).
31. Ann C. Baker, "Receptive Spaces for Conversational Learning," in Baker, Jensen, and Kolb, *Conversational Learning*, 109.
32. David Boud and Alison Lee, "'Peer Learning' as Pedagogic Discourse for Research Education," *Studies in Higher Education* 30, no. 5 (2005).
33. Roger C. Schank, *Tell Me a Story: A New Look at Real and Artificial Memory* (New York: Charles Scribner's Sons, 1990), 194.
34. John Seely Brown, Stephen Denning, Katalina Groh, and Laurence Prusak, *Storytelling in Organizations: Why Storytelling Is Transforming 21st Century Organizations and Management* (Boston: Elsevier Butterworth-Heinemann, 2005).
35. Swap et al., "Using Mentoring and Storytelling."
36. For more on storified learning as a separate discipline, see Brown et al., *Storytelling in Organizations*.

37. Metacognition can be broadly understood as thinking about thinking. In the learning sciences, it describes self-regulation of cognitive activity in a learning process. See Marcel V. J. Veenman, Bernadette H. A. M. Van Hout-Wolters, and Peter Afflerbach, "Metacognition and Learning: Conceptual and Methodological Considerations," *Metacognition Learning* 1, no. 1 (2006). See also Alan Collins, John Seely Brown, and Susan Newman, "Cognitive Apprenticeship: Teaching the Craft of Reading, Writing, and Mathematics," Center for the Study of Reading Technical Reports, University of Illinois at Urbana-Champaign, Champaign (1987).

38. John Seely Brown, Alan Collins, and Paul Duguid, "Situated Cognition and the Culture of Learning," *Educational Researcher* 18, no. 1 (1989).

39. Ann E. Austin, "Cognitive Apprenticeship Theory and Its Implications for Doctoral Education: A Case Example from a Doctoral Program in Higher and Adult Education," *International Journal for Academic Development* 14, no. 3 (2009).

40. Ryan Riley et al., *2013 Center for Army Leadership Annual Survey of Army Leadership (CASAL): Main Findings* (Fort Leavenworth, KS: Center for Army Leadership, 2014).

41. Ron Lawrence, "Executive Mentoring: Turning Knowledge into Wisdom," *Business Strategy Series* 9, no. 3 (2008), 127.

42. Terri A. Scandura and Ethlyn A. Williams, "Formal Mentoring: The Promise and the Precipice," in *The New World of Work: Challenges and Opportunities*, ed. Cary L. Cooper and Ronald J. Burke (Malden, MA: Blackwell, 2002).

43. Snider, "The U.S. Army as Profession."

44. Kathy E. Kram and Lynn A. Isabella, "Mentoring Alternatives: The Role of Peer Relationships in Career Development," *Academy of Management Journal* 28, no. 1 (1985).

45. Lillian T. Eby, "Alternative Forms of Mentoring in Changing Organizational Environments: A Conceptual Extension of the Mentoring Literature," *Journal of Vocational Behavior* 51, no. 1 (1997).

46. Cynthia D. McCauley and Victoria A. Guthrie, "Designing Relationships for Learning into Leader Development Programs," in Ragins and Kram, *The Handbook of Mentoring at Work*.

47. George Reed, Craig Bullis, Ruth Collins, and Christopher Paparone, "Leadership Development: Beyond Traits and Competencies," in Snider and Matthews, *The Future of the Army Profession*.

48. Nancy Dixon, Nate Allen, Tony Burgess, Pete Kilner, and Steve Schweitzer, *Company Command: Unleashing the Power of the Army Profession* (West Point, NY: Center for the Advancement of Leader Development and Organizational Learning, 2005).

49. Raymond A. Kimball, *The Army Officer's Guide to Mentoring* (West Point, NY: Center for the Advancement of Leader Development and Organizational Learning, 2015).

50. Scandura and Williams, "Formal Mentoring: The Promise and the Precipice," in Cooper and Burke, *The New World of Work*.

51. Ellen A. Ensher and Susan Elaine Murphy, "E-mentoring: Next-Generation Research Strategies and Suggestions," in Ragins and Kram, *The Handbook of Mentoring at Work*.

52. Betti A. Hamilton and Terri A. Scandura, "E-Mentoring: Implications for Organizational Learning and Development in a Wired World," *Organizational Dynamics* 31, no. 4 (2003).

53. Ellen A. Ensher, Christian Heun, and Anita Blanchard, "Online Mentoring and Computer-Mediated Communication: New Directions in Research," *Journal of Vocational Behavior* 63, no. 2 (2003).

54. Stavridis, Rokke, and Pierce, "Crafting and Managing Effects."

55. Paulette R. Gerkovich, *Women and Men in U.S. Corporate Leadership: Same Workplace, Different Realities?* (New York: Catalyst, 2004).

56. James G. Clawson and Kathy E. Kram, "Managing Cross-Gender Mentoring," *Business Horizons* 27, no. 3 (1984).

57. Amy E. Hurley and Ellen A. Fagenson-Eland, "Challenges in Cross-Gender Mentoring Relationships: Psychological Intimacy, Myths, Rumours, Innuendoes and Sexual Harassment," *Leadership & Organization Development Journal* 17, no. 3 (1996).

58. Carol McKeen and Merridee Bujaki, "Gender and Mentoring: Issues, Effects, and Opportunities," in Ragins and Kram, *The Handbook of Mentoring at Work*.

59. ICF International, "2013 Demographics: Profile of the Military Community," Office of the Deputy Assistant Secretary of Defense, Military Community and Family Policy, Washington, DC (2014).

CHAPTER 10

The Army Profession from Macro to Micro
How Individual Effort Is More Important Than Sweeping Initiatives

Steven Foster

No one is more professional than I.
I will not only seek continually to improve my knowledge and practice
of my profession.
I am an expert and I am a professional.
          US Army's Non-Commissioned Officer, Officer, and Soldier Creeds

Introduction

The above lines are words that members of the Army are not only expected to learn, but to live. Each line includes a word that has been debated for decades—"profession"—centering around the question, "Is the military truly a profession?" This is not a new question by any means.[1] In fact, it has been posed numerous times over the past several decades. In the wake of military conflicts in Iraq and Afghanistan, as well as of the numerous scandals that have rocked the moral and ethical foundations of the armed forces, the level of critique in recent years has increased. Some see the military as an organization that upholds the highest professional and ethical standards. Others, however, see an organization in decline, one whose moral and ethical foundation must be examined. The uncertainty many feel concerning the military's status as a profession has caused not only open criticism but also multiple instances of top-down programs to instill a professional ethic in the armed forces.

In his 1962 commencement address, Gen. Douglas MacArthur told the cadets at the United States Military Academy, "Yours is the profession of arms."[2] If you ask any senior military leader if that statement still holds, you would in most cases hear an unequivocal "yes." This positive

view is especially held by the leaders who work at organizations charged
with the promotion of ethics and professionalism in the military, specifically the Center for the Army Profession and Ethic (CAPE). For nearly a
decade CAPE and its predecessor, the Army Center of Excellence for the
Professional Military Ethic, has served "[as] the proponent for the Army
Profession, the Army Ethic, and Character Development, strengthens
America's Army as a military profession that inspires trusted Army professionals to honorably fulfill their oaths of service."[3] This not only brings
back to the forefront of the discussion the first question posed above but
also leaves us to ask, have the institutional efforts to build professionalism
in the Army (and the military as a whole) achieved their desired effect?
Furthermore, if the military is a profession, why must they be told that
they are?[4] All these difficult questions and increased scrutiny reveal yet
another opportunity for the military to look more closely at its efforts to
inspire a professional identity and ethical baseline within its personnel,
to truly capture the essence of its culture, and to discover that the most
effective solution is often found within the actions of those at the lowest
levels of the military's hierarchical structure.

Defining Professionalism

To effectively evaluate the "Profession of Arms Campaign" as an institutional effort, it is important to remember that words matter.[5] A simple Internet search of the question "What is a professional?" will bring
up myriad different articles and definitions, each with varying degrees of
veracity. Most definitions of the word "professional" fall along the lines
of Merriam-Webster's online dictionary: "participating for gain or liveli-
hood in an activity or field of endeavor often engaged in by amateurs" and
"exhibiting a courteous, conscientious, and generally businesslike manner
in the workplace." Simple enough. One article from the *Harvard Business
Review* begins with a poignant caution that it is "easy to fall back into
the 'I'll know it when I see it' argument."[6] This is especially true when
evaluating the professionalism of military personnel, because the achievements of members of the armed forces are often marked by skill badges
and awards worn on the uniform and displayed for all to see.

   In the Army, successful completion of airborne, air assault, ranger,
and similar training courses are important marks of achievement, each
vital for unique occupational specialties and leadership positions. These
courses, however, do not alone a professional make. Likewise, further

research of the definition of professionalism might result in a list of simple tasks that are expected of even the military's most junior members: be on time, be reliable, be flexible, and speak up when something is wrong.[7] Again, this is not a one-size-fits-all definition of professionalism, and most would agree that the inherent qualities of a professional far exceed these simple criteria. For example, in chapter 1, Pauline Shanks-Kaurin discusses the basic principles of ethical codes of conduct and occupational expertise that form the basis of military professionalism. Likewise, in chapter 6, Rebecca Johnson examines those similar characteristics against the mutual obligations of the clients that professionals serve. Both authors take a critical look at the defining criteria that should be applied when examining the military profession. Without doubt, however, the Army's own defined standard should serve as the evaluative baseline for examining professionalism across the institution. According to CAPE and *Army Doctrine Reference Publication 1, The Army Profession*, a profession has five dimensions, or aspects:

1. Professions provide a unique and vital service to the society they serve, one society cannot provide itself.
2. Professions provide this service by applying expert knowledge and practice.
3. Professions earn the trust of the society because of effective and ethical application of their expertise.
4. Professions self-regulate, and police the practice of their members to ensure it is effective and ethical. This self-regulation includes the responsibility for educating and certifying professionals.
5. Professions are therefore granted significant autonomy and discretion in their practice of expertise on behalf of the society.[8]

Examining the Army profession through these doctrinal dimensions exposes many areas that require further attention and change if the services are to achieve the objectives of the *Profession of Arms* campaign. In 2012 the Army released an *Annual Report on the Profession of Arms Campaign* and highlighted several focus areas.[9] Beyond those identified shortfalls, however, this chapter will examine the roots of professionalism in the military, those areas that inhibit a culture of professionalism and ethical behavior, institutional attempts to create a culture of ethics and professionalism, and alternatives to stewardship of the profession, principally from a bottom-up driven focus.

What Are the Foundations of Professionalism in the Military?

Military professionalism is established in time-honored doctrine, tradition, and historical precedent, the legal statutes that drive organizational frameworks for ethics and professional behavior, and individual moral and ethical beliefs. Historically, military professionalism can be traced back over several centuries from before the birth of the United States; it has continued to evolve through numerous revolutions in military affairs. In *The Soldier and the State*, Samuel Huntington describes the evolution of military education between the Civil War and World War I, and how the service academies moved away from an environment of technicism to one of military professionalism that required an awareness of the external forces influencing and shaping military conduct.[10] This significant period of military reform was led by Secretary of War Elihu Root, who spearheaded efforts to broaden the experiences of the officer corps, requiring line offers to spend time in staff departments and railing against the patronage system that closed off the staff departments from the remainder of the service. Furthermore, Huntington outlines an era of challenge prior to the civil war, where military professionalism had difficulty taking root in the United States, particularly in the wake of challenges federalism faced in the early United States. Huntington also describes how in the post–Civil War era, leaders of military education reform often analyzed the methods of German institutions such as the Kriegsakademie to find influence for shaping the path of military professionalism in the United States.[11]

Legally, the birth of the American military profession finds its roots in the establishment of the United States and the ratification of the Constitution in 1788. The Constitution charges the government with raising and supporting an army, an army subservient to its civilian leadership. Accordingly, the Constitution is backed through legal statute in Titles 5, 10, and 32 of the United States Code, which provide the authority for the military profession to support and defend the United States.[12] Additionally, Title 10 explicitly outlines what it terms "standards of exemplary conduct" for commanding officers and others in positions of authority:

- To show in themselves a good example of virtue, honor, patriotism, and subordination;
- To be vigilant in inspecting the conduct of all persons who are placed under their command;
- To guard against and suppress all dissolute and immoral practices, and to correct, according to the laws and regulations of the Army, all persons who are guilty of them; and

- To take all necessary and proper measures, under the laws, regulations, and customs of the Army, to promote and safeguard the morale, the physical well-being, and the general welfare of the officers and enlisted persons under their command or charge.[13]

These standards not only further support the professional standards outlined in *The Army Profession*, but they also codify and legally mandate specific criteria expected of those in positions of trust and authority within the uniformed services. In 2016 this mandate for higher standards of conduct expanded when the Army implemented Army Directive 2016–26, which "requires that [all] officers who are selected for promotion be vetted for mental, physical, moral, and professional fitness and meet the standards for exemplary conduct before their names are forwarded to the secretary of the Army for certification."[14] Extending from these legal requirements is the trust of the American public, also a vital component of the foundation of the military profession. In fact, a 2011 report by the Army Center for Army Leadership referred to trust as a "strategic advantage."[15] As stewards of the profession, it is fundamental that members of the military remain cognizant of their duty to support the defense of the American people and way of life as outlined in the Constitution. As a profession, the military serves under the trust of the American population through elected officials, as directed by law, to accomplish the nation's strategic objectives. Every failure of personnel and the institutions to uphold the standards of conduct not only undermines the basis for military professionalism but also breaks down the relationship of trust between the public and the military. Ultimately, as will be discussed later, this degradation in trust of military institutions leads to increased scrutiny and oversight of the military's ability to self-regulate by the legislature.

Upon entering military service, both commissioned officers and enlisted personnel swear oaths to support and defend the Constitution of the United States. Implicit in these oaths is the duty to uphold the tenets of military professionalism, as well as an inherent characteristic of subservience to the chain of command, to faithfully execute the duties of the office held, and to uphold the institutional values of the organization or branch of service being entered. According to *The Army Profession*, the "professional's oath to support and defend the Constitution requires strict adherence to the law. No order can set aside this obligation."[16] Likewise, the institutional values and cultural norms the Army upholds as expectations of professional conduct are articulated through the creeds recited by soldiers, NCOs, officers, and civilians. These creeds are intended to serve as an outward statement of the internally held values, beliefs, and guiding principles of the military profession.

All these defining principles of the military profession should and do presuppose the moral and ethical vision of individuals who join the service. Just as members of civilian professions subscribe to the professional and ethical standards of their respective vocations, members of the military swear solemn oaths to do the same. As Tufts University professor of international politics and noted author Daniel Drezner described, "This is what a profession does. . . . Regardless of political or personal proclivities, professionals do their job based on their training, guided by the codes and standards of the discipline. In the military, this means that soldiers respect the chain of command and adhere to their honor codes."[17]

Subscribing to the cultural influences of the military invokes an obligation to avoid the moral and ethical relativism that often pervades society. While there is a perception that moral relativism remains pervasive in civilian society, the military should not be subject to its effects, because the military's organizational culture is the driving force behind professionalism. Management expert Edgar Schein describes this phenomenon quite astutely in his book *Organizational Culture and Leadership,* a text used not only in business and educational circles but in professional military education as well. Schein states, "cultural forces are powerful because they operate outside our awareness. . . . Most importantly, understanding cultural forces enables us to understand ourselves better."[18] Looking at the Army through this lens, we see that members of the profession of arms are all subject to the effects of the cultural dynamics of the organization in which they serve. As Don Snider, a leader of the renewal of the study of professionalism in the military, and his colleagues state, "A strong culture exists when a clear set of norms and expectations—usually as a function of leadership—permeates the entire organization."[19] However, a range of factors that can inhibit professional and ethical behavior exist, and all serve to challenge the inherent culture and trust of the profession of arms.

Obstacles to Professionalism

America remains the strongest military power on earth. Beyond its technological overmatch; its unprecedented tactical, operational, and strategic comparative advantages; and the skill and expertise of service members, the armed forces pride themselves on maintaining an all-volunteer force made up of the best of America's people. Unfortunately, the military recently has again uncovered a series of moral and ethical breakdowns, sexual assault scandals, senior level officer humiliations, and a growing trend of experienced personnel attrition. The convergence of these factors has a profound effect on the military's efforts to embed and sustain a culture of professionalism in its personnel.

Lying to Ourselves: The Effect of Bureaucracy on the Profession

Ethical and professional degradation in the Army received a high-profile exposure in early 2015, when the Army War College's Strategic Studies Institute published the monograph *Lying to Ourselves: Dishonesty in the Army Profession*, a scathing examination of numerous ethical shortfalls occurring frequently at all levels of the Army organization. In fact, the authors of the report, Leonard Wong and Stephen Gerras, point out how the Army may be "inadvertently abetting the behavior it deems unacceptable."[20] The essence of their argument is that the overwhelming bureaucratic requirements of the Army's training management system have forced officers to violate the codes of ethics to avoid undue scrutiny. Their thesis describes a system that demands subordinate leaders to accomplish more tasks than are physically possible in a given training year. Beyond the standard individual soldier skills training and collective mission essential task training that must be accomplished on an annual basis, their system includes other priorities such as classes on suicide prevention, sexual harassment and assault prevention, substance abuse, ethics, and resilience, just to name a few. Wong and Gerras note that an Army War College analysis in 2002 determined that commanders are tasked with accomplishing an average of 297 days' worth of annual training requirements, with only 256 days available to complete them. This flood of training tasks forces commanders to willfully report inaccurate statistics or to purposefully not comply with the requirement, a tolerance of decided breaches of integrity that undermines the very foundations of the profession.

Unfortunately, this problem is not new. In 1970 Chief of Staff of the Army Gen. William Westmoreland directed researchers at the Army War College to study the Army profession. Sadly, the results of the 1970 *Study on Military Professionalism* were strikingly similar to the findings of *Lying to Ourselves*, pointing out "inaccurate reporting" and a "preoccupation with the attainment of trivial short-term objectives even through dishonest practices that injure the long-term fabric of the organization."[21] While both these reports focused specifically on the Army, the overarching point is not intended to imply that the problems of professionalism highlighted in its pages are not found elsewhere in the joint force.[22]

Breaking the Army: The Effects of Sustained Combat

A decade and a half of war has forced the military to adapt itself doctrinally, organizationally, and operationally to the effects of sustained combat operations worldwide. Likewise, the increased operational demands of soldiers, sailors, airmen, and Marines, coupled with declining force structures and resources, have produced tremendous strain on the profession. While these burdens are recognized at every level of military leadership, articulating their effect on the profession poses a challenge. Consequently, the solutions to properly address the effects often prove elusive as well. In 2006 the chief of staff, Gen. Peter Schoomaker, warned a congressional committee of the potential effect of repeated, extended deployments on the Army. His seemingly prophetic description highlighted the impending risk of breaking the force: he argued that the limited downtime units were given between combat rotations further increased the strain on members of the Army. For example, during the peak of the wars in Iraq and Afghanistan, professional military education was often deferred or waived for officers and NCOs, later placing mid-grade and senior leaders in positions of tremendous responsibility without proper training and development.[23]

Likewise, in 2010 Lt. Gen. Robert Caslen and Maj. Erik Anderson addressed the looming challenges of an era of persistent conflict in their *Military Review* article, "Reconnecting with Our Roots: Reflections on the Army's Ethic."[24] Citing numerous lapses in ethical judgment and professional discernment, Caslen highlights how the strain of combat operations can degrade judgment, leading to decisions that fall outside the military's espoused professional guidelines. Similarly, in 2012 Don Snider predicted that through his examination of the state of the profession, the chairman of the Joint Chiefs of Staff would find "that our Armed Forces have, under the pressures of the last decade of war, actually abetted the moral corrosion of war by perpetuating a very unbalanced approach to their most important resource—their uniformed personnel."[25] His assertion has been substantiated again and again in the years since he wrote it. These lapses in professionalism not only undermine the moral, ethical, and legal basis under which the military exists as an institution, but they also risk degrading the trust placed on the military by the public and civilian leadership of the government, a fundamental aspect of the profession.[26] That trust is especially imperative in the current era of Gray Zone conflict where the risk of escalation is woven throughout many aspects of military and nonmilitary engagements and demands exceptional professional discernment in the non-kinetic domain to avoid the unintended consequences of lapses in professional judgment.[27] A far cry from the bipolar world of state-on-state conflict of Huntington's era, the transregional and multidomain challenges of the current and emerging conflict spaces demand developing and retaining leaders that can manage more than simply the province of violence.[28]

Bleeding Talent: Experienced Personnel Attrition

The loss of talented leaders across the military has been a concern for both uniformed and civilian leadership for several years; this loss serves as an impediment to promoting professionalism in the armed forces. While every member of the military is expected to serve as a steward of the profession, leaders are expected to bear the standard for professional performance and ethical conduct above all, a point repeated throughout Don Snider and Lloyd Matthews' *The Future of the Army Profession*.[29] What is not addressed in this text, however, is the retention of leaders who will carry the mantle for the profession. In his book *Bleeding Talent*, veteran and author Tim Kane decries the current system of personnel management in the military, and how its inability to retain and promote the best leaders is creating an environment where great leaders are produced, but then are forced to leave for better opportunities.[30] If Kane is correct, the military is driving its professionals to seek other opportunities through personnel mismanagement forced by the Defense Officer Personnel Management Act of 1980, further eroding the capacity to enhance professionalism.[31] The legislated requirements for career management do little to encourage expanded development beyond the assignment, position, and education gates that leaders must pass through for promotion and advancement. Consequently, leaders are advanced through the military with few opportunities to broaden their experiences. Those who do, or who seek out such opportunities, are often discouraged out of fear for their career timeline. Often, another result is that these leaders leave the service, taking with them their talents, desire, and perspective for organizational improvement. Over time, this has created a damaging trend for the military. For example, at the senior level numerous officers selected for attendance at the Army War College choose to defer attendance in order to remain in assignments that they see as more beneficial to their promotion potential. Likewise, many officers choose a deferment as a way to determine if they are subsequently selected for promotion or command as some are chosen to attend the War College and are later not promoted.[32] The combination of these two factors creates a significant gap in strategic level education that degrades the structure of leadership at our most strategic levels, thus permeating throughout the force. This happens because the current personnel management and promotion system is built in a manner that institutionalizes such backward practices.

The trend of professional degradation resulting from personnel management practices is no secret. In 2009 Richard Kohn published an article in *World Affairs* titled "Tarnished Brass: Is the U.S. Military Profession in Decline?" In that article Kohn highlights a profession at risk of decline due to lapses in intellectual, ethical, and political variables. Furthermore, he questions the military's resolve in transforming itself in the wake of what he sees as a multilayered degradation in professionalism, stressing the importance of the military staying ahead of political leaders in policing its problems.[33] An organization that requires intervention from outside to correct itself, he says, is one in decline, and must either adapt or be forced into adaptation.[34] The recent attempts by congressional oversight committees led by Senator Kirsten Gillibrand (D-NY) to withhold the authority of commanders to prosecute sexual assault cases is one example of such outside intervention.[35] If the military fails to adapt in this scenario, and does not properly react to the trust given to control behavior within its own ranks, it opens the door for a situation that will create an expansion of scrutiny and an increase in the influence of civil law on the armed forces' ability to self-regulate. Ultimately this reform should come from within, something the military has attempted numerous times over the past four decades without realizing complete results.

Institutional Efforts to Enhance Professionalism in the Military

When Gen. William Westmoreland directed his 1970 review of the Army profession, the US was fighting the Vietnam War with a blended force of volunteers and conscripted personnel riddled with moral and ethical issues.[36] Leadership in the Army at that time was predominantly made up of professional officers, but the strain of what was then America's longest war, the loss of public support, and the pressures of leading a blended force combined to stress Army leadership at all levels. Westmoreland's study was followed later that decade by Gen. Bernard Rogers' "Assessing the Army" white paper, written in the wake of the end of the Vietnam War and the creation of the all-volunteer force.[37] The Army continued to search for its identity as a professional force throughout the 1980s and 1990s, and each successive chief of staff commissioned separate research efforts to evaluate the professionalism of the Army. Accordingly, each study was accompanied by strategic inflection points, such as the height of the Cold War, the force reductions of the mid-1990s, or the onset of the war on terrorism after the turn of the century, during which *The Future of the Army Profession* was published. Furthermore, the studies all led to requisite policies and programs that attempted to instill the culture of professionalism within the institution.[38] As the wars in Iraq and Afghanistan seemingly ended, institutional history would again repeat itself, bringing with it another reflection on the profession of arms.

In 2010 Gen. George Casey and Gen. Martin Dempsey (then the commander of the Army's Training and Doctrine Command) directed the establishment of the Army Profession of Arms Campaign, an effort to assess the effect of a decade of war on the profession and to determine how the Army could remain successful despite the strains. The Profession of Arms Campaign was also timed to follow the realignment of CAPE under the Training and Doctrine Command's Combined Arms Center, moving it from the control of the United States Military Academy and providing more institutional emphasis on the campaign's effect. One product of advancing that direction toward that end was the publication of *The Army Profession* in June 2013.[39] *The Army Profession* provides members of the Army the doctrinal directive of professionalism, serving as the institutional basis for training and teaching professional conduct across the force. Soon after its publication in 2014, General Dempsey (by then the Chairman of the Joint Chiefs of Staff) directed an evaluation of the Profession of Arms Campaign. Though the results of the evaluation have not yet been published at the time of this writing, in July 2014 Gen. Raymond Odierno released the *Army Ethic White Paper*, another document intended to evaluate the progress of the campaign and to synthesize and convey the organization's intent for the direction of training and teaching the Army. In the paper Odierno quotes Caslen as saying that "the profession and ethic are inseparable."[40] Clearly, the results of Wong and Gerras' study prove that Caslen is indeed correct, and the Army has work to do.

Beyond the Army, however, the work continues as well. In 2014 Secretary of Defense Chuck Hagel's appointment of Rear Adm. Margaret "Peg" Klein as senior adviser for military professionalism demonstrated that the concern for lapses in ethical and professional conduct extended to the military's civilian leadership. As Hagel stated, "Competence and character are not mutually exclusive. They are woven together, and they must be. And an uncompromising culture of accountability must exist at every level of command."[41] Culture is best cultivated at the lowest level of command and must be emphasized at that level to effect change.

Stewardship of the Profession from the Bottom Up

Professionals are granted certain permissions inherent to that title. With those permissions comes a commensurate set of expectations. Meeting or exceeding the expectations of a professional starts at the individual level. When individual members of a profession adopt and demonstrate the expected values, norms, and behaviors of their chosen profession, it permeates the very fabric of the organizational culture. As outlined in Schein's text, those cultural forces eventually become so ingrained that they go beyond an individual's awareness, becoming second nature. This is where the individual and institutional dimensions of professionalism intersect, and where stewardship of the profession is maximized.

Looking back to the definition of professions outlined in *The Army Profession*, the Army provides a unique and vital service to the United States, one that its people cannot provide themselves except through military service. As the proponent for the application of swift, sustained, and dominant strategic land power in the armed forces, no other entity can match this capability. Foundationally the Army must lead and be led by experts in the application of land-based combat operations. However, the current and emerging operating environments demand more. Army leaders—and leaders in all military services—must be able to create effects across all domains, not just those their service specializes in.[42] This changing environment creates a demand for a new level of military expert, one far different from what Huntington expected when he wrote *The Soldier and the State* in 1957, and even from when Snider and Matthews published *The Future of the Army Profession* in 2002. The path to this level of military expert is not easy and highlights the sort of professional needed in the Army of the next generation.

Expertise is built through a multifaceted approach at training, education, and most important extensive efforts at self-development. A professional should, as Machiavelli says in *The Prince,* "read histories and consider in them the actions of excellent men, should see how they conducted themselves in wars, should examine the causes of their victories and losses, so as to be able to avoid the latter and imitate the former."[43] The study of history, strategy, and the conduct of military operations occurs at every level of professional military education and should serve as a guidepost to shape the critical thought required to serve as a professional leader in the Army. The described anti-intellectual bias, neglect of the duty to develop and educate young professional officers, and dogmatic doctrine undermine professionalism at the lowest levels.[44] Moreover, the perceived distinction between thinkers and doers further exacerbates the anti-intellectual trend and de-emphasizes the importance of education in these vital focus areas of personal study. As Lloyd Matthews states, "The army that rejects seminal thinkers, thereby depriving itself of innovative ideas and the instruments for continuous self-renewal, will ultimately be an extraneous army."[45]

While there is a disheartening lack of focus on the intellectual side of professionalism, which cripples leader development and stifles innovative thought at all levels, anti-intellectualism is not isolated to the military, but rather reflects American society at large. Nevertheless, the purpose of the military is not solely to educate its professionals for education's sake. Rather, as Prussian general and strategic theorist Carl von Clausewitz stated in his magnum opus *On War,* "The whole military activity must therefore relate to the engagement. The end for which a soldier is recruited, clothed, armed, and trained, the whole object of his sleeping, eating, drinking, and marching is simply that he should fight at the right place at the right time."[46] Education of military professionals should serve the purpose of preparing for battle. By doing this, the military intends to create a culture of profession and ethics formed of habituation and focused on its sole purpose of supporting and defending the Constitution of the United States. Building on the moral baseline of its personnel, combined with professional ethical standards that are both institutionally driven and individually developed, habits and behavior are created and ingrained in professional military personnel.

This leads to self-regulation. Professions police themselves and do not rely on outsiders to do it for them.[47] Rather than decry the problem, recent years demonstrate a few notable examples of mid-grade officers working outside their day-to-day duties to enhance professional development opportunities for themselves and others with social media platforms, blog sites, writing programs, and professional conferences. The increase in the use of military blogs has led many young officers to branch into professional writing, guided reading, and historical discussion programs. Professional online publications like *The Strategy Bridge*, *The Military Leader*, and the joint venture between the Center for Company-Level Leaders at the US Military Academy at West Point and the Kings of War, a blog of the Department of War Studies, King's College London, are just a few great examples of mid-grade officers working outside their day-to-day duties to enhance professional development opportunities for themselves and others. Such programs are a promising sign that many of our officers see the seriousness of self-study, personal accountability for development, and policing our own, and are being embraced by senior military leaders across all services. There is no reason these innovative development initiatives cannot and should not be implemented within individual units, to enhance learning for leaders of all levels.

Conclusion

Despite decades of effort on the part of the Department of Defense, there is little doubt that the professional and ethical standing of the military remains in question. In the wake of the continued debate of the military's professional status, and particularly the publication of *Lying to Ourselves*, the Department of Defense must take a hard stance on improving professionalism across the joint force. As Lt. Gen. (Ret.) David Barno and Nora Bensahel wrote in an article,

> Their damning findings cry out for a top-to-bottom institutional soul-searching on the state of military ethics in an era of information and requirements overload. This ethical crisis will not be resolved by another catchy program or new Pentagon office. It can only be addressed by strong senior level leadership, marked by candor and transparency. Junior officers deserve public acknowledgement of the irreconcilable ethical conflicts they confront daily and must participate in building the changes needed to reconcile these impossible tensions. Their leaders must now demonstrate the moral courage to acknowledge the depth of this

corrosive problem, to listen and seek advice from their subordinates, and to lead their force to a solution. But most importantly, the nation expects—and deserves—complete honesty and integrity from its military upon which so much of the nation's security depends. Anything less will ultimately put the nation at risk by deeply eroding the foundations of its future strategic choices.[48]

Barno and Bensahel's analysis of the findings reflects the type of candid assessment needed to truly spark a reform in military professionalism. A key point to their argument is that the "ethical crisis will not be resolved by another catchy program or new Pentagon office."[49] To be frank, the last thing the military needs is another layer of bureaucracy to work through in order to make improvements. In fact, the numerous layers of bureaucratic requirements are at the heart of the problem highlighted by Barno and Bensahel's article, which echoes Wong and Gerras' *Lying to Ourselves*.

Ultimately, the excessive reporting demands and layers of bureaucratic influence will not disappear overnight. However, the military should look closely at itself and devote as much institutional effort on studying how to streamline the requirements it places on commanders as it does on its ethics programs. By doing this, it can resolve the twofold dilemma of advancing ethics while reducing the bureaucracy that is crippling the profession. Moreover, professional military education institutions have a role in helping solve the problems plaguing the profession. As the tip of the spear for leader development, the military's NCO academies, service academies, officer training programs, staff colleges, and war colleges all must focus on underscoring the moral and ethical obligations of members of the armed forces. Furthermore, they must also continue to promote the individual characteristics needed to maintain and cultivate those individual leadership and stewardship traits needed to advance professionalism within the ranks.

Improved personnel management practices will be an integral component of advancing a professional culture in the military. For more than a decade, the armed forces have been engaged in persistent conflict around the world. For more than thirty years, personnel practices have created a culture that rewards mediocrity and discourages innovation and professional entrepreneurship. The government must finally undertake pragmatic reform of the Defense Officer Personnel Management Act and the

Goldwater-Nichols Department of Defense Reform Act of 1986 to minimize or eliminate the requirements that stifle rather than encourage professional development. With the limited career flexibility and reduced
incentive for exceptional performance that current personnel policies
mandate, true advancement of the profession from individual leaders will
not occur. It is past time to reform personnel management in the military.

Finally, leader development programs at all levels must focus on
increasing trust and autonomy. Subordinates must be given latitude to
learn, without fear of retribution or overly risk-averse leadership behavior.
This extends from training, to off-duty activity, and regrettably to combat
as well. While leaders must be cognizant of the activities of subordinates
to a degree, autonomy and discretion must be employed as well. When
leaders are trusted to lead, and subordinates trusted to act, an environment of professionalism can finally be fostered.

The expectation is that those who wear the uniform at all levels
have become some part of the profession of arms, and likewise should
exhibit the level of expertise, conduct, and stewardship commensurate
with their rank, role, and responsibility. There are heartening examples
of professionalism in our ranks today, but the armed forces still have
work to do. For decades, sweeping initiatives driven down from the military's highest levels have generated extensive studies but limited results.
For more than a decade, the armed forces have fought admirably, demonstrating the resilience, adaptability, and professionalism expected. However, they have also exhibited the effects of the strain such a demand has
placed on them. As a result, the military yet again is at a strategic inflection point and must continue to look for innovative ways to advance
professionalism in its ranks or risk becoming a force that is hollow in
both ethics and capabilities.

Notes

1. John Mattox, "The Moral Foundations of Army Officership," in Snider and Matthews, *The Future of the Army Profession*, 389.
2. Quoted in Martin Dempsey, "America's Military—A Profession of Arms White Paper,"
   http://www.jcs.mil/Portals/36/Documents/Publications/aprofessionofarms.pdf, 3.
3. "Mission & Intent | CAPE," http://cape.army.mil/mission.php.
4. Thom Shanker and Elisabeth Bumiller, "Panetta and General Dempsey to
   Review Military Ethics," *New York Times*, 15 November 2012, http://www.nytimes.
   com/2012/11/16/world/panetta-and-general-dempsey-to-review-military-ethics.
   html. General Dempsey stated, "If we really are a profession—a group of men and

women who are committed to living an uncommon life with extraordinary responsibilities and high standards—we should want to figure it out before someone else figures it out for us."

5. Center for the Army Profession and Ethic, press release, 14 December 2010.

6. Gretchen Gavett, "What Does Professionalism Look Like?," *Harvard Business Review*, https://hbr.org/2014/03/what-does-professionalism-look-like.

7. Alison Green, "What Does It Mean to Be Professional at Work?—US News," *US News & World Report*, http://money.usnews.com/money/blogs/outside-voices-careers/2013/07/22/what-does-it-mean-to-be-professional-at-work.

8. Department of the Army, *Army Doctrine Reference Publication 1, The Army Profession*, Headquarters, Department of the Army, June 2015, 1-1.

9. US Army, Doctrine Command, "US Army Profession Campaign," 2012, http://data.cape.army.mil/web/repository/CY11ArmyProfessionAnnualReport.pdf

10. Huntington, *The Soldier and the State*.

11. Huntington, *The Soldier and the State*, 237.

12. "Doctrine & Policy, Center for the Army Profession and Ethic, CAPE."

13. US Code, "Title 10–Armed Forces," Sub-Title B–Army, Part I–Organization, 1997, http://uscode.house.gov/view.xhtml?req=(title:10%20section:3583%20edition:prelim).

14. US Army, "New Directive: Officers Must Be Vetted before Promotions Are Confirmed," http://www.army.mil/article/173782/new_directive_officers_must_be_vetted_before_promotions_are_confirmed.

15. James P. Steele, *Army Trust: A Multi-level Review* (Fort Leavenworth, KS: Center for Army Leadership, US Army Combined Arms Center, 2011).

16. US Army, *Army Doctrine Reference Publication 1: The Army Profession* (2013).

17. Daniel W. Drezner, "What Do the Academy and the Military Have in Common?," *Washington Post*, 15 January, 2015, http://www.washingtonpost.com/posteverything/wp/2015/01/15/what-do-the-academy-and-the-military-have-in-common/.

18. Edgar H. Schein, *Organizational Culture and Leadership* (San Francisco: Jossey-Bass, 2010).

19. Don M. Snider, Paul Oh, and Kevin Toner, *The Army's Professional Military Ethic in an Era of Persistent Conflict*, Vol. 1 (Carlisle, PA: Strategic Studies Institute, 2009).

20. Wong and Gerras, *Lying to Ourselves*, 3.

21. US Army War College, *Study on Military Professionalism* (Carlisle Barracks, PA: US Army War College, 1970), 13, 20. This study was an early iteration of nearly four decades of successive attempts at the institutional level to determine the causes and potential solutions to ethical breakdowns in the Army.

22. In the wake of the cheating scandals that were uncovered in the Air Force's and Navy's nuclear officer corps, drug and alcohol abuse, sexual assault incidents at basic training locations, theft and bribery in combat zones, and numerous incidents of misuse of government travel cards, evidence suggests that breakdowns in professionalism are far from isolated to the Army alone.

23. Charles D. Allen, "The Impact of a Decade of War," *Armed Forces Journal* (May 2011): 14–16, 36.

24. Robert L. Caslen Jr. and Erik Anderson, "Reconnecting with Our Roots: Reflections on the Army's Ethic," *Military Review* (1 September 2010): 110.

25. Don Snider, "The Moral Corrosion within Our Military Professions," http://www.strategicstudiesinstitute.army.mil/index.cfm/articles//The-Moral-Corrosion-within-Our-Military-Professions/2012/11/27.

26. Snider, "The U.S. Army as Profession," 25.

27. Michael J. Mazarr, *Mastering the Gray Zone: Understanding a Changing Era of Conflict* (Carlisle, PA: Strategic Studies Institute, 2015), 57.

28. Stavridis, Rokke, and Pierce, "Crafting and Managing Effects," 18.

29. George Reed, "Leadership Development: Beyond Traits and Competencies," in Snider and Matthews, *The Future of the Army Profession*, 597.

30. Tim Kane, *Bleeding Talent: How the US Military Mismanages Great Leaders and Why It's Time for a Revolution* (New York: Palgrave Macmillan, 2012).

31. Tim Kane, "Why Our Best Officers Are Leaving," *The Atlantic*, February 2011, http://www.theatlantic.com/magazine/archive/2011/01/why-our-best-officers-are-leaving/308346/.

32. Charles D. Allen, "Redress of Professional Military Education: The Clarion Call," *Joint Force Quarterly*, no. 59 (2010), http://www.au.af.mil/au/awc/awcgate/jfq/allen_clarion_call.pdf.

33. Looking back at the definitions listed throughout the book and in this article specifically, the mark of a profession is self-regulation. By this defining characteristic alone, Kohn is questioning the professional status of the military.

34. Richard Kohn, "Tarnished Brass: Is the U.S. Military Profession in Decline?," *World Affairs Journal*, Spring 2009, http://www.worldaffairsjournal.org/article/tarnished-brass-us-military-profession-decline.

35. "Congressional Record—114th Congress—THOMAS (Library of Congress)," http://thomas.loc.gov/cgi-bin/query/F?r114:1:./temp/~r114K17DyC:e341796.

36. US Army War College, *Study on Military Professionalism*.

37. Charles D. Allen, "Assessing the Army Profession," *Parameters*, Autumn 2011, 74. This also led to the very first *Field Manual 100–1* (later *Army Doctrinal Publication 1*), *The Army*, which not only described what the Army was for, but how professional soldiers should act, and what their obligations to the profession are. A section on "The Profession" has been in *The Army* since this publication was created.

38. Allen, *Assessing the Army Profession*.

39. Allen, 74.

40. Raymond Odierno, *Army Ethic White Paper* (West Point, NY: Center for Army Profession and Ethic, 2014), 7.

41. Jennifer Hlad, "Hagel Appoints Top Ethics Officer," *Stars and Stripes*, http://www.stripes.com/news/hagel-appoints-top-ethics-officer-1.274483.

42. Stavridis, Rokke, and Pierce, "Crafting and Managing Effects," 6.

43. Niccolo Machiavelli, *The Prince*, 2nd ed., trans. Harvey Mansfield (Chicago: University of Chicago Press, 1998), 60.

44. Lloyd J. Matthews, "Anti-Intellectualism and the Army Profession," in Snider and Matthews, *The Future of the Army Profession*, 79.

45. As quoted in Don Snider, "Strategic Insights: Whiskey Over Books, Again? Anti-Intellectualism and the Future Effectiveness of Army 2025," http://www.strategic studiesinstitute.army.mil/index.cfm/articles//Whiskey-Over-Books-Again/ 2016/02/23, 82 (quote).

46. Carl von Clausewitz, *On War* (Princeton, NJ: Princeton University Press, 1989), 95.

47. Don M. Snider, *Once Again, the Challenge to the US Army During a Defense Reduction: To Remain a Military Profession* (Carlisle, PA: Strategic Studies Institute, 2012), 23.

48. David Barno and Nora Bensahel, "Lying to Ourselves: The Demise of Military Integrity," War on the Rocks, http://warontherocks.com/2015/03/lying-to-ourselves-the-demise-of-military-integrity/.

49. Barno and Bensahel, "Lying to Ourselves."

CHAPTER 11

The Military Is Not the Sole Profession on the Battlefield

Holly Hughson

Introduction

The military is not the sole profession on the battlefield. In parallel, another profession is mobilized to respond in a lateral capacity, and to mitigate the impact of war on civilian noncombatants often caught in the literal crossfire. Humanitarian aid workers are first responders who work based on need, to alleviate human suffering where life-saving assistance is required. Both professions have a shared protection mandate and often a commonly desired end-state: a stable community that poses no threat abroad or to itself. The traditional battlefield, with uniformed combatants and lines drawn along national borders, fostered a clear line of demarcation between military action and humanitarian response. The world wars of the twentieth century mobilized the international community with a conviction and consensus that now, in the twenty-first century, appears elusive, if not impossible. Achievements in international humanitarian law, largely contained in the four Geneva Conventions of 1949, sought to limit the effects of armed conflict. In the post–World War II security environment, these international agreements provided structure and guidance for the military and humanitarian professions, both of which undertook efforts to professionalize in the second half of the twentieth century.

This chapter examines the US military and international humanitarian response in deployment through the lens of a direct witness to both professions in action. The operational reality inherent in the changing character of conflict in the twenty-first century has blurred the lines of responsibility and poses existential questions to both professions. When a deployed military force faces an enemy indistinguishable from the civilian population, aid workers are threatened equally by their work being indistinguishable from the foreign policy and national security objectives of that force. Just as the identity of the threat fractures into a thousand non-state pieces, so are the battlefield professions forced to adapt to a new, uncomfortable reality: the profession charged with the management of violence no longer operates in isolation from the profession charged with the mitigation of that violence.

Witness

As one who made the nontraditional decision to support civil-military coordination while serving as an aid worker, I was afforded the opportunity to see the military as an outsider while having insider access. This perspective reinforces my observation that soldiering is a battlefield profession.[1] It is, however, not the only battlefield profession.

I have had many opportunities to speak to college students about humanitarian aid work. Often, they perceive my work as limited to non-threatening environments. This compels me to provide a clearer understanding of this role: "I want to tell you about a friend of mine, a guy named Jason. Over the past decade, Jason has served in both Iraq and Afghanistan. He spent over a year in Iraq, and two years in Afghanistan. His life was constantly under threat and sometimes, direct fire. Thankfully, Jason is now safely home. But he's had some challenges since he got back."[2]

At this point in my lecture, I asked if anyone could guess what some of those challenges are. The students responded with sensitivity to what many veterans have faced on return from combat deployments: symptoms of post-traumatic stress, trouble finding employment, and the challenge of reintegrating back into a society. Next I asked, "Do you have any ideas how he could get some help?" They suggested that he could seek help through existing services from the government and private sector, including counseling available through veterans' benefits, and the Montgomery GI Bill to study or train for a new type of work. "The only problem is that Jason isn't a combat soldier or a marine. He is not even in the military. He is a humanitarian aid worker. He led the emergency response team into Iraq in 2003 for an international non-governmental organization [NGO]. Years later in Afghanistan, he served as the Country Director, in charge of hundreds of staff all working unarmed and under the constant threat from insurgents and opportunistic criminals who often targeted anyone partnering with the Afghan or Iraqi governments, and foreign military or international aid organizations. He lost colleagues in both countries."[3]

At this point the classroom was quiet. The students had presumed Jason was in the military. They had not considered the service of humanitarian aid workers, who also respond in times of war.[4] These responders include nurses, doctors, logisticians, engineers, epidemiologists, and generalist project managers, among others, all charged with the organization and delivery of life-saving assistance to populations trapped or displaced by conflict. The students' perceptions mirror those of our broader society that associates battlefield service predominantly with a military uniform.

Problem Set

Significant changes in twenty-first-century warfare have challenged the conventional postures and identities of both the military and humanitarian professions. In the second half of the twentieth century and post–World War II security environment, both the US military and international humanitarian practitioners evolved considerably to professionalize.

For the US military, the record of professionalization was a response to specific threats from distinct enemies and tough lessons learned in the aftermath of the Vietnam War. The strategic logic was that victory would be determined by the side with a superior arsenal of conventional weapons combined with the best-trained and resourced fighting force. As chapter 3 outlines, the Cold War paradigm, which justified the first large, standing, peacetime military in US history, triggered a debate about what defined the profession of arms. The cornerstone of this debate was Samuel Huntington's seminal work, *The Soldier and the State* (1957). Huntington's thesis that the military needed to be a profession was an attempt to preserve it as a politically neutral force in relationship to its civilian control. More relevant for this discussion, Huntington identified the core competency of the military profession as "the management of violence."[5]

For the humanitarian community, the reference point for professionalizing was the International Committee of the Red Cross/Red Crescent's (ICRC) Code of Conduct. The founding principle of the Code of Conduct is that the humanitarian imperative—the right to receive humanitarian assistance—is a fundamental human right that applies universally without exception. The obligation to provide humanitarian assistance wherever it is needed is predicated on the understanding that aid is not a partisan or political act. Counterpart to the military profession, the mandate for humanitarian action on the battlefield is to mitigate the impact of war and conflict on the civilian noncombatants.

As the professions charged with management and mitigation of violence evolved in the late twentieth century, they did so in reference to international humanitarian law. International humanitarian law is the body of rules governing relations between states in armed conflict. This framework is largely contained in the four Geneva Conventions of 1949, and nearly every state in the world has agreed to be bound by them. International humanitarian law, and the expectation of war as an act of aggression by one state toward another, provided clear direction for the concept and development of the military and humanitarian professions.

In the twenty-first century, however, unprecedented changes have affected both professions. The pace of technological change and the scale and pace of information flows have fostered a world dis-order where chaos and disruption are force multipliers. In this security environment, the power of the individual has never been so great. Empowered by the information age, agents of change are no longer obviously or exclusively the establishment elite or the uniformed combatant. Rogue individuals or other non-state groups can now exploit the vulnerability of civilians with impunity and at a speed hitherto impossible. In the twenty-first century the state, and by extension its security forces, no longer maintains a monopoly on violence.

In his monograph *The Strategic Logic of the Contemporary Security Dilemma*, Max Manwaring suggests a fundamental paradigm shift has taken place. The security dilemma has evolved from a determination of what is or is not aggression and is now a question of why, when, and how to intervene to protect people and prevent egregious human suffering. Manwaring reasons that this question "in turn encompasses more than a redefinition of security. It is nothing less than a redefinition of sovereignty."[6] The reality of this evolution has blurred the lines so carefully drawn in the twentieth century and poses existential questions to both the military and humanitarian professions on the battlefield.

Security in the modern world is increasingly defined as a combination of characteristics and broad concerns, rather than the traditional measurements construed along national lines. Twenty-first-century threats to international security are now largely intrastate and driven by an amorphous collection of non- and/or quasi-state actors with frontlines constantly shifting. Modern conflict is a broad spectrum and complex, often involving the entire population, either directly or indirectly. The actors and means extend far beyond the traditional concepts of a battle space with clearly defined and identifiable combatants. While diplomatic lines of effort continue to rely on twentieth-century conventions and international laws, and the UN is yet the forum for discussing threats to international security, the operational reality of conflict bears little correlation to this outdated framework.

The protracted war in Syria painfully demonstrates how the international community has lost the ability to agree and mobilize to end conflict despite a mass humanitarian disaster, which has spread violence and suffering across a region and contributed to the global migration crisis. Tragically, the UN Security Council has not been able to enforce its own resolutions on Syria, leaving another twentieth-century achievement ineffectual in the long run.

The operational reality inherent in the changing character of conflict today has blurred the professional lines and poses existential questions to both professions. Chapter 3 describes the US Army's changed definition of a profession, which now focuses heavily on the moral and ethical aspects of its work and which tracks with Manwaring's reframed security dilemma. As these decisions are pushed down to tactical-level military leadership, the expanded scope of the military profession is taking on the mitigation of violence. This mitigation is a requirement of today's battlefield as witnessed in both Iraq and Afghanistan. Huntington's language of the management of violence no longer captures what is being asked of the military.

Closer to the humanitarian profession, the paradigm is now broader than national borders; it is global in its consideration. Just as the identity of the threat fractures into a thousand non-state pieces, so are the battlefield professions (and training) forced to adapt to a new uncomfortable reality: the profession charged with the management of violence no longer operates in isolation from the profession charged with mitigation of that violence. The paradigm of civil–military coordination needs to be expanded beyond the military's relationship to its civilian governance. Facing a security dilemma of why, when, and how to intervene to protect people, it would appear the next and most important effort for both professions is in education and training. Dialogue and understanding is needed more than ever before to mobilize appropriate combinations of resources, skillsets, and influence in the twenty-first-century security paradigm.

What Is a Profession?

There are several synonyms for the term "profession," including "occupation," "business," and "work." These can apply both to the military and humanitarian communities, but essentially encompass every kind of employment. More interestingly, the list of synonyms for profession includes "vocation," "calling," and "mission." These words suggest an existential component to a profession and echo themes of service and personal sacrifice, which both military and humanitarian aid communities uphold as their foremost raison d'être. That kind of motivation is not easily measured, because it is routinely an internal response to core values and/or a sense of personal obligation.

When the United States made the strategic decision to maintain a large standing military in the post–World War II security environment, the subsequent implications for civilian control mark the contemporary origins of the military as a profession of arms. Questions posed by Samuel Huntington and Morris Janowitz sought to define profession to ensure political or partisan neutrality. The phrase "civil–military coordination" emerged to capture the relationship and line of communication between the executive (commander in chief) and legislative (budgetary approval) branches and the military professionals charged with ensuring the state maintains its monopoly on violence.

In *The Soldier and the State*, Samuel Huntington framed his definition of military professionalism as a vocation: "The distinguishing characteristics of a profession as a special type of vocation are its expertise, responsibility, and corporateness." Huntington breaks down the components of this definition of profession as specialized knowledge and skill combined with a responsibility to society, whose members "share a common sense of organic unity and consciousness of themselves as a group apart from laymen."[7]

What is different about the decision for the military way versus an individual in possession of equivalent knowledge and skills is the motivation that these skills, specialized knowledge, and systems to advance education in their field might serve a broader, overarching mission or goal. This is not to suggest that all members of the military are professionals. After all, not everyone in the military conceives of their military service as a vocation or calling. Equally, not all military members who conceive of their service as a calling or vocation do so with honorable intent. As framed here, the military is a profession in the sense of an individual pursuit, a conscious journey beyond one's inherited circumstances, willingly offering one's skills, courage, and potentially life for the sake of strangers or comrades in harm's way. Both the military and humanitarian communities share this sense of profession. In the case of the military personnel, the strangers they are defending are, first, their fellow citizens and colleagues and, second, allied foreign populations. For the aid worker, specialized skills and knowledge are combined with the responsibility to protect the vulnerable citizens of the world based on their threatened humanity; the aid worker's sense of organic unity as a responder is akin to the physician's Hippocratic oath. Put another way, the humanitarian profession is principled action taken in fulfillment of an overarching responsibility for humanity to ensure basic human rights for all. Just like the military profession, this traditional posture is being tested by the operational reality in the twenty-first century.

The Humanitarian Profession

The humanitarian profession is perhaps best understood as an organic merging over time of three traditions, which evolved from human instinct to formalized response. First is the basic human instinct to protect and respond to human suffering by attempting to provide care. Next, with the evolution of tribal allegiances into systems of governance and attempts to codify values into ethical obligations, is the tradition of politically directed relief; the Marshall Plan is the most successful contemporary example of this second tradition. The third tradition was born with the idea of the Red Cross. In 1859 Swiss businessman Henry Dunant witnessed a bloody day between the armies of Austria and the Franco-Sardinian alliance at the Battle of Solferino, Italy. At the sight of 40,000 men dead or dying without medical attention, he organized local people to care for the wounded. The experience led him to call for the creation of national relief societies to aid those wounded in war. "Would there not be some means, during a period of peace and calm, of forming relief societies whose object would be to have the wounded cared for in time of war by enthusiastic, devoted volunteers, fully qualified for the task?" he wrote.[8] The Red Cross was born four years later, in 1863.

The humanitarian profession has been historically guided by the principles of humanity, impartiality, independence, and neutrality. Assistance is given based on lifesaving need, without discrimination. These principles draw on the Hippocratic oath held sacred by the medical profession for more than two millennia: treatment is given based on need to the best of one's ability. In the modern era, these humanitarian principles formally date to the First Geneva Convention, 1864.[9] The Convention established the framework that all parties to the conflict have an obligation to provide medical care, without discrimination, for wounded and sick military personnel, and to protect marked medical personnel, transport, and equipment.

Following World War II, the framework established by the First Geneva Convention was expanded from military and medical personnel to include all human life. The "Universal Declaration of Human Rights," 1948, was the first attempt in history for a universal statement outlining the basic rights and dignity that each human being deserves, without discrimination.[10] Humanitarian action and the professionals who deliver it are guided by this tradition. Today, these humanitarian principles are protected by UN General Assembly resolutions.[11] The General Assembly and growing body of international humanitarian law have guided humanitarian action and its practitioners who strive to operate based on these principles rather than on extensions or tools of foreign policy.

The broad international consensus in the decades following World War II that humanitarian assistance was to be impartial, independent, and apolitical reflected the vivid, living memory of the horrors of two devastating world wars. It further reflected the clear-cut lines of the Cold War allegiances in the twentieth century. What it did not reflect, however, was the nature of funding that was largely from individual governments or pooled resources through UN coordination. While most government donors try to separate humanitarian assistance funding from foreign policy objectives, the operational reality has never been straightforward, and much less so today as the speed and scale of humanitarian crises has far outstripped available resources, both financial and human.

Just as the military profession is no guarantee of the professionalism of its individual members, neither is there any guarantee of the professionalism of individual aid workers. Coordination in humanitarian response is ultimately voluntary, although donors as a condition of funding can compel it. In place of an obligatory chain of command and allegiance to a state, there are global initiatives for minimum standards and coordination. Although legally nonbinding, the Code of Conduct for the ICRC and nongovernmental organizations engaged in disaster relief provides a set of common standards in humanitarian terms for organizations engaged in humanitarian activities, including a commitment to the humanitarian principles. As of this writing more than 492 organizations have signed the Code of Conduct.

Without question, the voluntary nature of humanitarian coordination is an inherent vulnerability of the profession. In terms of deployment, there is no humanitarian organizational equivalent to the US military's combat training centers, which host military readiness exercises qualifying individual units as being fit/unfit for deployment. Humanitarian response is by nature intense, chaotic, and full of rapid change and uncertainty. It is an emergency, like a burning building, and aid workers are the firefighters rushing in to help. Only they do not go through a systemwide recruitment process or basic training to establish a common, minimum qualification before their assignments begin.

The humanitarian profession also faces the challenges of quickly developing in-country program rapid requirements and follow-on rapid recruitment, often leading to a high turnover of staff. Like the military unit, which has trained meticulously for combat, faces a different level of reality on the ground, so too does the humanitarian organization face an unavoidably steep learning curve and a highly fluid situation. Even with professional staff that has prior operational experience on the ground, most teams are formed at short notice with multiple national and international actors, each with varying levels of technical and language capacity and proficiency. The better-funded organizations maintain established global emergency response teams, which improve the quality and efficiency of their rapid response to crises. The dynamics of deployment and the adrenaline highs of putting your knowledge and skills to the ultimate test in the field are familiar to both professions. A unit commander and country director face a similar task of getting teams to maintain order. Leadership in a humanitarian organization has the added hurdle of getting a diverse team to collaborate voluntarily across varying levels of experience, field credibility, and a chain of command to check individuals' personality for fitness and suitability. The key difference is that the military has, often, trained as a cohesive unit prior to deployment; it is during training that trust and common purpose are established.

Professions at the Intersection

At the strategic level, both civilian and military responders have a protection mandate, and both work to reinstate security for the respective populations at risk, whether foreign or domestic. Whether the goal is countering a specific terrorist threat through direct military action or through providing humanitarian assistance, the objective is the same in the long term: creating a safe, stable community that poses no threat abroad or to itself.

At the tactical level, the posture could not be more different and more critical. After the initial invasions in both Iraq and Afghanistan, the military routinely faced an amorphous enemy that was often indistinguishable from the civilian population, an enemy that adapted constantly to its environment. Reflecting this identification challenge, the minimum requirements for escalation of force and authorizing airstrikes have grown more stringent because of increasing concerns for civilian casualties amid the reality that the civilian population might directly or indirectly support, assist, or even become the enemy. Meanwhile, enemy forces, both state and non-state actors, have exploited these operational concerns and requirements by deliberately using the civilian population for the protection and concealment of their fighting forces, weapons, and supplies.

For humanitarian aid workers the operational environment has unquestionably changed. The twenty-first-century record for attacks against aid workers is on a disturbing trajectory. The Aid Worker Security Database records major incidents of violence against aid workers from 1997 to the present. Major incidents are defined as killings, kidnappings, and attacks that result in serious injury. According to the Aid Worker Security Database, in 2000 there were 41 significant attacks on aid workers. By 2014 that number had risen to 190. In those 15 years more than 3,000 aid workers were killed, injured, or kidnapped.[12] According to Humanitarian Outcomes' "Aid Worker Security Report 2014," the previous year a record was set for violence against civilian aid operations, with a 66 percent increase in the number of victims from 2012.[13] In 2014 there were 190 reported incidents where 329 aid workers were victims with 121 killed, 88 wounded, and 120 kidnapped.[14]

Not surprisingly, this dramatic increase in the threat has occurred in locations where there has been an implosion of governance and subsequent power vacuum: Afghanistan, Libya, Pakistan, Somalia, South Sudan, Sudan, and Syria. Just as, increasingly, the rules of conventional warfare do not apply in such locations, neither does the traditional protection offered by international humanitarian law for nonparties to the conflict (i.e., noncombatants), including aid workers and journalists. In addition to absent representative governance, it is no accident that locations where aid workers have been most vulnerable are also the sites of foreign military interventions. Led by the United States and Western allies, the wars in Iraq and Afghanistan have contributed heavily to a polarizing paradigm that has fueled the rhetoric and power of violent extremist groups and governments hostile or opposed to the Western-led military intervention. Neither theater proved a straightforward fight, but rather fomented full-scale insurgencies countered with protracted occupations and a large foreign military footprint.

Unfortunately, counterinsurgency operations in both theaters did not prove decisive. In the eyes of the humanitarian aid community, the decisions to allocate funding to the military to "win hearts and minds" dangerously blurred the traditional lines separating humanitarian action for the protection of civilians who do not take part in the fighting as codified in international humanitarian law. Counterinsurgency projects designed to stabilize communities and win hearts and minds were uncoordinated with humanitarian and development activities and were often directly disruptive and duplicative of taxpayer-funded projects by US- and coalition-partnered governments and implementing partners. This strategy put a military face on the very same activities implemented by nongovernmental organizations and eroded the perception of aid workers as neutral and impartial to the conflict. Worse yet, the very enemy it was designed to defeat manipulated the counterinsurgency approach. The large military occupation footprint along with stabilization projects played right into the hands of the insurgents and the emergent tactic of warfare by spoiler: "In AQI [Al-Qaeda in Iraq] the Task Force faced less a hostile military organization, however decentralized, and rather a militant organism. They weren't just fighting AQI, they were fighting in a vicious circle where the very footprints of coalition forces and reconstruction projects designed to win hearts and minds created endless targets of opportunity. The unexamined logic of the invasion and end-state of defeating the enemy was security. This fed perfectly into the emerging organism that was the counterinsurgency of which AQI was part."[15]

The character of conflict in the first two decades of the twenty-first century is clear. When a deployed military force faces an enemy indistinguishable from the civilian population, aid workers in their area of operations face the threat of their work not being distinguished from the foreign policy and national security objectives of that military force. Because vulnerable civilian populations are disproportionately affected by the actions of a violent minority of state and non-state actors, both journalists and aid workers find themselves increasingly targeted as suspected spies or perceived agents of Western-imposed ideas, policies, and values.

However, the greatest challenges often hold the greatest opportunities. One result of this changed operational environment—where conventional military tactics can be ineffectual and traditional humanitarian space is threatened—is an opportunity for both civilian and military organizations to look inward for the solution, defending their historic strengths or principles while adapting to current realities. The instinctive reaction for organizational self-preservation is to retrench and reinforce identities, as they have been known. Retired general Stanley McChrystal exposed this reaction within the tribal nature of the US Joint Special Operations Command Task Force in Iraq, but the default tendency equally applies to the humanitarian profession: "We tend to become so cohesive that nobody is as good as you and so you are not really comfortable dealing with anyone but you."[16]

When security is the goal and operational effectiveness is the means, military personnel and aid workers often idealize the past, a detriment to responding and overcoming new complexities presented in contemporary conflict. What can the deployed military and humanitarian responders learn from their mutual professions of service?

It is important to understand how humanitarian civil–military coordination and relations differ during conflict and following natural disasters. It is equally important to understand how the delicate, sensitive, and very complex civil–military coordination dynamic carries over into the postconflict relations and activities, particularly when the scenario includes counterinsurgency and unconventional warfare elements, and what the subsequent consequences or effects might be.

Operating in a very complex environment that includes a host of military actors and non-state operatives, it is imperative to separate, but coordinate, humanitarian and military operations. The humanitarian organizations' and beneficiaries' safety and security concerns, due to the affiliations, are real. For example, Al Shabaab in Somalia has repeatedly accused the UN of serving US interests. On 19 June 2013 Al Shabaab attacked the UN Development Program compound in Mogadishu, resulting in thirteen killed. Several Al Shabaab militants live-tweeted messages during the attack including, "Serving #US goals, the #UN is a monolithic block in the path towards the establishment of Allah's Law on earth & must therefore be dislodged."[17]

On 11 July of the same year South Sudanese soldiers ransacked a residential compound that housed international staff from several aid organizations. Despite appeals for help by phone and text to the UN peacekeeping mission located only 1 kilometer away, for more than four hours the government soldiers beat and robbed people, carried out mock executions, shot dead a local journalist for his ethnicity, and raped several foreign women. Significantly, the soldiers singled out Americans and accused them of supporting opposition forces. It appears the soldiers were part of a faction of South Sudan's army, which is already divided from three years of civil war. Salva Kiir, South Sudan's president and leader of its army, acknowledged that not all his soldiers were "completely subordinate to the authority of a civilian government."[18]

Both security incidents illustrate a changed security paradigm where international laws and principles hold little sway and the breakdown of authority and subsequent power vacuum have resulted in distributed networks of competing and questionable legitimacy. This post-sovereign fragmentation is characterized by isolationism and deteriorating security fueled by the unchecked transmission of information. On these battlefields, two professions are forced to adapt and evolve from the safety of their traditional posture and identity.

Conclusion

With very different tools and approaches to conflict, both humanitarian practitioners and the deployed military accept vulnerability, uncertainty, and risk. Both are willing to leave the relative safety of home with a mission to serve and protect strangers. Whether the goal is countering a specific terrorist threat or providing humanitarian assistance to protect the vulnerable, the objective is shared in the long term: a safe, stable community that poses no threat to others or to itself. Both military and humanitarian actors seek the near- and long-term protection of civilians; in places with weak or failed governments contested by non-state actors, however, neither military nor humanitarian objectives can be achieved in isolation. Failure in one disrupts the other. Persistent success in complex conflict environments can be achieved only through a nuanced understanding of the operational realities faced by both the military and humanitarian professions. This understanding is enhanced by the symbiotic relationship of our respective professionals.

On the ground, the fundamental differences of identity, mandate, and mobilization between the military and humanitarian aid workers are real and need to be understood. Certainly, there is substantial common ground between the two professions and much to be learned from the other's knowledge, skills, and perspective.

Professional soldiers, and aid workers like my friend Jason, are not forced into combat zones. They volunteer. In parallel, the members of the military and humanitarian aid community have made the decision that there is something higher and more important than who they are and what they can achieve in their own self-interest. At cursory glance, and from the view of the twentieth century, humanitarian and military organizations have diametrically opposed mandates. They do not have comparable training, resources, or chains of command. Yet they also have mutually enviable qualities and assets. Depending on their approach to the nuanced, complex goals of enabling safe, secure, and stable environments, there is a compelling argument to be made that the professions possess a complementarity. In some instances, the access and influence of one profession can enable the other to achieve more through a coordinated, collaborative, and inclusive plan and common desired end state.

The twentieth century thesis of security driven by disciplined, hierarchical organizations of the nation-state accountable to the growing body of international humanitarian law fostered a clear line of demarcation between military and humanitarian action on the battlefield. This thesis is met with the twenty-first-century antithesis of intrastate conflict driven by amorphous non-state actors and nation-states that both disregard international humanitarian law with impunity. The dynamic of information-based, globalized societies that distribute authority along self-selected channels has fundamentally disrupted mechanisms for international dialogue and accountability. When nation-states and non-state actors disregard both mechanisms for dialogue and accountability to international humanitarian law, the lines of identity are blurred between the combatant and the non-combatant, and the management and the mitigation of violence. Returning to Manwaring, "In this security environment, war, the power to make war, and the power to destroy or manipulate personal security of human beings, and radically change nation-states, and even the international security system, is now within the reach of virtually any kind of violent non-state actor."[19]

As twentieth-century training, tactics, and international laws and conventions routinely fail to hold up to operational reality, this new era calls for bold synthesis drawn from a shared and honest acknowledgment of new interdependencies, as well as a common desired end state between the humanitarian and military professions. Because threats to security are broad spectrum and transnational, the solutions need to be holistic and, at times, trans-professional. This reality is evidenced in the growing inclusion of protection of civilians in military operations.

The current number of forced migrants internationally is the highest since World War II. Today, the magnitude of this human mobility is arguably pushing existing norms, funding, and personnel to the extremes. The global migration crisis suggests a dialogue over fault lines, violations, and trans-professional accountability is well overdue. This broader interpretation of civil–military coordination at the international level holds the potential for new means of response. At issue is not only the protection of civilians but also the identification of viable durable solutions. For the past 150 years protection of civilians has traditionally been enshrined in the ICRC and UN High Commissioner for Refugees mandates. Clearly, though, protection of civilians is evolving and is more visible in both the military doctrine as well as political rhetoric, if by no means with a consensus on that response (i.e., responsibility to protect doctrine, European Union's response to the migrant crisis of 2016).

Protection of civilians in the recent record of military interventions, such as those in Libya and Iraq, as part of their own operational objectives is a positive development, if one that suggests a need to reflect carefully on the less-well-navigated waters of humanitarian and military professions working toward a shared security mission. The challenge begs for dialogue beyond the interagency concept of civil-military relations and instead treats potential threats to the traditional twentieth-century postures as opportunities to adjust the current approach to protection by both professions in conflict.

Just as international humanitarian law appears to be threatened across the planet, the two expeditionary professions charged with obligations to uphold it are culturally and structurally disinclined for dialogue. Twenty-first-century leaders of the military and humanitarian professions require a combination of both vision and operational realism. The two professions no longer operate in isolation, and the new instruments of power are intelligence, public diplomacy, media, time, and flexibility.

Manwaring's response to the changed tactical level paradigm identifies the "process of developing a new strategic-level paradigm for conflict is educational."[20] With education as the aim of this level of civil-military dialogue, what are some concrete steps that would begin to build familiarity leading toward understanding of each other's mandates, mutual challenges, and the ultimate prize: trust?

First, overlapping security and humanitarian missions require a more technical understanding between the professions and call for a more structured set of offerings by both. One model of information and educational exchange is the US Agency for International Development's (USAID's) Office of Foreign Disaster Assistance (OFDA) Joint Humanitarian Operations Course. This two-day course was developed to teach key US military personnel how the US government responds to international disasters. Learning objectives for participants include becoming familiar with OFDA structure, mandate, and role in humanitarian assistance; disaster relief responsibilities; and learning to identify areas of coordination and cooperation between USAID and the US military.

In the spirit of the Joint Humanitarian Operations Course, US military-civil affairs could offer a course to humanitarian professionals on civil affairs' mandate for engaging the population; and specialized training in researching, planning, coordinating, and conducting operations to support stabilization, reconstitution, and reconstruction activities.

Second is accountability. Mistakes will continue to be made that undermine trust between the military and humanitarian professions. Despite proactive actions to deliver coordinates of hospital locations, human and technological errors will continue to occur, particularly with the willful use of human shields and increasing manipulation of humanitarian assistance as a weapon of war. Civil-military dialogue can be used to identify failures in the application of existing procedures and highlight any existing room for action on the part of practitioners and organizations. Huge strides in building goodwill would begin if both professions agreed to independent inquiry after mistakes are made.

Third, direct coordination in conflict remains highly problematic if not life-threatening for humanitarian aid workers, given their unarmed status and their posture working as they do, often in isolated locations among the populations they are there to assist. Examples listed above demonstrate how vulnerable aid workers are in twenty-first-century conflict zones. However, the purpose of this chapter has been, in part, to demonstrate the respective and mutual value of the professions.

Arguably, therefore, joint operations centers outside conflict zones are needed for civil-military dialogue and operational coordination, whereby civilian organizations, both governmental and nongovernmental, can meet with military counterparts without compromising their forward-deployed staff. Sensitivities are real and will have to be respected. If necessity is the mother of invention, it follows that the reality of the changed operational environment can foster a new era of relationship between the professions, to include:

- open exchange of ideas and discussion,
- better understanding of strengths and limitations,
- establishment of common goals,
- establishment of methods of accountability,
- establishment of independent review of mishaps, and
- establishment of schedule of meetings.

Today's battlefield threatens global stability; the professions charged with a shared mandate to mitigate violence and protect civilians face the possibility that the greater the disaster, the greater the opportunity.

Notes

1. My perspective on the military as a profession is informed by my firsthand experience of working with the Army light infantry and the Marines both in and training for deployment. As boots on the ground, they are the military counterparts to the aid worker I reference in this article. The principles underlying my case for counterpart professions on the battlefield could apply equally to all military branches.
2. Holly Hughson, guest lecture delivered 1 January 2015 to Macro Social Work course, at Pacific Union College, Angwin, California.
3. Hughson, guest lecture.
4. For purposes of this discussion, humanitarian aid worker or aid worker refers to those individuals who have adopted an attitude and commitment to the profession as combination of technical skills, willingness to be sent into harm's way, and willingness to operate according to humanitarian principles of humanity, neutrality, independence, voluntary service, unity, and universality.
5. Huntington, *The Soldier and the State*, 7.
6. Max G. Manwaring, *The Strategic Logic of the Contemporary Security Dilemma* (Carlisle Barracks, PA: US Army War College, 2011), 7 (quote).
7. Huntington, *The Soldier and the State*, 8 (first quote), 10 (second quote).
8. IFRC, "The Formation of the IFRC," http://www.ifrc.org/en/who-we-are/history/.
9. International Committee of the Red Cross, "Convention for the Amelioration of the Condition of the Wounded in Armies in the Field," Geneva, 1864, https://ihl-data

bases.icrc.org/ihl/52d68d14de6160e0c12563da005fdb1b/87a3bb58c1c44f0dc
125641a005a06e0.

10. Unites Nations, "Universal Declaration of Human Rights," http://www.un.org/en/
documents/udhr/.

11. General Assembly resolution 46/182 adopted in 1991, which also established the role
of the emergency relief coordinator; and 58/114 adopted in 2004.

12. Aid Worker Security Database, "Humanitarian Outcomes," https://aidworkersecurity
.org/. For a brilliant, interactive page capturing each incident, see http://archive.irin
news.org/aid-worker-security-map/dataviz.html.

13. Abby Stoddard, Adele Harmer, and Kathleen Ryou, "Aid Worker Security Report
2014—Unsafe Passage: Road Attacks and Their Impact on Humanitarian Operations,"
Humanitarian Outcomes, https://aidworkersecurity.org/sites/default/files/Aid%20
Worker%20Security%20Report%202014.pdf.

14. Gregg Zoroya, "American Described as Aid Worker Killed in Kabul," USA Today,
https://www.usatoday.com/story/news/world/2015/12/21/american-described
-aid-worker-killed-kabul/77706570/.

15. Holly Hughson, "Warfare by Spoiler: #Reviewing 'Team of Teams,'" The Strategy Bridge,
https://thestrategybridge.org/the-bridge/2015/12/28/warfare-by-spoiler-reviewing
-team-of-teams.

16. Stanley McChrystal, "Leadership Is a Choice," Stanford Graduate School of Business, https://www.youtube.com/watch?v=p7DzQWjXKFI.

17. Jessica Chasmar, "Somali Militants Live-Tweet Deadly Attack on U.N. Compound," Washington Times, 20 June 2013, https://www.washingtontimes.com/news
/2013/jun/20/somali-militants-live-tweet-deadly-attack-un-compo/.

18. Max Bearak, "The U.N. Faces Intense Scrutiny in South Sudan after Failing to Stop a
Brutal Attack on Foreign Aid Workers," Washington Post, https://www.washingtonpost
.com/news/worldviews/wp/2016/08/18/the-u-n-faces-intense-scrutiny-in-south-
sudan-after-failing-to-stop-a-brutal-attack-on-foreign-aid-workers/?utm_term=.
e3ae3a768c6e.

19. Manwaring, Strategic Logic, 5.

20. Manwaring, xi.

CHAPTER 12

Born of Insubordination
Culture, Professionalism, and Identity in the Air Arm

Brian Laslie

And make no mistake, this is a profession. We are professionals.
Air Force Little Blue Book, 2015

Introduction

The US Air Force is, and has always been, led by parochial officers who were better at succeeding in their own career field than in understanding the organization as whole. This has proven a perfectly acceptable way to run the business. Air Force officers are divided into dozens of different specialty career fields, commonly referred to as stove pipes. It is more important to look at the Air Force's stove-piped officer development than at the organization as a whole to understand Air Force professionalism. It is impossible to study the Air Force as a monolithic entity. While the Air Force has long struggled to break down these stove pipes, these stove-piped career fields, each with its own identity and culture, provided the correct avenues for solving problems within the service.

The US Air Force was born on 18 September 1947, but in several of its communities, its members' identity and culture predate this date. The fact that the Air Force's identity and culture predate its official date of birth has an impact on how members of the Air Force perceive their service. There is no one-size-fits-all model of professionalism for the Air Force; rather, each career field has a unique history that impacts the way it addresses problems. Finally, there is also an insubordinate streak in Air Force officers that traces its roots to Brig. Gen. William Mitchell. This streak is fundamental to understanding how the Air Force reacts to internal problems and how one might define professionalism in this service. The professional officer corps of the US Air Force is both a victim and a success of this insubordinate streak and its need to separate officers into functional stove pipes.

Any discussion of professionalism inevitably begins with Samuel Huntington. In *The Soldier and the State*, Huntington stated, "Officership is strongest and most effective when it most closely approaches the professional ideal; it is weakest and most defective when it falls short of that ideal."[1] What, then, is the ideal professional Air Force officer? The answer is that it depends largely on what career field that officer serves in. While the Air Force Core Values—integrity first, service before self, and excellence in all we do—are an excellent starting point, the Air Force has a long and storied history of professional airmen solving problems in unique ways. I would also like to point out that what follows is only a snapshot in time. Even as this book goes to press there continues to be much fluctuation in Air Force career fields, which impacts how these career fields perceive of their profession inside the "Big Blue" Air Force.

Someone who fell far short of the Air Force officer ideal was Brig. Gen. William Mitchell. No history class on the Air Force is complete without some discussion of Mitchell, his theories, and his works. There is no doubt that Mitchell had a disobedient streak. In 1925 he was tried and court-martialed for insubordination after he stated that the senior leaders in the military were guilty of "incompetency, criminal negligence and almost treasonable administration of the national defense."[2] As a result of that trial, Mitchell became the very embodiment of the (existing) insubordinate streak found in the officers of the air arm. In a way, Mitchell and the airmen who followed him mirrored an insubordinate and revolutionary streak found in the greater American culture, which is why these rebels have been embraced and elevated. The trial was a major scandal, covered in newspapers, and even resulted in the 1955 film starring Gary Cooper, *The Court-Martial of Billy Mitchell*. The trial would have paled in comparison to Mitchell's personal affairs that are often glossed over in histories written about Mitchell. Historian Alfred F. Hurley said in his biography, *Billy Mitchell: Crusader for Air Power*, that Mitchell's transfer overseas to visit other air forces was done in part to head off a "bitter struggle that could have erupted into a major scandal. To repeat the details of that struggle here would serve no significant purpose."[3] The potential scandal that Hurley refused to cover was that Mitchell shot his wife in a drunken rage—she survived.[4]

Although Mitchell is remembered as much for his thoughts and theories on air power as he is for his insubordinate streak, it would not be a stretch to say that the Air Force was born out of this insubordination, and that the entire service was born with a chip on its shoulder. To better frame this argument, instead of the word "insubordinate" this chapter will use the term "pragmatic professionals." These are the men and women whose identity, culture, and concept of professionalism are tied to something stronger than the Air Force as a whole. An entire generation of Mitchell's acolytes brought air-mindedness from a nascent fighting force to a global strategic air force. While Mitchell's popularity as an iconic figure in the Air Force has ebbed and flowed over the past ninety years, professional military education schools still include him in curriculum. In fact, his book *Winged Defense* is required reading for officers attending such courses in-residence.[5] Although no organization is entirely monolithic or entirely fractured, the Air Force does not have a unifying linkage for its officer corps the same way the US Army and US Marine Corps do. In the Corps, every Marine is a rifleman; this common ground gives all Marines an understanding of how they contribute to combined arms battle. Rather than long-held and long-accepted concepts of identity in the other services where every Marine is a rifleman or the Army's ubiquitous identity of being a soldier, members of the Air Force generally cannot agree on who they are. There is no widely accepted completion to the sentence "Every airman is a . . . ."

Mitchell's identity as a leader of air force theory and doctrine is interesting due, in no small part, to his court-martial. The fundamental problem with Mitchell as an iconic figure in the Air Force is that he cannot be considered to have been professional in either his work or his personal life. Despite the existence of a unique air-mindedness perspective to quoting Billy Mitchell, the founding father of the US Air Force was unprofessional. While this might strike a chord with members of the Air Force or be viewed as a somewhat heretical statement, it is nonetheless true. Therefore, it begs the question, How professional can an organization be when the US Air Force's primary historical figure was put on trial for unprofessionalism? Simply put, the Air Force is a service born from insubordination. Its heroes have long been mavericks and outside-the-box thinkers.[6]

Does this make the Air Force an unprofessional service? Not by any stretch of the imagination. It does, however, indicate that insubordination might be in the Air Force's DNA, and that the issue of professionalism—or being professional—is an issue the Air Force continues to grapple with well into the twenty-first century. What does this portend for the modern Air Force? This chapter will dually show how outside-the-box thinking or actions might have caused the issue of professionalism in the USAF but also how that same determinist streak used by pragmatic professionals to solve the problems enabled the Air Force to fix the problems discussed herein as well. This chapter has two sections. Section 1 explores Air Force identity and culture. Section 2 uses case studies as examples of Air Force stove pipes that find solutions to problems. This chapter explores Air Force identity and culture as a lens through which to view Air Force professionalism and that independent, and some might argue subversive, streak that the air service continues to bear today. Finally, this chapter focuses on regaining professionalism in the face of adversity through analysis of three contemporary case studies: the grounding of the entire F-22 fleet in 2011 and 2012, the 2014 cheating scandal that rocked the Air Force's assumptions about itself in the missile career field, and the rise of a professional drone pilot corps.

A Note on Air Force Culture

In my book *The Air Force Way of War* (2015), I noted that the air service has long suffered from an identity crisis. This comes in the form of arguments over strategic versus tactical, or operators versus support personnel; the Air Force has long struggled with a cohesive identity and culture that could be shared throughout the ranks and through its many Air Force specialty codes. That work was not the first to note that the Air Force seemed to struggle with identity. Perhaps the most famous work was Carl Builder's *The Icarus Syndrome.*[7] It has long been recognized that the Air Force has struggled, and continues to struggle, with its own identity. Before diving into the case studies on professionalism in the air arm, it is important to note that the Air Force is not a monolithic entity; all attempts at creating a shared understanding of its history, doctrine, and operations have failed. To this end, I will first look at Air Force training in the officer corps, the identity and concept of the word "airmen," the stove pipes of the officer corps, and, finally, the Air Force's inability to achieve, write, consolidate, or find an agreed-on history.

The Failure of Shared Culture and Identity

In 1996 Chief of Staff of the Air Force Gen. Ronald Fogleman started a program called the Air and Space Basic Course. The mission of this course was to bring new Air Force lieutenants, commissioned from the US

Air Force Academy, Officer Training School, and Reserve Officer Training Course, to Maxwell Air Force Base to unite the disparate commission sources with an understanding of the previously mentioned concepts. Obviously, the concept of the Air and Space Basic Course was based on the Marine Corps Basic Course. The course never fully met the Air Force's intent. Bad reviews from attendees, disparate Air Force specialties unable to see their place in the fight, and financial constraints forced the Air Force to shutter the course in 2011. One senior leader did state that the course accomplished its mission, but since the Air Force did not stop commissioning officers, one wonders how a unifying curriculum to link lieutenants could ever be declared "mission accomplished."[8]

The now defunct website for the closed course stated that it was initially designed to create airmen who were "inspired to articulate and advocate what the Air Force brings to the joint fight."[9] The website highlighted four mission areas: to have them comprehend air, space, and cyber operations; understand service history, doctrine, and capabilities; adopt the service's Core Values; and value airmen as a team and the role of officers in leading that team. The course highlighted an existing problem for the Air Force writ large. Its officers saw themselves as their specialty code (i.e., their job) first and Air Force officers second, which is commonly referred to as stove piping. As an example, Air Force finance officers would be shown how their career field aided and enabled putting warheads on foreheads, as the colloquial saying goes, but it was an extreme stretch for certain Air Force career fields to see how their particular stove pipe fit into the overarching identity of war making. This further highlighted two other problems in the Air Force: the rank versus the identity of airmen, and the origins of the Air Force itself.[9]

The Rank of Airmen vs. the Identity of Airmen

There are many images connected with the US Air Force; the most well-known of these are, of course, the aircraft themselves. America's air arm is most obviously identified by the equipment used to carry out its missions: fighters, bombers, rotary-wing, and airlift aircraft flying through the skies. Many Americans grew up attending local air shows and were afforded the opportunity to get up close and personal with the technological wonders that the Air Force employed in achieving its mission. It is therefore no wonder why, flyers or not, the first question often asked of any airmen is, "What do you fly?" though only a very small percentage of Air Force personnel fly or even maintain aircraft. Americans associate the Air Force with machines and not personnel. Furthermore, this association affects the identity of Air Force members. Most Air Force officers do not identify themselves as airmen.[11]

The concept that everyone in the Air Force is an airman is a recent advent. In 2004 Chief of Staff of the Air Force Gen. John Jumper dictated that all members of the US Air Force were airmen; he emphasized this by stating the word would always be spelled with a capital A. The fact that all members of the Air Force were now airmen, coupled with the fact that airmen denoted the lowest enlisted ranks of the service, caused enduring problems. In a 2015 seminar at the Air Force's Air Command and Staff College for majors, an officer bemoaned that the term "airmen" was not representative of the officer corps and that identity was more closely held, again with a mentality of job first, Air Force second.[12]

Therefore, the identity of Air Force members is more closely associated with their job. If you ask a member of the Air Force what she does, you are more likely to be answered with a specific job than an overarching definition of airman. To that end, the identity of Air Force members comes in their job first; each of these jobs comes with its own identities and cultural norms. There is no Air Force identity or culture; responses to challenges within the service are linked to each individual's place in the stove-piped hierarchy. So, what does this portend for professionalism in the air arm? It all depends on the culture in which you are brought up. At the most basic level the Air Force is divided into operations and support. Beyond that, unique cultures develop in different areas: flyers, missile men, and support officers; and each of these would have a different concept of professionalism. As will be shown, approaches to professionalism are largely dependent on career field rather than the entire Air Force as a whole. Also, the way in which certain career fields approach solutions to problems would not work for the Air Force as whole. The pragmatic professionals, due to the insubordination in their DNA, will deduce solutions to problems more rapidly than the business end of the Air Force.

In this chapter I have divided the Air Force into support, operations, and missile functions for simplicity. The support functions inside the Air Force—personnel, logistics, civil engineers, and so on—have long taken on a culture more closely structured on what could be called business model professionalism. Despite rising numbers of support functions being deployed since 2001, the home station existence of these personnel is office-centric, technically focused, and program-management oriented.

The operations function composed of flyers might be called pragmatic professionalism. These individuals tend to take a very tactical, mission-first orientation. The very small Air Force special operations community would also fall into this operations category, and they are perhaps the most pragmatic and tactically oriented. The missileer career field is the last vestige of the Strategic Air Command professionalism model. Despite the establishment of all Air Force bombers under Global Strike Command, the missile officers in their silos still maintain a deterrence-focused, checklist-always professional posture. I am not alone in seeing the stark differences between operations and support professionals. Col. Jeffrey J. Smith noted in his 2014 work *Tomorrow's Air Force* that he believed Air Force officers could be categorized into five separate identities: pilot, space, intelligence, missile, and support.[13] Before we turn to the case studies, a note on accepted Air Force history is important as one final element to the airmen's identity.

Although I have chosen to view the Air Force through a functional lens, there is also a very real class system inside the Air Force's officer corps with pilots sitting atop and support functions at the bottom. It is not the purpose of this chapter to demonstrate where each career field might fall in a class system, though it is important to denote that it does indeed exist.

Accepted History

Since 1947 the US Air Force celebrates its independence on 18 September. On this date, Stuart Symington was sworn in as the first secretary of the Air Force. I would argue that the Air Force celebrates its independence and not its birthday; to begin Air Force history from this date marginalizes and obfuscates the true history of the service and all that occurred prior to independence. There are many dates one could consider as the birthday of America's air service. Official unit histories from dozens of Air Force squadrons trace their own identity to dates prior to American involvement in World War II. These squadrons, primarily fighter, bomber, and reconnaissance units, view their history and heritage as existing before the Air Force, and their cultural identity more closely aligns at the unit level than with the Air Force itself. Even these pilots, all linked by the bonds of flying, rapidly separated in the postwar period into separate stove pipes, each stove pipe advocating for its particular airframe's contributions to air warfare. Even as recently as 2015, the Air Force has attempted to reinforce its identity, culture, and heritage through rather unremarkable publications.[14]

These issues of identity and culture and their impact on professionalism continue to play out. Instead of concrete measures, such as the defunct Basic School, the Air Force has issued what can only be described as treatises, as attempts to link its members into a cohesive whole. On 28 August 2015 Secretary of the Air Force Deborah Lee James and Chief of Staff of the Air Force Gen. Mark Welsh issued a new pamphlet titled "America's Air Force: A Profession of Arms." This small twelve-page book opened by telling airmen, "This book serves as a guide to the principles that make us so strong. Wherever you are in your Air Force career, it is a reminder to the meaning of service in our profession. . . . The Profession of Arms." While this might not, on the surface, indicate any form of massive identity and cultural problem within the Air Force, it does demonstrate a continuing need by Air Force senior leaders to remind members of the service where they stand. If this were not enough, Air Force senior leaders go on to issue an emphatic reminder by stating, "And make no mistake, this is a profession. We are professionals." The directive nature of the statement immediately draws into question whether this is a reminder or an attempt to convince the organization that this is a true statement. The pamphlet then goes on to list the Core Values, which are themselves even then broken down further, and taking what were initially meant to be three easily understood concepts that did not need explanation and adding un-needed layering. Three Core Values became nine problematic issues facing the organization. The pamphlet itself was received with mixed emotions.[15]

Three Contemporary Case Studies

The history, identity, and culture issues that continue to plague the Air Force represent unique perspectives from which to approach problems. Since this chapter is about professionalism in the air arm of the US military, the case studies will be pulled from a more operational perspective vice support functions, itself contentious terms for airmen and their identity. As previously mentioned, any other case study looked at through the eyes of a support function in the Air Force might be considerably different. The three case studies demonstrate that solutions to the Air Force problems come not from an overarching identity, but rather from the stove-piped career fields that possess their own cultural norms and identities. These case studies also raise the question about just how monolithic and united the Air Force is if these tribes or communities attempt to solve their own problems. Does this mean there is not a single profession?

Debate among officers and policymakers about the idea of additional separate service for space, cyber, or other identifiable career fields continues.
For this chapter I take the stand that it is entirely unlikely, given current
budgetary conditions and political willpower, that we will see a separate
US space or cyber force.[16]

A final note before delving into case studies: these three case studies
are contemporary, as I intended. These case studies are the professional
problems facing the service today.

Case Study 1: The F-22 Fleet in 2011 and 2012

The F-22 Raptor, much like its sibling the F-35 and its older relatives
the F-15 and F-16, was mired in developmental problems as the aircraft
reached its full operational capability throughout its first years in active
service. However, these developmental problems paled in comparison to
a series of events that occurred between 2009 and 2012. In short, there
seemed to be a problem with the aircraft's on-board oxygen generating system that was causing pilots to become hypoxic (oxygen deprived) while
in flight. This culminated in 2011–12 when the entire fleet of aircraft
was grounded. It was eventually determined that a single valve on the
pilots' upper pressure garment was not adequately doing its job, leading to
cases of severe hypoxia. Luckily, even though the Air Force determined as
many as twenty-four hypoxic incidents related to this issue, there was no
loss of life. After the pilots were again allowed to fly and prior to official
determination of the problem, the Air Combat Command commander,
Gen. Gilmary Hostage, took the time to become qualified in the jet in
an attempt to show the community, but also the public at large, that he
was taking the situation seriously and was prepared to personally face the
dangers that seemed to be inherent in flying the Raptor. Not only did Air
Combat Command ground the entire fleet, but the situation also became
bad enough for that command to include an aerospace psychologist in the
task force studying the problem.[17]

On the heels of the grounding and recertification of the aircrews,
the Air Force was hit with an additional scandal, some might say an
act of insubordination, when two pilots of the 192nd Fighter Wing of
the Virginia Air National Guard went public with their fears of flying
the aircraft on 60 Minutes and ABC Nightly News. The story was subsequently picked up by other major news outlets and gave the appearance
that many—if not most—of the F-22 pilots were afraid of the aircraft and
were concerned the Air Force was not doing enough to protect its pilots.

The whistleblowing was not well received by the other flyers. The pilots going public went against the ethos and culture of problem solving that linked airmen flyers back to World War II. Inside the fighter squadrons, it was the typical maverick attitude taken too far. The mood at Langley Air Force Base and the relations between the active component flyers and national guardsmen became hostile.[18]

The pilot culture was very important to the greater oxygen system issue, both in terms of what the pilots were to do while grounded and in finding a solution to the problem. The fighter pilot culture aided in the maintaining and regaining of professionalism in the face of adverse conditions. As mentioned earlier, the practical or pragmatic professionalism of the operations class in the Air Force is marked by its tactically focused, mission-oriented mind-set. Despite the myriad problems facing the jet and the pilots, F-22 pilots refused to allow the grounding of the aircraft to keep them from accomplishing their jobs. Furthermore, it was the identity of being fighter pilots—that unique culture—that helped them get through the issues they faced.[19]

The F-22 was officially ordered to stand down operations in May 2011. The jets did not fly again until September of that year. And when the jets did take back to the sky the pilots faced the dual problem of regaining all their qualifications while managing pressures on the home front from spouses who were not confident in the equipment their significant others were flying. At the time Col. Peter "Coach" Fesler was the squadron commander of the 27th Fighter Squadron at Langley Air Force Base, part of the 1st Fighter Wing, the unit he later commanded in 2015. He had this to say about flying the aircraft in the fall of 2012: "The pilots were under tremendous pressure at home. Some of them had even increased their life insurance. There was a lot of pressure on these guys, both in the squadrons and at home. These guys were 100% committed to doing their job and flying that jet in the face of pressure from above and impressions in the media that they didn't want to fly the jet. They wanted to fly, but they were highly skeptical of being told how to do their job."[20]

The five months they spent grounded were not idle time for the pilots. Wing leaders at the various Raptor bases did all they could to increase their pilots' knowledge of their weapon system when not flying during this period. The first step was an increase in the use of simulators at home stations, but many of the pilots were also afforded the opportunity to visit the Lockheed

Martin Plant in Marietta, Georgia, to fly Lockheed's even more advanced simulators. Pilots visited the Boeing plant in Seattle to discuss software development and test-beds for the aircraft, the Boston Pratt and Whitney plant, BAE systems, and Hanscom Air Force Base. In short, pilots took this time to develop relationships with the men and women who designed their fighter and its many systems. At Langley Air Force Base in Virginia, members participated in a unit compliance inspection from higher headquarters. They also took the time to fix administrative issues that had fallen by the wayside during normal operations. As another pilot said, "We did what we could . . . but we wanted to fly." Despite the problems with the Raptor, the flyers remained "100% committed to mission accomplishment." Even with the huge strain faced at work and in their home lives, these pragmatic professionals wanted to figure out what was wrong with their aircraft and the only way they could do that was by flying it.[21]

Many of the mid-grade officers came together to put forth a plan to get the pilots back in the air and regain the qualifications that were falling off the charts the longer the pilots stayed grounded. In the first few months of the grounding, pilots lost their air combat training (a demanding mission currency that pilots are required to maintain), but quickly also lost basic requirements including instruments, takeoff and landing, and ready aircrew program sorties per experience. By the ninety-day point not a single F-22 fighter pilot was rated as combat mission ready.

Lt. Col. "Deeq" Abba and Lt. Col. "Coach" Fesler, both squadron commanders, experienced pilots, and weapons school graduates, along with the operations officers Lt. Col. "Bigbee" Hinds and Lt. Col. "Caveman" Craddock, put together the risk mitigation plan to be enacted once the grounding was lifted. It was a building-block approach to getting the jets back in the air and the pilots requalified. Beyond regaining qualifications and getting their flyers combat mission ready again, the squadron commanders and operations officers knew there was the very real possibility another hypoxia event would take place. Exposure to oxygen deprivation was included as part of the training program they put together. This meant exposing the pilots to the effects of hypoxia on the ground to ensure the pilots would be able to recognize the symptoms. This training became a required recurrent annual event. This problem solving at the tactical level indicated that the pilots recognized a problem and determined a way to deal with it.

In the spring of 2012 an internal investigation identified the upper pressure garment valve as the root cause of the problem leading to the cases of severe hypoxia during missions. It was not the oxygen system at all, but something the pilots wrapped themselves in to handle the demanding pressures of flying at high-G's.[22] From start to finish, the culture and professionalism of the fighter pilot community are what held the small-knit fold of Raptor pilots together. This is not to place the solution on a mythical idea, but rather a well-developed and understood identity, culture, and unique perspective on professionalism.

The solution to the hypoxia issues was not found in the Air Force's Core Values. It was not found in a code of conduct, a creed, an oath, or the *Little Blue Book* of professionalism. It was found in a disciplined approach to mission accomplishment where risk mitigation could protect individuals only to a point. The fighter community traces its roots to the pursuit pilots of World War I, where life expectancy was measured in weeks, but they still flew knowing the risks. This acceptance of risk and willingness to face it have not changed. Despite attempts to unify the Air Force under a common ideal, the mentality and DNA of the fighter pilot remain linked to the identity of their predecessors more than any other career field in the Air Force. The pragmatic professionals of the flying community continue to identify more with Billy Mitchell, Eddie Rickenbacker, and Raoul Lufbery than they do with fellow non-flyer officers in the support communities today. Conversely, the support officers identify with their own stove-piped career field and have trouble speaking to members of the larger defense community about what the Air Force brings to the table in the joint environment.

Case Study 2: The 2014 Cheating Scandal in the Missile Career Field

There is a unique missileer culture at work inside America's missile men and women. They represent the last true vestige of the old-line Strategic Air Command–trained killer mentality. The Strategic Air Command was responsible for two-thirds of America's nuclear triad: the ground-launched nuclear missiles and the air-launched nuclear weapons flown on Air Force nuclear-capable bombers, most notably through Strategic Air Command's venerable B-52 bomber. While many Air Force flying squadrons no longer have a nuclear mission, the crews in the missile field have continued an uninterrupted tradition since the earliest days of Strategic Air Command. The checklist-heavy Strategic Air Command mentality made famous by Gen. Curtis LeMay can still be found in the missile fields today. Rather than causing a loss of professionalism, it was this mentality that was helping to right the career field even as this chapter goes to print.

In the mid-1990s the Air Force combined the missile career field with the space career path. Clearly, missile operations needed many junior officers with significantly fewer field grade officers. The opposite was true for space operations and staff work, which required more field-grade officers than company-grade officers. It became clear to the missileers that they should abandon their initial operational tours as soon as possible. The fall of the Soviet Union created another problem: the existential threat of a nuclear attack from abroad abated. As new generations of officers joined the space and missile career field, they did not grow up with the shared identity and understanding that came with those children of the Cold War who went before them. Although the importance of the nuclear deterrence has not gone away, it became clear that the possibility of direct confrontation between the two superpowers no longer existed.

As opposed to bomber pilots, where there are definable and executable missions below the nuclear threshold, maintaining integrity inside the missile career field requires the missileers to believe there remains a valid instance in which they would be called on to perform their duties. This has been a challenge, not only in a post–Cold War Air Force but also in an Air Force that has been removed from threat of imminent Soviet attack for more than quarter of a century. Many missileers simply cannot imagine a valid scenario in which they would be called on to launch. They also function within a career path where it is expected that they leave the nuclear missile portion of their career at the first opportunity. Was it this lack of shared understanding of the existential threat that led to recent scandals?

In 2014 a major news story broke about an ongoing and massive cheating scandal within the Air Force's space and missile career field, specifically among the junior officers charged with monitoring and, if necessary, launching America's ground-based nuclear missiles. Hundreds of officers were caught up in the scandal and nearly a dozen more senior officers were relieved of command or fired from their positions of authority. The junior officers in the space and missile career field were from a generation different from the generation of men who monitored and prepared to launch the missiles during the Cold War. Many of these officers had not even been born when the old Strategic Air Command was inactivated in 1992. How the Air Force went about maintaining and regaining professionalism in the missile wings was a fascinating reinvigorating of the Strategic Air Command mentality inside the career field.[23]

The issues plaguing the nuclear triad, especially in the Air Force, were cause for concern long before the cheating scandal broke. In the late 2000s, the Air Force recognized that malaise had set in and the bomber and missile wings had allowed skills to atrophy. An early solution was the establishment of Global Strike Command in 2009 to place the two legs of the nuclear triad into one major command from which it could be organized, trained, and equipped. It was in January 2014 that nearly one hundred junior officers spread across all three of the Air Force's nuclear missile wings were implicated in the cheating scandal. Although not all one hundred officers actively emailed or texted answers to missile procedure tests, they were all aware that this was going on. The cheating was brought to light as part of a separate investigation in which junior officers were alleged to be using synthetic marijuana, called spice. Between the initial investigation into the drug charges and the later, much more inclusive cheating scandal, the Air Force realized it had a serious problem inside its officer corps of missileers.[24]

The Air Force reacted quickly. By March nine officers had been fired. Separate from the nine officers, Col. Robert W. Stanley II, commander, 341st Missile Wing, chose to resign. In his letter of resignation to the members of the wing he wrote, "We've seen the reputation of our beloved wing and America's ICBM [intercontinental ballistic missile] mission tarnished because of the extraordinarily selfish actions of officers entrusted with the most powerful weapon system ever devised by man."[25] Stanley had already been nominated for the rank of brigadier general, but he would never see the stars of a general officer. He resigned from the service as part of leaving his wing leadership position. Below Stanley at the Malmstrom missile wing, the Air Force fired all three missile squadron commanders as well as the operations group commander and his deputy. It was a complete house cleaning of the missile leaders in one wing.

The commander of Global Strike Command, Lt. Gen. Stephen Wilson, stated after the firings, "We're not just putting a fresh coat of paint on these problems. We're taking bold action." This "bold action" included the creation of the Nuclear Deterrence Operations Service Medal in order to demonstrate "a clearly visible way to recognize the dedication and professionalism of our Airmen who are the guardians of our nation's nuclear deterrence."[26] The medal was retroactive only to December 1991. It would take further bold action along the lines of Strategic Air Command to restore professionalism in the atrophied missile wings.

The missileers continue to face the problem of maintaining professionalism in a world where the operational officers simply have difficulty
believing they will ever execute their mission. This will be, for the fore-
seeable future, a continuous problem of a military professional organization that is unlikely to ever be called up to execute its mission. The Air
Force has moved these missiles back under the Global Strike Command
and has reintroduced a Strategic Air Command mentality into this missile career organization. With the stand-up of Global Strike Command
and a reintroduction of the old Strategic Air Command way of doing
business, morale and professionalism should increase in the near term.
Even a revanchist Russia might help increase morale and a sense of mission in the near term. The stove-piped missile career field needs to lean
heavily on the identity of Cold War missileers. Significant unit identi-
fications and Cold War–era identifying uniforms, not worn in decades,
should be returned to the career field. The career field should embrace its
historical individual characteristics. Ironically, for the Air Force to fix the
missile career field, it needs to allow the career field to wear those trade-
mark insignias and uniforms that set them apart from the rest of the Air
Force during the Cold War. In other words, the US Air Force needs to
let the career field be stove piped and allow it to use its own history and
heritage to right itself. These additions might seem prescriptive, but by
marrying the current missile operators to LeMay, the Cold War, and the
historic mind-set of Strategic Air Command, the Air Force might create
a self-policing organization. There should be no doubt that the Air Force
needs a long-term strategic vision and career progression for its missileers
if the career field is to remain relevant and a place desired by junior officers entering the service.

Case Study 3: The Rise of a Professional Drone Pilot Corps

It has gone by many names in a relatively short life span: unmanned aerial
vehicles, unmanned aircraft, remotely piloted vehicles, and more commonly simply drones. Although in use since the mid to late 1990s, drone
aircraft in the US military have played an increasingly important role
in the nation's conflicts since 2001. They have progressed from providing intelligence, surveillance, and reconnaissance to providing almost
continuous overwatch to combatant commanders and lower-level headquarters, as well as to troops in the field. Their operations have become
such a part of ongoing conflict that it has become an accepted norm that
they will be overhead. In recent years, and with much consternation to

political leaders and members of the public, these drones have been used to provide armed support to troops on the ground and as attack aircraft. The very term "drone wars" has become synonymous with modern conflict, leading to conversation as to whether the day of manned aircraft is coming to an end.

With this rise in drone aircraft comes a new identity problem for the Air Force. What should it do with the drone pilot? Where does she fit in with Air Force identity and culture? Despite having enormous impact on combat operations, it is not even possible to recognize these men and women with a separate combat medal. In 2013 uproar over the proposed Distinguished Warfare Medal caused the USAF to entirely scrap the award designed to mark the drone pilot's service. Conceived of to honor extraordinary impact on combat operations for drone and cyber-operations, the medal was met with enormous criticism. It seemed that the US Department of Defense as a whole could not come up with an acceptable warfare medal for those not on the field of battle . . . or even in the same theater.[27]

The inability to recognize a deserving service to the nation, an acute shortage in drone pilots, difficulty in retaining trained drone pilots despite increasing bonuses all while facing increasing operational demand around the globe has led the Air Force into uncharted territory. The Air Force has increasing difficulty meeting an in-demand, critical mission. This Air Force now faces the question of how to instill professionalism in a career field few want to join.

The Air Force's answer to this question has been money, but not a significant amount and certainly not enough to fix a problem in morale. The bonuses for agreeing to a commitment of either five or nine years of dedicated service ranged from $10,000 to $20,000, relatively little compared to what pilots receive in flight pay. The Air Force was even considering allowing enlisted airmen to pilot drones, although this seems unlikely to move beyond a hypothetical consideration. However, monetary incentives do nothing to fix the stigma surrounding drone operators in the military today. Even the satirical *Duffel Blog* (duffelblog.com) routinely pillories drone operators, but this satire strikes at the heart of the problem that the Air Force is facing: drone operators are not accepted as professional members of the force. This is not a generalized editorial opinion, but rather a fact that drone operators themselves cite.[28]

A 2014 Government Accountability Office report found that drone pilots dealt with issues including lack of legitimacy and acceptance in the wider force. The report stated that despite being the "most in-demand capabilities the Air Force provides to battlefield commanders," the Air Force would continue to "face challenges recruiting officers to serve as RPA [remotely piloted aircraft] pilots because of a negative perception that some in the Air Force associate with flying RPAs."[29] Perhaps the biggest problem facing the men and women flying drones is one they are incapable of solving: their lack of a shared identity and culture from which to derive a solution to their current problem.

The drone corps is not one of the Air Force's stove-piped professional organizations previously mentioned. There is currently very little history and heritage to fall back on, and the remotely piloted aircraft officers certainly find themselves at the bottom of the Air Force's pilot-pecking order despite the tremendously important burden and mission placed on their shoulders. This is not the fault of those who now find themselves flying Reapers and Predators; rather, it is the fault of transferred pilots from another platform or new officers, directly accessed and assigned to fly drones. The members of this community truly are in one of the few career fields being asked to do too much with too little. The drone squadrons do not have the history and heritage of the flying community or the space and missile community. Therefore, they do not have the same identity and culture that helped sustain other career fields through times in crisis. Their adolescent age is working against them. Despite many of these units being bestowed with lineage and heritage from reconnaissance and surveillance squadrons dating back to World War II, this is not the same as the uninterrupted lineage and history of the flying community. As an example, that continued identity can be found in the reconnaissance squadrons operating U-2 reconnaissance planes today.

Conclusion

The Air Force's unique history dating back to World War II affects how many of its members today view their careers. From its earliest days, the Air Force had numerous independent thinkers held up as icons. Outside Italian general Guilio Douhet (imprisoned) and Billy Mitchell (court-martialed), Army Air Corps, Army Air Forces, and finally US Air Force leaders have not been afraid to speak their mind on the future of air power operations often to the detriment of their careers. For an organization that strives to remind its members that it is a professional organization, the Air Force does not hesitate to hold up the slightly less-than-professional icons of its history. The Air Force cannot escape the fact that it was a service founded as much on insubordination as it was on innovation. The unique stove pipes of Air Force career fields have allowed Air Force members to overcome the challenges plaguing the service throughout its more than one hundred years of existence. Rather, it was the culture and identity of the fighter force or Strategic Air Command mentality of the missile career field, the unique strains of professionalism found in the stove-piped career fields of the Air Force that aided these career fields in finding solutions to problems. As a professional military organization, the US Air Force needs to accept that stove pipes work: culture, identity, and heritage in stove pipes might not be the identity the Air Force wants to embrace, but it is the identity the air service needs.[30]

Notes

1. Huntington, *The Soldier and the State*, 11.
2. Alfred F. Hurley, *Billy Mitchell: Crusader for Air Power* (Bloomington: Indiana University Press, 1964), 101 (quote).
3. *The Court-Martial of Billy Mitchell*, dir. by Otto Preminger (Burbank, CA: Warner Brothers, 1955); Hurley, *Billy Mitchell*, 71 (quote).
4. Huntington, *The Soldier and the State*, 11; Phillip S. Meilinger, "The Inadvisability of Posthumously Promoting Billy Mitchell," *Air and Space Power Journal*, Summer 2007, http://www.airpower.maxwell.af.mil/airchronicles/apj/apj07/sum07/meilinger .htm; Hurley, *Billy Mitchell*, 71, 101.
5. Billy Mitchell, *Winged Defense* (Mineola, NY: Dover Publications, INC.2006).
6. In addition to Mitchell, I would add many members of the Air Corps Tactical School who were acolytes of Mitchell, many of whom felt no compunction with bucking the system when necessary to advance the arguments of the air arm. One could also argue that Guilio Douhet and Col. John Warden fall into the category of air-minded leaders willing to advance air power by any means necessary and against the status quo.
7. Brian Laslie, *The Air Force Way of War: US Tactics and Training after Vietnam* (Lexington: University Press of Kentucky, 2015); Carl Builder, *The Icarus Syndrome: The Role of Air Power Theory in the Evolution and Fate of the U.S. Air Force* (London: Routledge, 2002.
8. Scott Fontaine, "Leadership Training to End for Lieutenants," *Air Force Times*, 30 July 2011, http://archiveis/20131031005645/www.airforcetimes.com/article/20110730/ NEWS/107300316/#selection-1475.0–1475.42.
9. Fontaine, "Leadership Training."
10. Air Force Historical Research Agency (AFHRA), Maxwell Air Force Base, Organizational Records, Air and Space Basic Course, http://www.afhra.af.mil/factsheets/ factsheet.asp?id=13012.
11. Jeffrey J. Smith, *Tomorrow's Air Force: Tracing the Past, Shaping the Future* (Indianapolis: Indiana University Press, 2013), xii–xiii, 181. Smith's book goes to great lengths

to note that the author identifies himself as an airman after he first identifies himself as an officer, a graduate of the School of Advanced Air and Space Studies, with a doctoral degree from Washington State University. Furthermore, Smith's work demonstrates a clear divide of Air Force officers into the following groupings (and not as airmen): pilot, space, intel, missile, support.

12. Author's notes, Air Command and Staff College, seminar meetings, academic year 16, August 2015; Lisa Horn, "General Jumper Decrees Airmen Be Spelled with a Capital 'A,'" *Stars and Stripes,* 22 May 2004, http://www.stripes.com/news/general -jumper-decrees-airman-be-spelled-with-capital-a-1.20174; General John P. Jumper, Chief of Staff, "Airmen with a Capital 'A,'" USAF Official Website, http:// www.af.mil/News/Commentaries/Display/tabid/271/Article/142333/airman-with-a-capital-a.aspx.

13. Smith, *Tomorrow's Air Force,* 180,181.

14. As an example, America's oldest fighter squadron, the 27th Fighter Squadron, traces its roots to 15 January 1917, and Eddie Rickenbacker's 94th Fighter Squadron, the Hat-in-the-Ring Gang, was established on 20 August 1917. Air Force Historical Research Agency, Organizational Records, http://www.afhra.af.mil/organizational records/squadronsandflights.asp

15. Headquarters Department of the Air Force, "America's Air Force: A Profession of Arms," (Department of the Air Force, 2015), 2 (first quote), 3 (second quote).

16. For calls for separate, independent forces see Michael C. Whittington, *A Separate Space Force: An 80-year Old Argument* (Maxwell AFB, AL: Air War College, 2000); Benjamin S. Lambeth, *Mastering the Ultimate High Ground: Next Steps in the Military Uses of Space* (Santa Monica, CA: RAND, 2003); Adm. James Stavridis, "Time for a U.S. Cyber Force," *Proceedings* 140, no. 1 (January 2014): 1,331.

17. Brian W. Everstine, "Breathing Free?," *Air Force Magazine,* November 2015. Although there was a single crash of an Alaska-based F-22 in November 2010 that resulted in the death of pilot Capt. Jeffrey Haney, it was determined that this incident was not related to the later hypoxia issues. Spencer Ackerman, "Pentagon: Blame Tight Vests, Not Stealth Jets, for Choking Pilots," *Wired Magazine,* http://www.wired .com/2012/07/f22-valve/; Air Combat Command, Office of History, *History of Air Combat Command* (2012), 157–58, copy obtained by David Axe as part of a 2015 Freedom of Information Act request.

18. Air Combat Command, *History of Air Combat Command,* 157–58; interview by Leslie Stahl, *60 Minutes,* "Is the Air Force's F-22 Fighter Jet Making Pilots Sick?," http:// www.cbsnews.com/news/is-the-air-forces-f-22-fighter-jet-making-pilots-sick/2/; ABC *News,* "Fighter Pilots Claim Intimidation over F-22 Raptor Jets," http://abcnew .go.com/Blotter/fighter-pilots-claim-intimidation-22-raptor-jet-concerns/story ?id=16294011.

19. Peter Fesler, 1st Flight Wing commander, interview with author, 24 Aug 2015, notes in author's collection.

20. Fesler, interview 24 Aug 2015.

21. Fesler, interview 24 Aug 2015 (including quotes).

22. G-force is the force of gravity on a pilot's body during high-speed maneuvers. When speed and turns combine it exerts higher gravity on the pilot. In some cases, it exerts

several times the actual force of gravity, which can lead to blackouts if pilots do not wear protective measures and equipment.

23. The Air Force does not deactivate organizations. Instead, it inactivates organizations until such a time when they might be reactivated as part of a new unit or reestablished unit. Strategic Air Command was inactivated in 1992, but when Global Strike Command was established in 2009 the history and heritage of Strategic Air Command was bestowed on Global Strike Command. Air Force Historical Research Agency, Organizational Records, http://www.afhra.af.mil/factsheets/factsheet.asp?id=15047

24. Jim Miklaszewski, Courtney Kube, and Elizabeth Chuck, "92 Nuclear Missile Officers Implicated in Cheating Scandal, Air Force Says," *NBC News*, 30 January 2014, http://usnews.nbcnews.com/_news/2014/01/30/22508088-92-nuclear-missile-officers-implicated-in-cheating-scandal-air-force-says?lite.

25. Jenn Rowell, "Malmstrom commander Stanley resigns," *Great Falls Tribune*, 27 March 2014, http://www.greatfallstribune.com/story/news/local/2014/03/27/malmstrom-commander-stanley-resigns/6962809/.

26. *Air Force Magazine*, http://www.airforcemag.com/MagazineArchive/Pages/2014/May%202014/0514world.aspx; *USAF News*, "AF Releases Criteria for New Service Medal," 10 October 2014, http://www.af.mil/News/ArticleDisplay/tabid/223/Article/507416/af-releases-criteria-for-new-service-medal.aspx.

27. Ernesto Londoño, "Pentagon Cancels Divisive Distinguished Warfare Medal for Cyber Ops, Drone Strikes," *Washington Post*, 15 April 2013, https://www.washingtonpost.com/world/national-security/pentagon-cancels-divisive-distinguished-warfare-medal-for-cyber-ops-drone-strikes/2013/04/15/62335492-a612-11e2-8302-3c7e0ea97057_story.html.

28. Gordon Lubold, "Air Force Will Offer Bonuses to Lure Drone Pilots," *Wall Street Journal*, July 14, 2015 http://www.wsj.com/articles/air-force-will-offer-bonuses-to-lure-drone-pilots-1436922312.

29. Government Accountability Office, "Air Force: Actions Needed to Strengthen Management of Unmanned Aerial System Pilots," GAO Report 14–316 (April 2014).

30. While the Air Force officially recognizes 1947 as its year of birth, this chapter has noted that many aspects of culture in certain Air Force units trace their organizational records to before World War I; this accepted history has shaped how these members have reacted to problems within their service. I therefore submit that the term "hundred years" allows for a more applicable understanding of Air Force history, culture, and professionalism.

The Modern Military Profession

Nathan K. Finney and Tyrell O. Mayfield

A cross this volume we have revisited the foundational twentieth-century thinkers on military professionalism, including Huntingon, Janowitz, and Hackett. Analysis from many perspectives found that while many of the attributes outlined in their theories on professionalism still ring true, new ways of thinking about the issue are emerging. Additionally, new domains of operation, demanding innovative approaches to warfare, are altering the battlefield, and naturally affecting the professionals that fight on it. Much has changed since these works were presented half a century ago, and the question of professionalism is perhaps more complicated than it was at that time. Small, volunteer, standing armies seem to have permanently replaced their larger conscripted counterparts of the nineteenth and twentieth centuries. Just as the character of warfare and the armies that engage in it evolve, so too must the professionalism of the forces that encounter this crucible of combat. For just as conscripted, Western forces were stymied by ethical shortfalls in the Korean and Vietnam Wars, the professional all-volunteer force confronting non-state actors in the twenty-first century remains dogged by ethical failures. This has undoubtedly contributed to the elusive political and strategic effects—including international order, regional stability, and enduring national security—sought by Western forces since World War II.

Huntington, Janowitz, and Hackett would surely recognize many of the preconditions for cultural change today; they are in some ways very similar, and yet in other ways opposites, to what the militaries of the 1950s and 1960s faced. The cycle of wartime expansion and postwar drawdowns will repeat itself. Western military forces are continually expanding and contracting to meet political demands and fiscal realities. With that said, professional militaries are inherently more efficient and effective than their massive, conscripted counterparts of the past, due largely to the increased leveraging of technology, quality of accessions, and improved training methods. Professional militaries are also staggeringly expensive to maintain. The procurement of increasingly complicated and expensive weapons systems—designed to leverage advantages in capability over quantity—is intended to offset the long-term reduction in the overall size of standing military forces while maintaining or improving a base level of capability. The increasing technical requirements inherent in today's forces and the changing character of the battlefield add new dynamics to the question of military professionalism. For instance, some technological advancements such as unmanned aerial vehicles offer the advantage of completing missions without placing personnel in harm's way while also increasing the ambiguity of ethical considerations in the use of force. New technologies and the ethics involved in their use will continue to be issues the military must address as its code of ethics evolves along with the changing battlefield.

One clear result of this shift away from conscription to a technologically focused force is that fewer and fewer members of society—the very population with which the military must maintain trust—have any personal connection with the military or any exposure to conflict in a meaningful way. This abstraction of military service has resulted in an ever-widening gap between the professional armies of the West and the societies they serve. This gap has not resulted in the calls for change and demands of accountability that drove change in the mid-twentieth century, an amazing occurrence given the starkly ambiguous strategic and political results of the past decade and a half of war. Instead, the pendulum seems to have swung to its opposite point: today's military personnel are held in high regard and are widely respected by the societies they serve. Western society's distance from its militaries appears to have reduced their vested interest in success or failure and replaced it with acceptance of the status quo and muted demands for the continued professionalization of the force and its accountability. Could this cultural distance be the reason why no twenty-first-century Huntington, Hackett, or Janowitz has appeared?

It appears that, at least in the case of the United States, the Vietnam War and its effects on societal consciousness created one enduring impact; society seems to have deliberately partitioned its thoughts and support for a war from its warriors. The unquestioned support from average citizens seems to be eroding their ability to critically evaluate an organization as diverse and arcane to contemporary society as a modern military. As is true in most Western nations, the military remains the most trusted institution in the United States—a very positive aspect when considered alone—but there is a danger that Western societies have placed their militaries on too high a pedestal.[1] This combination of unquestioned support and mental partition seems to have separated the professionalism of the military from the evaluation of ethics in war and the metrics used to evaluate the professionalism of the force.[2] When people stop asking questions, standards can start to slip. An oft-quoted maxim of NCOs is that soldiers do those things that leaders check. This idea is true at the macro level as well.

Pauline Shanks-Kaurin's chapter acknowledges this necessity for constant evaluation by arguing that a professional status is contingent not only on self-ascribed standards for entrance to the community but also on the acceptance of the military's standards of behavior and ethical responsibilities by the citizenry it serves. In her estimation, the military is only as professional as its political leaders demand and their constituents overtly require. Therefore, while broad support for the military reflects a healthy relationship and general satisfaction with the profession, the military's absolutism in the face of enduring conflict provides room for stagnation and reduced oversight. If this book has illuminated anything, it is that critical evaluation of the military—from diverse sectors of society— remains necessary for the maintenance and continued development of a professional force.

On the Arc of Professionalism

The modern, professional army is a young thing when compared side by side with its raison d'être—the conduct of warfare. Advances in professionalism seem to be positively correlated with advances in technology and the increasing specialization they require. As technology improves, war fighting becomes more complex. With each iteration of technology— from catapults to artillery, horse-mounted cavalry to armored vehicles, sails to steam, hot air balloons to fixed-wing flight—militaries developed new core competencies. Driven by technology, these new core competencies required an equal development of technical understanding within the professional force that fields them. Simon Anglim's outline of the arc of professional military education serves to demonstrate the West's acute realization of the necessity of technical proficiency, as well as the discipline and ethics it requires. Today's military continues to pursue the professionalization of its force through education and training, though as William Beasley demonstrated with an example from the US Navy, this has not always been the case; the focus on professionalism ebbs and flows with both institutional demands and society's familiarity with the military and its capabilities.

There is more to being a professional than education or specialization, however. In contrast to the other authors in this work, Tony Ingesson argues that there remains ample room to dispute the professional status of military personnel and that identifying them all as professionals perhaps goes too far. By removing individuals from the point of decision and action on the battlefield, those individuals become distanced not only from the actual act of war but also from the professional status Huntington envisioned. This speaks, in part, to the increasingly remote nature of warfare for many and minimizes the reality of warfare for all but the very few who see combat with their own eyes. There can be little question that the taking of a life through the lens of a camera and over the top of a rifle are two very different experiences, both providing unique perspectives and consequences for the participants. But the question remains: Is it indeed the act of taking a life that delineates the professionals from those who support the profession?

This certainly is not the position of the US Army, which has sought to both define and achieve its own professional status; these efforts include substantial work by Don Snider and other scholars.[3] This effort culminated with the publication of *Army Doctrine Reference Publication 1: The Army Profession* as discussed in Casey Landru's chapter. For Landru, the relationship between soldier and state is a unique burden of trust that goes beyond the application of force and includes a responsibility for military professionals to manage human and fiscal resources as part of their professional obligations. Mike Denny carries this thesis one step further, taking the position that being a true professional supersedes both trust and the authority a professional derives from society. Instead, Denny argues that the mark of a professional is possession of expert knowledge and a secure ethical foundation from which to knowingly violate rules and regulations—or even orders—for the good of the mission or the troops, or even to succeed in a conflict. Brian Laslie's chapter on the insubordinate culture of the Air Force takes Denny's argument to an institutional level, describing how pragmatic professionalism has created the profession we see today.

The possession of expert knowledge is one of the attributes of a profession that the military shares with some of its civilian professional counterparts and seen in the chapter by Jo Brick. To be fair, there is a great deal of technical knowledge maintained and developed by the military in the application of its unique weapons systems. And while the nature of war perhaps has not changed over time—it is still humans struggling violently against other humans—the environment and attributes of this struggle continue to change and rarely manifest themselves in the same manner twice. How then can military personnel be rated as experts in the execution of an unknown event? They may well be experts in the conduct of the last war, but this knowledge rarely prepares them for what comes next. Unlike law or disease—both of which are relatively static and predictable in nature—the notion of future warfare forces military experts to imagine what shape the next threat might assume; lawyers and doctors rarely work in such an ambiguous environment. There seems to be very little science in the preparation for the next conflict, and an inordinate amount of what many would call art.

It is in this realm of art—the practicing of a developed technical skill that requires imagination—that the issue of ethics again arises. For in war, as in the making of art, there are times when the artist-practitioner finds herself with a blank piece of stone and only an image in her head. What then? How does one direct a destructive force toward the making of something better without rules or guidance? It is in this ethical composition that the moral compass plays such a pivotal role in the actions of the practitioner of war. What is to be done when the problem cannot be described or bounded by rules of engagement or strategy and its presence represents a real and imminent mortal threat to the practitioner and those who she is sent to protect? This ethical component could be found and explained by those that have been there before or have studied deeply—from mentors. Ray Kimball addresses this aspect of the military profession by analyzing related identity formation processes, such as experiential learning and cognitive apprenticeship and makes suggestions for the practical implementation of these processes. For Steven Foster, the answer comes in the institutionalization of the profession from the bottom up, because the greatest effects are seen through individual and small-unit collective efforts. In an even more imaginative application, Holly Hughson compares the work of aid workers in combat zones to that of soldiers, postulating that neither civilian nor military organizations can operate in isolation on the modern battlefield and therefore their mutual recognition as professions adds import to both the understanding of those who operate in spaces affected by war and success in conflict.

The ethical obligations of modern militaries have always been obliquely alluded to and enforced through means of military justice, though their inclusion in military formal education has been largely overlooked. In fact, the inculcation of ethics into the military ethos through formal education is a relatively new phenomenon. The most prominent milestone on the ethical path for the American military may indeed be the *Study on Military Professionalism* directed by General Westmoreland and conducted by the Army War College at the apogee of the Vietnam War experience and the arguable nadir of American military professionalism. As discussed by Casey Landru, this report "added a code of behavior to Huntington's three-fold definition of professionalism, elevating it from a facet of 'corporateness' to equal footing alongside expertise and responsibility."[4] As discussed by Rebecca Johnson, ethics and the education that provides them are the preventive measures taken by the military to guide its professionals. Military justice, policy, and regulations serve as the corrective when ethics fail. Perhaps by increasing the emphasis on ethics during both civilian and military education society might produce more professional forces that require less reactive justice and fewer restrictive policies and regulations.

A Modest Contribution

Huntington stretched his definition of professionalism across a three-sided framework of expertise, responsibility, and corporateness.[5] Janowitz presumed that the militaries of Western democratic states were professional and predicted their necessity to become smaller, more technologically focused, and more politically attuned.[6] Hackett enshrined the concept of unlimited liability in the concept of the professionalism, postulating that unlike any other profession, "The whole essence of being a soldier is not to slay but to be slain."[7] By this, he meant that the demands of the military profession were significantly more all-encompassing than any other. Between these three essential theorists of the military profession there is a foundational balance that is struck; Huntington planted firmly in historical context, Hackett describing the realistic, even functional, role sacrifice and loyalty play in the profession, and Janowitz looking forward, predicting a continued revolution in military affairs and a changing context of military engagements.

The military itself has not remained passive in the discussion of professionalism. From Westmoreland's study at the end of the Vietnam War to the doctrine of the Army and the Joint force, the conversation and analysis of the military as a profession—and what that means for our warriors and society as a whole—have continued, if less analytically or diligently than the conversation following the Korean War.

What the authors of this edited volume have offered is a contemporary look at the profession of arms and the development of its ethic. Taken from different perspectives and based on varied experiences and education, the work provides a starting point for discussing the future of the military profession. Though this discussion has encompassed an entire book, the conversation is far from over. That we have a collection of essays produced by company and field grade officers, as well as academics and civil servants from other branches of government, that spans three continents is in our estimation a good thing. It indicates that the conversation is ongoing, that it is broad, and perhaps most important, that it includes military members, other recognized professionals, and citizens from the society that they serve. So long as the conversation continues, the pursuit of a military composed of individual professionals remains alive and the balance between civil authority and military capability allows for the maintenance required in free, democratic societies.

Notes

1. Jeffrey. M. Jones, "Confidence in U.S. Institutions Still Below Historical Norms," Gallup, http://www.gallup.com/poll/183593/confidence-institutions-below-historical-norms.aspx.
2. Huntington, *The Soldier and the State*, 62.
3. Don Snider's extensive research and writing on the Army as a profession includes these: Snider and Matthews, *The Future of the Army Profession*; Snider, *Forging the Warrior's Character*, 2nd ed. (New York: McGraw-Hill, 2008); Snider, *The Army's Professional Military Ethic in an Era of Persistent Conflict* (coauthor with Paul Oh and Kevin Toner; Carlisle, PA: Strategic Studies Institute, 2008); Snider, *American Civil–Military Relations: The Soldier and the State in the New Era* (Baltimore: Johns Hopkins University Press, 2009).
4. US Army War College, *Study on Military Professionalism*, 6 (quote).
5. Huntington, *The Soldier and the State*, 84.
6. Janowitz, *The Professional Soldier*, (New York: Free Press, 1960) 21, 35, 164.
7. Hackett, *The Profession of Arms*, 63; U.S. Army Center of Military History, Publication 70-18, 40; Lieutenant General Sir John Winthrop Hackett, quoted in Gwynne Dyer, *War: The Lethal Custom* (New York: Carroll & Graff), 129 (quote).

ABOUT THE CONTRIBUTORS

Volume Editors

Nathan K. Finney is an officer in the US Army and the creator, cofounder, and first executive director of the nonprofit The Strategy Bridge. He has also been a visiting fellow at the Australian Strategic Policy Institute, a term member at the Council on Foreign Relations, a non-resident fellow of the Daniel K. Inouye Asia-Pacific Center for Security Studies, and a non-resident fellow at the Modern War Institute at West Point. He is a PhD candidate in history at the University of Kansas and holds master's degrees in public administration from Harvard University and the University of Kansas, as well as a BA in anthropology from the University of Arizona.

Tyrell O. Mayfield is an officer in the US Air Force and a cofounder and board member of the nonprofit The Strategy Bridge. He has published photography and has written in a number of online forums, magazines, newspapers, and peer-reviewed journals. He holds master's degrees in international relations from the University of Oklahoma, national security studies from the Naval Postgraduate School, and strategic studies from the US Army War College, as well as BS in criminal justice from Illinois State University. He is currently writing a memoir about his time in Kabul.

Contributors

Simon Anglim is a teaching fellow in the Department of War Studies at King's College London, and is the author of two books on Major General Orde Wingate and over a dozen papers in referenced journals, as well as a regular contributor to *The Strategy Bridge*. He previously spent five years as a historian with the British Ministry of Defence.

William M. Beasley Jr. is an attorney with Phelps Dunbar, LLP. He graduated Phi Beta Kappa from the University of Mississippi with a BA and MA in history and a JD from the University of Mississippi School of Law, where he served on the editorial board of the *Mississippi Law Journal*. Prior to joining Phelps Dunbar, he worked as a research consultant with the Potomac Institute in Arlington, Virginia. He is a member of the Center for International Maritime Security (CIMSEC), and his work on maritime history and security has appeared in U.S. Naval Institute *Proceedings*, at *The Strategy Bridge*, and the *US Naval Institute Blog*.

Jo Brick is a legal officer in the Royal Australian Air Force. She served in Australian Defence Force operations in Iraq and Afghanistan and has extensive experience providing legal support to combined and joint air operations, cyber security, detainee operations, and military justice. She is a graduate of the Australian Command & Staff College and recently graduated from the Australian National University with a master's degree (advanced) in military and defence studies (hons). Her research interests are in Australian civil-military relations, strategy, military ethics and the laws of war, air power, and armoured warfare. She is an associate editor at *The Strategy Bridge*, and a member of the Military Writers Guild.

Hugh Michael Denny Jr. is an officer in the US Army National Guard. Formerly he served as a field artillery officer on active duty with two deployments to Afghanistan. As a civilian, he is a management professional in a government agency. He is a regular contributor to *Task & Purpose*, *The Strategy Bridge*, and other outlets. He is a member of the Military Writers Guild.

Steven L. Foster is an officer in the US Army, has extensive experience in logistics, and specializes in operational and strategic planning. He holds a masters in of public policy with emphasis in national security policy from George Mason University. His interests include policy, strategy, and history, and he is a senior editor at *The Strategy Bridge*. He also has experience in the private sector in business management and a strong interest in leader development and talent management. He is a member of the Military Writers Guild.

Holly Hughson is a senior advisor and trainer, having worked for almost two decades in high-stakes crisis response, humanitarian action, and civil-military coordination. Working on the frontline of twenty-first-century conflict, she has seen firsthand the disruption to the twentieth-century norms of security, power, profession, and identity. In addition to organization and leadership development consulting, she is a visiting scholar at Sarum College in the UK and a member of the Military Writers Guild.

Tony Ingesson is an assistant professor of political science at Lund University, Sweden, where he teaches political science, intelligence analysis, and peace and conflict studies. His research is primarily focused on decision-making under stress at the tactical level. In his dissertation, he studied the impact of subcultures on strategic outcomes, using case studies from 1939 to 1995. He has previously served in the Swedish Army, Air Force, and Navy.

Rebecca Johnson is dean of academics and deputy director of the Marine Corps War College. Her research focuses on military ethics and leader development. She also serves as adjunct faculty at Wesley Theological Seminary.

Raymond A. Kimball is an officer in the US Army with service from the tip of the spear to echelons above reality. He has an abiding interest in leader development and decentralized learning and is a regular contributor to *The Strategy Bridge*. He is a member of the Military Writers Guild.

Casey J. Landru is a mechanical engineer and former US Army officer. During his service he was a rifle platoon leader, company executive officer, and scout platoon leader with the 2nd Battalion, 27th Infantry Regiment, at Schofield Barracks, Hawai'i, from 2010 to 2013. During that time he deployed to Afghanistan for a year. He has contributed to *The Strategy Bridge* and is a member of the Military Writers Guild. He holds a BS in mechanical engineering from the United States Military Academy.

Brian Laslie is the deputy command historian for the North American Aerospace Defense Command (NORAD) and US Northern Command and an adjunct professor of history at the US Air Force Academy. After spending six years in the US Air Force, where he served as a logistics officer and instructor, he left active duty to get his PhD in military history from Kansas State University. He is the author of *The Air Force Way of War: US Tactics and Training after Vietnam* and *Architect of Air Power: General Laurence S. Kuter and the Birth of the US Air Force*.

Pauline Shanks-Kaurin holds a PhD in philosophy from Temple University and is a specialist in military ethics, just war theory, social and political philosophy, and applied ethics. She is currently the Admiral James B. Stockdale Chair in Military Ethics at the Naval War College in Newport, Rhode Island. Recent publications include: *When Less is not More: Expanding the Combatant/Non-Combatant Distinction; With Fear and Trembling: A Qualified Defense of Non-Lethal Weapons;* and *Achilles Goes Asymmetrical: The Warrior, Military Ethics and Contemporary Warfare* (Routledge 2014).

INDEX